Quality Matters in Children's Services

Series Editor: Mike Stein

Consultant Editor: Caroline Thomas

The provision of high quality children's services matters to those who use and provide children's services. This important series is the result of an extensive government-funded research initiative into the *Quality Protects* programme which aimed to improve outcomes for vulnerable children, as well as transform the management and delivery of children's services. Focussing on current challenges in making every child matter, titles in the series are essential reading for all those working in the field.

Mike Stein is a research professor in the Social Work Research and Development Unit at the University of York. He has researched the problems and challenges faced by vulnerable children and young people for 25 years and contributed to the development of policy and practice in the UK and internationally. He acted as an academic adviser to the *Quality Protects* research initiative. Caroline Thomas is Senior Research Fellow at the Department of Applied Social Science, University of Stirling, UK. She is an academic adviser to the Department for Children, Schools and Families.

in the same series

Child Protection, Domestic Violence and Parental Substance Misuse
Family Experiences and Effective Practice
Hedy Cleaver, Don Nicholson, Sukey Tarr and Deborah Cleaver
ISBN 978 1 84310 582 4

The Pursuit of Permanence
A Study of the English Child Care System
Ian Sinclair, Claire Baker, Jenny Lee and Ian Gibbs
ISBN 978 1 84310 595 4

Kinship Care
Fostering Effective Family and Friends Placements
Elaine Farmer and Sue Moyers
Foreword by Brigid Daniel
ISBN 978 1 84310 631 9

by the same author

Children's Homes Revisited
David Berridge and Isabelle Brodie
ISBN 978 1 85302 565 5

Quality
Matters
in **Children's**
Services

Educating Difficult Adolescents

Effective Education for Children in Public Care or with Emotional and Behavioural Difficulties

▶ David Berridge
▶ Cherilyn Dance
▶ Jennifer Beecham
▶ Sarah Field

Jessica Kingsley Publishers
London and Philadelphia

First published in 2008
by Jessica Kingsley Publishers
116 Pentonville Road
London N1 9JB, UK
and
400 Market Street, Suite 400
Philadelphia, PA 19106, USA

www.jkp.com

Library of Congress Cataloging in Publication Data
Educating difficult adolescents : effective education for children in public care or with emotional and behavioural difficulties / David Berridge ... [et al.].
p. cm.
Includes bibliographical references.
ISBN 978-1-84310-681-4 (pb : alk. paper) 1. Teenagers with social disabilities--Education--Great Britain. 2. Teenagers--Institutional care--Great Britain. 3. Foster children--Education--Great Britain. I. Berridge, David.
LC4096.G7E25 2009
371.940941--dc22

2008014728

British Library Cataloguing in Publication Data
A CIP catalogue record for this book is available from the British Library

ISBN 978 1 84310 681 4

Printed and bound in Great Britain by
Athenaeum Press, Gateshead, Tyne and Wear

Contents

List of Figures, Tables, Boxes and Case Studies

Contents

List of Figures, Tables, Boxes and Case Studies

Acknowledgements

We are grateful to the Department for Children, Schools and Families (DCSF) for funding the research which formed the basis to this book and providing overall support. We are especially indebted to Caroline Thomas who, as ever, provided an effective link to the department. Mike Stein was a capable academic co-ordinator of the overall *Quality Protects* research initiative of which this was a part; always a source of wise advice, encouragement and friendship.

We would also like to take this opportunity to thank Harry Daniels and Ted Cole, who were each involved in the original design of the study and were available to the team for consultation throughout the life of the project, particularly concerning special education and residential special schools.

Members of our advisory group gave unselfishly of their time and expertise: Cathy Ashley, Robert Beattie, Nina Biehal, Isabelle Brodie, Sarah Byford, Robert Cassen, Tony Dewhurst, Tommy Foley, Alex Kirwan and Ruth Sinclair. We are also grateful for the advice and support from our university colleagues. Any limitations in the report, of course, remain our responsibility.

Most importantly, we could not have completed the study without the agreement of the managers of local authorities and schools. We are obliged to the many carers, social workers, residential staff, teachers and other care and education professionals who individually contributed to the work. Our final word of thanks must go to the young people we met, who were prepared to share their thoughts and feelings with us, in the hope that we all might learn from their experience. We hope they would feel that our efforts have been worthwhile.

Chapter 1

Introduction

Considerable attention has been paid to social policy for children over the past decade. Government made the ambitious pledge to halve child poverty by 2010. Early-years services have received a welcome boost, especially in disadvantaged communities under the *Sure Start* initiative where over 500 projects have been established. Government also embarked on a more general modernisation programme for children's social services, aimed particularly at offering greater protection for children from abuse and neglect, raising the quality of care provided for looked after children ('in care') and improving the life chances of children who need social services support (DoH 1998a).

Government's measures to improve children's social services were brought together under the *Quality Protects* initiative starting in 1998. This was announced initially as a three-year programme with £375 million of extra resources, subsequently extended to 2004, intended to tackle problems of attitudes, standards, management, service delivery and training. A number of aims were included under the *Quality Protects* initiative, including: improving adoption services with a view to increasing the number of adoptions; ensuring greater placement stability for looked after children with fewer moves between foster and residential homes; strengthening services for care leavers; and improving the health and education of looked after children. Various performance targets were established, which were monitored annually. A research initiative was mounted in 2002 to evaluate the achievements of *Quality Protects* and this book outlines the findings from a study undertaken into its educational objectives. It has a particular focus on older pupils. We begin first by sketching more of the background.

Education and looked after children

Positive educational experiences are increasingly seen as essential in a rapidly developing society, for a competitive and skills-based economy, and for reasons of personal fulfilment. In a context of generally improving educational standards and pupil achievements, there are specific groups of children and young people whose lack of adequate progress arouses concern. One such group is children experiencing family breakdown and being looked after by councils, mainly in foster and residential homes, as a result of abuse or neglect, family dysfunction, absent parenting or related factors. If the state intervenes owing to unsatisfactory parenting it is considered unacceptable if children continue to make inadequate educational progress. However, since Jackson's (1987) pioneering work two decades ago, it has long been recognised that looked after children as a group continue to perform poorly at school. Indeed, this has become something of a litmus test of the perceived inefficiency of children's social services as a whole; and appears to have been one of the key elements behind the drive to 'modernise' the sector. For example, the 1998 White Paper contained the following:

> Too many reports and inquiries have highlighted cases where social services have failed vulnerable children. Children in the care of local authorities have been abused and neglected by the care system that was supposed to look after them...the majority of looked after children leave care with no educational qual-ification at all, many of them at great risk of falling into unemployment, home-lessness, crime and prostitution. (DoH 1998a, p.41)

Though parts of the White Paper might be seen as a rhetorical statement from an incoming government committed to welfare reform, the above extract reflects widely held public and professional views on the inadequacies of the care system.

Such observations are often based on statistics published annually by the relevant central government department. A more detailed analysis is included in Chapter 2; however, initially Table 1.1 summarises the most recent GCSE results of Key Stage 4 (Year 11, 16-year-old) looked after children compared with all pupils in England. When the poor educational performance of looked after children is discussed, these are the statistics that are most often used. The figures include only pupils who have been looked after for at least a year, as councils have little opportunity to influence the achievements of more recent entrants. The table shows that, in 2006, 63 per cent of Year 11 looked after pupils achieved at least one GCSE (or GNVQ) compared with nearly all pupils in England – 98 per cent. In other words, almost four in every ten looked after pupils obtained no GCSEs at this stage. Furthermore, 41 per cent obtained five GCSEs at any grade (91% for all pupils); while only 12 per cent managed five 'good' GCSEs grades A*–C (59 per cent for the whole group). The comparative low academic achievement of this group is striking.

The proportion of looked after pupils achieving at least one GCSE had previously been below half. As a consequence, the government had earlier set the target that the proportion of *care leavers* (not the same as the above) aged 16 and

Table 1.1 Comparative GCSE or GNVQ results of Year 11 pupils who were looked after for more than a year and all pupils in England, 2002–2006

	Looked after children (%)					All children (%)				
	2002	2003	2004	2005	2006	2002	2003	2004	2005	2006
Proportions obtaining at least:										
one GCSE grade A*–G or a GNVQ	53	53	56	60	63	95	95	96	96	98
five GCSEs (or equivalent) at A*–G	36	37	39	41	41	89	89	89	89	91
five GCSEs (or equivalent) at A*–C	8	9	9	11	12	52	53	54	56	59

Source: Department for Education and Skills (DfES) (2005, 2006c), Department for Children, Schools and Families (DCSF) (2007b) Table C. Percentages in this table and elsewhere in this book are rounded to the nearest whole number.

over with a GCSE or GNVQ qualification would rise to at least 50 per cent by 2001 and to over 75 per cent by 2003. However, these targets were being missed and were subsequently revised in 2003 to include the proportion obtaining five GCSEs at grades A*–C rising by at least four percentage points each year since 2002; and to ensure that in all authorities at least 15 per cent of young people in care achieved this level of qualifications. We can see from Table 1.1 that the proportion of pupils achieving five good GCSEs has, in fact, barely changed. Permanent exclusions of looked after pupils, although declining slightly, remain about eight times the national rate. Therefore, although generally some modest improvement is reported in the official statistics, the low educational achievement of looked after pupils persists.

Why might this be? The authors have researched the educational experiences of looked after pupils, in various guises, over the past decade, and contributory factors are now better understood. We have reviewed the research literature elsewhere (Brodie 2005; Harker *et al.* 2004). For example, inadequate corporate parenting has previously been reported, in particular the failure of social services and education departments to work together adequately. Communication and co-ordination have often been poor, and joint working and information-sharing have been difficult. Information on children's educational progress, in particular that held by social services, has been incomplete and inaccurate. Direct contact between schools and social services has been problematic, and carers' responsibilities for children's education have been unclear. It will be interesting to see the extent to which this has changed now that local councils' social services and

education departments have been brought together in children's services departments. Problems may also have been heightened by aspects of central government
education policy, which have emphasised schools' independence from local
authorities and the publication of academic results. Some schools, therefore, may
not have welcomed low-achieving, looked after pupils. (Policy developments are
discussed later in this chapter.)

In addition, there has sometimes been a failure to prioritise education for
looked after children. Social workers have tended to emphasise placement issues
and social and emotional factors rather than educational considerations. Looked
after children comprise a tiny proportion of most schools' populations, and they
may not receive the special attention they require. Schools have greater problems
elsewhere. Linked to this, teachers, social workers and carers may have low expectations for looked after children, which can depress achievement. There is a body
of educational literature showing that teachers' perceptions of pupils' abilities
may be self-fulfilling (Hargreaves 1967) and this may be occurring here.

A further contributory factor to poor educational achievement may be
placement instability: too many children move between placements, and this
fluctuation undermines application, concentration and establishing positive
relationships with teachers and peers. Some 12 per cent of looked after children
have been reported to experience more than three placements in a year (CSCI
2005) and there have been concerns in the past that changes may occur for
agency- or carer-related factors rather than on the basis of children's needs
(Berridge and Cleaver 1987). At its most extreme, placement changes may also
necessitate school transfer (Morgan 1999). Placement change *per se* is not necessarily harmful. It affects groups differently and is necessary at times but, in
general, instability should be avoided (Berridge 2000; Sinclair *et al.* 2006).
Incongruously, the likelihood of placement breakdown increases with age just as
key GCSE examinations draw near.

Disrupted schooling may occur in other ways, too. Periods of education may
be missed on entry to care and school absenteeism may have been a contributory
factor, or consequence, of family breakdown. One in six looked after pupils has
reported truanting regularly (Meltzer *et al.* 2003). They may be more likely to be
diverted to alternative provision in pupil referral units (PRUs), which can be perceived as stigmatising, or be allocated to special needs schools even if their
problems are less severe than those of many pupils in mainstream schools
(Gordon, Parker and Loughran 2000).

The care environment

Another key influence on looked after children's educational experience and success is the care environment. Focusing on outcomes for children now receives greater priority from government (DfES 2004a), although it is a complex area for researchers (Parker *et al.* 1991). For looked after children, there are questions about how best to capture any subtle changes which might occur and, especially for older groups, what degree of change is it realistic to expect? The care population is not a homogenous group and we need to know more about the distinguishing factors between children who succeed educationally and those who do not (Jackson 1998). In understanding the relationship between educational success or failure and the care system it is therefore important that attention is given to everyday practices within placements, as well as to structures and procedures. Little detailed attention has been given to the relative impact of different types of care placement on educational achievement (Borland *et al.* 1998). The evidence suggests that individual placements can make a difference to care objectives in the short term, even if longer-term outcomes are more difficult to influence: if the current environment can have an impact then so, presumably, may those that follow (Sinclair and Gibbs 1998; Sinclair *et al.* 2006).

Two-thirds (24,400) of older children who are looked after are living at any one time in foster homes (DfES 2006b). (Official statistics are presented in such a way that this includes those ten years of age and above.) About five in every six of these children are living with unrelated carers rather than with family or friends, and one-third are placed outside their council's boundaries. Fifteen per cent (5490) of older looked after children live in children's homes, almost half of whom now are based outside the local authority. There has been a significant shift in placement patterns from residential to foster care, with a reduction in the overall children's homes population of two-thirds over the past 20 years (Berridge and Brodie 1998). This has occurred for various reasons, including the perceived risk of institutionalisation, cost, problems associated with managing young people's behaviour, staffing and scandals involving the physical and sexual abuse of residents (Stein 2006a).

Foster and residential homes have not always been educationally stimulating, with insufficient encouragement of reading, literacy and homework (Social Exclusion Unit 2003). There has been very little detailed research in the UK on foster care and education (Wilson *et al.* 2004). Foster carers' own educational attitudes and achievement have not traditionally been important features in their recruitment and selection. It has also been reported that foster homes often lack the basic supports for education, including quiet study facilities, essential books and access to computers (Martin and Jackson 2002).

Most heads of children's homes participating in the study by Sinclair and Gibbs (1998) prioritised residents' education but, nevertheless, felt that they achieved limited success. Previous research on children's homes found that staff identified education as a major difficulty, second only to problems with behavioural management (Berridge and Brodie 1998). Most of the homes visited in the mid-1990s for participant observation were felt to be unexciting and there was little to do ('somewhat dull places in which to live'; Berridge and Brodie, p.110). Books, magazines and daily newspapers were scarce. Television was seldom watched and its educational potential was unexploited. But, overall, staff encouraged school attendance, asked children how the day at school had gone and encouraged and (usually) checked homework. A range of activities and trips out was organised and most homes, despite tight budgets, tried to ensure that all children had an annual holiday. Links between residential homes and schools were variable, and there were few contacts with other educational services such as educational psychology or education welfare. Some private homes ran their own educational units and these risked isolation from mainstream education in the local authority as well as educational support services. Many pupils did not attend school regularly; on investigation, few were formally excluded, although staff believed that they were (see also Brodie 2001). Workers were unclear how they were expected to occupy residents out of school who were present during the day and clear policies were lacking.

In addition to foster and children's homes placements, the research on which this book is based also included residential special schools for pupils 'with behavioural, emotional and social difficulties' (BESD, formerly referred to as 'EBD'). We have long been interested in this sector: a significant number of residents in special schools are legally looked after and it is felt that there are some similarities between their pupils and those living in foster care and children's homes (Grimshaw with Berridge 1994). Yet the special schools adopt a quite different approach to meeting children's needs and it is interesting to compare the implications for quality of care and education, outcomes and costs. Estimating the size of this residential special schools sector is problematic as detailed statistics are not collated by the Department for Children, Schools and Families from the independent sector. The largest group of pupils boarding in maintained and non-maintained (excluding independent) schools are those with BESD – 35 per cent or 2061 children (Pinney 2005). Many residential schools also cater for day pupils, while some mainly day schools have a small boarding component. Cole, Visser and Upton (1999) estimated that in England approximately 12,000 pupils,

mainly adolescents, were attending BESD schools, with almost one-third of them boarding for at least part of the week.

Interestingly, despite catering for a group of pupils numerically probably not far short of the children's homes population, the residential BESD sector has attracted much less research attention. There has been sociological interest in the assessment of BESD, the rate of which varies considerably between local authorities – suggesting that it is as much a function of professionals' decisions and local resources as of children's intrinsic needs (Daniels and Porter 2007; Galloway, Armstrong and Tomlinson 1994). Indeed, Malek and Kerslake (1989) wrote of 'system spillage' suggesting, to some extent, that service users may be interchangeable (between the care system and residential BESD), whereas economists have similarly written of 'cost-shunting' to displace financial responsibility (Knapp 1984). However, our earlier work (Grimshaw with Berridge 1994) identified important differences between the residential BESD group and the children's homes population, although it will be useful here to reconsider these findings (see also Cliffe with Berridge 1994). The study by Triseliotis et al. (1995), of social work services for teenagers, reported positive findings for residential special schools: compared with foster and children's homes, they provided the greatest degree of stability and improved young people's educational achievements and self-esteem. For these reasons, residential BESD schools strike us as an interesting and important sector and, when considering the education of looked after adolescents, a fruitful area for comparative study.

The 'Taking Care of Education' initiative

Although there are strong opinions, there are surprisingly few detailed, up-to-date empirical studies on the educational experiences of looked after children. As we have seen, this applies particularly to foster care, which nowadays is the main experience (Heath, Colton and Aldgate (1994) is an exception). Residential homes are generally easier to access than foster care: they are more 'public' environments, social workers tend to be less protective and residential staff, in our previous experience, have been more research-minded than foster carers (Berridge 1997). One of us has also been engaged, in association with the National Children's Bureau, in a detailed parallel study of what is known as the *Taking Care of Education* initiative. This consisted of a development project with an accompanying evaluation. Funding was provided for three carefully chosen local authorities to develop a range of good practice tools and techniques, policies and practices to advance the educational achievements of looked after children. The intention was to examine, in optimum circumstances, whether improvements could be made and, if so, what lessons could be learned (Harker et al. 2004).

The initial stage of the evaluation focused both on the nature of organisational change as well as educational outcomes for children. A sample of 80 looked after children over 10 years of age was identified across the three authorities and a two-year follow-up occurred. Key adults and, wherever possible, young people themselves were interviewed, and standardised tests were used. Detailed local analysis revealed that annual government statistics on educational outcomes for looked after children at different key stages were an unreliable indicator of attainment over time, as the groups changed considerably year on year, in terms of school exclusion, absenteeism and rates of special educational needs. Numbers in certain groups were also quite small, leading to erratic results.

Encouragingly, however, it was concluded that there were signs of positive change in the education of children in the evaluation sample, measured both in terms of their own subjective ratings and in the opinion of key adults in their lives, as well as by use of standardised tests. This was possibly the first detailed study of the education of looked after children in the UK – if not research literature more generally – to report positive results. Young people attributed much of the improvement to the degree of encouragement for education provided by carers: the communication of an educational ethos within foster and residential placements, and the perception that carers were interested in, and willing to support, young people's education. The quality of relationships between young people and carers influenced placement stability and feelings of emotional security. Educational resources in placements improved over time; for example, purchases of books, mobile library visits and the availability of computers. Achievement award ceremonies were popular with young people and there seemed to be advantages in authorities having a local co-ordinator or 'champion' for the education of looked after children. The particular approach and contribution of schools were also key factors, a dimension that has been overlooked in much previous child welfare research.

Policy change

It was clear from the *Taking Care of Education* research that the situation in other authorities had not stood still and it is complicated in evaluations to attribute improvements to specific policy initiatives (such as *Quality Protects*) rather than to general change. Indeed, the government has introduced a range of measures designed to improve the education of looked after children. For example, at a general level, the government's *Opportunity for All* initiative expressed a clear commitment for a more inclusive society in which citizens have the opportunity to achieve their potential (DSS 1999). The eradication of child poverty and strengthening educational opportunities were key elements of this.

Means-tested education maintenance allowances (EMAs) have been introduced to encourage young people to continue with their education at school or college: at the time of writing it is estimated that about half of all 16-year-olds should be eligible for them, with weekly payments of up to £30. Reform is planned for the 14–19 curriculum and qualifications framework, which includes skills development, vocational education and stronger links between secondary schools and colleges of further education (DfES 2006e). School absenteeism and exclusion have also been addressed (Social Exclusion Unit 1998). Other general initiatives include *Education Action Zones*, *Excellence in Cities* and *Study Support* to promote learning outside school lessons. These schemes have been generally well-received, although commentators have criticised the contradictory elements in seeking to promote a more inclusive educational system while prioritising greater autonomy for schools, high academic standards and publication of results, which may encourage schools to concentrate on higher-achieving pupils (Blyth 2001).

Policy specifically to improve the education of looked after children was co-ordinated within the Department for Education and Skills (now the DCSF) *Education Protects* programme, which was implemented after the introduction of the joint guidance between the then Department for Education and Employment and the Department of Health (DoH). This highlighted six key principles of corporate parenting: prioritising education; raising standards through high expectations; changing attitudes and reducing the stigma of being looked after; emphasising continuity and stability; early intervention; and listening to children. *Education Protects* linked with the *Quality Protects* initiative described earlier.

In addition, the Children (Leaving Care) Act 2000 imposed responsibilities on local authorities to encourage education and training for those over 16 years old. Another important milestone was the Social Exclusion Unit (2003) report, which provided a detailed examination of the low educational achievement of looked after pupils and reviewed other policy measures, including the requirement for schools to have a designated teacher for looked after pupils as well as the use of personal education plans (PEPs) for this group. There was a duty in the Children Act 2004 for local authorities to promote the education of looked after children. Furthermore, powers were contained within the Education and Inspections Act 2006 for local authorities to direct a school to admit a looked after pupil, even if the school is already full, if that is felt to be the best setting to meet the pupil's educational needs.

Developments in the field of special education are relevant to our area of interest and this has also experienced much policy development. About one in every five pupils has a special educational need (SEN) at some stage of their school career and, at any one time, this applies to about three per cent of all pupils, including a quarter of looked after children (Social Exclusion Unit 2003). *The Report of the Special Schools Working Group* (DfES 2003c) emphasised the need for all special schools to deliver a high quality of education for their pupils within a wider policy of inclusion. Indeed, concerns over standards that require special measures occur more frequently in special schools than in mainstream primary or secondary schools. There have been changes in the population of SEN pupils, including a higher proportion of children being diagnosed with autistic spectrum disorder (ASD) and a growing number of children presenting severe behavioural, emotional and social difficulties (BESD). The Special Schools Working Group highlighted the importance of effective partnerships between health, education and social services in order to deliver integrated services for children and their families. Specific measures were recommended concerning leadership, teaching and learning, and funding and structures as well as support beyond the classroom.

Many of these points were reflected in the government's strategy for SEN (DfES 2004c), aligned with the Green Paper on the reform of children's services *Every Child Matters* (DfES 2003b). This emphasised a graduated approach to SEN, rather than preoccupation with the bureaucratic and resource-intensive process of 'statementing', and a greater prominence of personalised learning. SEN policy prioritised early intervention, removing barriers to learning, raising expectations and achievement, and bringing about improvements in partnership. The report questioned standards in some residential special schools:

> There are concerns about the high costs of such placements, the quality of some provision, patchy monitoring arrangements, and the lack of contact some children have with their families. (DfES 2004c, p.44)

The Department for Education and Skills (2003a) highlighted the need for more research on the outcomes for disabled children living in residential schools as well as the circumstances leading to their placement. We include these children in our research.

In the BESD sector specifically, initiatives included strengthening the *National Behaviour Strategy* and a new *Inclusion Development Programme*, involving, for example, guidance on effective classroom strategies and working in multi-disciplinary teams. The report highlighted problems for BESD pupils concerning school admissions and exclusions. The respective roles and relationships of PRUs, special schools and alternative provision were said to require clarification. The SEN strategy specifically raised issues for looked after pupils identified as having BESD, including school transfers mid-year, or even more seriously, mid-term, because of the need to change their care placement.

The other major policy development affecting looked after children has been the Green and White Papers *Care Matters*, resulting at the time of writing in the Children and Young Persons Bill (2007–2008). As this new legislation is so current, and the research outlined in this book fed into its development, it will be discussed in the concluding chapter. In particular, we shall consider the extent to which new legislation and policy are consistent with our findings.

Research objectives

From the above it may be seen that the education of looked after children, in particular their low academic achievement, is an important issue and one that has received a significant amount of policy attention. Our previous research has shown that some improvements have occurred as a result of targeted initiatives (Harker *et al.* 2004), but we need to consider whether there is evidence that these have now occurred more generally.

Preparatory phase

We began our research with a nine-month exploratory analytic phase to pave the way for the current more robust evaluative study (Berridge *et al.* 2002). As the intention is to contrast the care and educational experiences of children living in foster care, children's homes and residential BESD schools, it was important to consider the extent to which users of these services were comparable (Berridge *et al.* 2003). We also needed to consider carefully exactly how homes and schools would be selected. This initial phase, therefore, sought to clarify certain conceptual, methodological and practical issues, as well as generating empirical findings of interest in their own right. In particular, there was a need to develop an appropriate methodology and good quality costs information on the special schools sector and alternative educational provision.

Though increasingly protracted, access was successfully negotiated to four contrasting (at the time) social services and education departments, and procedures were agreed. Adolescents aged between 13 and 18 years were included in the preparatory study. For piloting purposes, we aimed to visit the three children's homes and three residential BESD schools most frequently used by each agency in the previous 12 months. Detailed organisational information was collected on the homes and schools to inform subsequent sample selection. The characteristics of the fostered population were analysed from central records – up to 50 for each authority.

In relation to results from the piloting, each of the homes and schools was well-used and none was felt to be so disorderly or idiosyncratic as to preclude their involvement in the following evaluative phase. Foster and children's homes accommodated a gender mix but most BESD schools admitted boys only. Similarly, there were few African-Caribbean (and Asian) teenagers attending residential schools, which seemed anomalous given the disproportionately high rate of school exclusions of black pupils (Osler 1997). We needed to address these points in sampling in our subsequent work so as to attempt to compare like with like. Average age across sectors was broadly comparable. The children's homes group had the most complex and problematic backgrounds. In order to ensure comparability for the evaluative phase, we developed a set of criteria to identify a subsample of 'difficult' adolescents related to antisocial behaviour: offending, school exclusion, regular alcohol or drug misuse, or going missing from the placement. This comprised 48 per cent of the overall group; surprisingly, therefore, about half were not considered 'difficult'.

Some issues emerging from the initial phase that were worth pursuing further were: on the face of it, residential BESD schools appeared a less costly option; children's homes catered for a more difficult group; and pupils tended to stay significantly longer in residential schools. We also did not explore quality of care, user satisfaction and outcomes in that initial work, which need to be set alongside costs information. The BESD schools contrasted in other ways with the preferred social services model: there was a much clearer focus on education, they had greater clarity of mission and there were also different attitudes to distance from home and parental contact. BESD schools were more professionally insular than foster and children's homes. In addition, authorities used a wide range of single external placements and we wondered how these were selected and how children's progress was monitored. Managers did not always have a strategic overview of external placements used.

Methodology

To reiterate, the main phase of the study described here was part of the *Quality Protects* research initiative and funded by the then Department for Education and Skills. It was undertaken between 2003 and 2006. More detailed discussions of our methodology and data analysis are contained in the Appendix but we summarise them briefly here. Overall, we sought to evaluate educational achievements, unauthorised absences and permanent exclusions of a sample of pupils derived from three contrasting social services and education departments. These were particular objectives of the government's *Quality Protects* initiative.

We focus particularly on adolescents presenting difficulties. Similar studies are required on younger pupils, but child welfare research is increasingly required to focus on specific subgroups rather than general populations. Modern society poses particular challenges for adolescents in domains such as family, relationships, school and work, and it is estimated that one in three children experiences mental distress while they are young (Coleman 2000). Regrettably, public sympathy for youth is often in limited supply (Young 1999) and, whatever advances have been made in children's social services generally, there are major concerns in the field of juvenile justice policy (Pitts 2001). The government highlighted some of these issues in 2007 in its *Aiming High* ten-year youth strategy.

Our study employed both quantitative and qualitative methods. Initially, we examined the corporate parenting role in the three councils, including development and implementation of policy related to the education of looked after pupils. This was achieved through scrutiny of local documentation and interviews with key managers. Secondary statistics were analysed on the progress of looked after children in the three locations. The part that was the most time-consuming was a detailed follow-up study of the care and educational experiences and outcomes of 150 pupils. This involved semi-structured interviews with young people, carers and teachers. We liaised with National Voice and the Family Rights Group to enhance service user perspectives, and gave detailed consideration to equality issues and to research ethics.

The 150 young people had experienced one of three broadly defined types of settings: foster care, children's homes or residential special schools for BESD pupils. They originated from three councils, which we term 'County', 'Metro' and 'Borough', and eight residential schools. We sought to gather information at two periods – Stage 1 and Stage 2 – approximately nine months apart. Nine months was chosen because that was the maximum duration possible within the research resources available and given that we wanted to adopt a broad perspective. In order to be eligible for our study, the sample of young people at Stage 1 needed to be between 11½ – 15½ years old and to have been living in their current setting for between three months and four years. Our pilot work had revealed that relatively few residential BESD schools cater for girls and there were often few pupils from minority ethnic groups. With this in mind, four of the eight BESD schools were selected because they educated a wider range of pupils.

To ensure a greater degree of comparability across the three settings, we focused particularly on pupils who presented behaviour that was 'difficult to manage'. We appreciate that this is hard to define and, sociologically speaking, deviancy (rather like beauty) is in the eyes of the beholder. 'Difficult behaviour' could consist of one of six forms: poor school attendance; behavioural problems in school; regular use of alcohol or drugs; conviction or caution for a criminal offence; self-harm; and aggression or violence. To be eligible for our sample, two of the above forms of BESD had to have been evident within the previous three months.

Following on from our work in the pilot study we included an economic perspective. Cost constraints play an important role in the provision of children's services, but research-based findings to inform choices between support options are in short supply (Beecham 2006; Beecham and Sinclair 2007). Education managers find it hard to work out how much is spent on education for pupils with BESD in mainstream school and, again, there is little research-based information (Ofsted 2003). We sought to calculate comprehensive support costs, covering all areas of care, education and health support, over the research period in a manner that would enable like with like comparisons across young people and their care or education locations. We also wanted to explore the extent to which costs were associated with the needs and circumstances of young people and their outcomes (see the Appendix for further details).

In summary, therefore, our research objectives were to:

- Analyse the secondary statistics concerning the educational progress of looked after children.

- Evaluate the educational and wider experiences of comparable samples of 'difficult' adolescents living in foster homes, children's homes and residential special schools for pupils with BESD.

- Analyse the comprehensive costs of care and education services delivered and compare these to outcomes.

All of this is set in the context of the development of policy and practice to meet government education objectives for the education of looked after pupils.

Research ethics

Undertaking research with vulnerable young people imposes particular ethical responsibilities. We also recognised from the outset that this group might not be easy to engage in the research process and potentially difficult to track for the follow-up. The start of our study predated the advent of the publication, *Research Governance Framework for Health and Social Care* (DoH 2005). However, we subscribed to the *Ethical Guidelines* of the Social Research Association (2005) and adhered to strict principles of confidentiality and anonymity. We had developed a procedure for situations in which young people divulged to us that they were at risk of serious harm. None did. Ethical approval was obtained via our university mechanisms, as well as during the initial phase of peer review. We were concerned that our rigorous ethical stance might lead to self-selection that could produce overly optimistic results. We were, therefore, anxious that the sample should be as broadly representative as possible of the groups of young people in whom we were interested. For this reason, where young people themselves declined to be involved with the research, we followed cases anonymously through discussions with social workers or other professionals.

Our screening procedure took place completely anonymously, young people being identified only by initials or a case number. Our procedure for engaging young people whom we wished to include in the research sample was to ask the professionals involved in their care (social workers, heads of care or case managers, in the case of young people in residential schools) to introduce, on our behalf, information about the study and advise us of the young person's decision. We had previously designed detailed, colourful, informative leaflets to give young people the necessary information and, it was hoped, to obtain informed consent. Wherever appropriate, we asked for information to be forwarded to young people's parents or guardians and, again, asked to be advised if permission was withheld. Where young people declined to participate directly in the study (or their parents or guardians refused permission), we used such information as was available on an anonymous basis; for example, we would know only what sort of care setting a young person was living in, but not the specifics of where he or she was placed.

Young people were offered a small reward in recognition of the time they had given to participate in an interview. Although this may have been an inducement to many, some young people emphasised that they did not contribute simply for the voucher but because they had something they wished to say in relation to their care and educational opportunities that might benefit others.

Theory

In this introduction to the study, we need to say something about our overall framework. It was Kurt Lewin, the early social psychologist, who said that nothing is as practical as a good theory. One of us has recently written about theory, and its limitations, in empirical child welfare research (Berridge 2007a). Theory in social research is important both in influencing which questions are posed and how, as well as to help identify and explain related elements in the social world. Our study was a complex one and we need to explain how it was approached and the assumptions that we brought to it.

The overall team comprised seven researchers who, at different stages during the course of the work, were located at seven different academic institutions. As a group, our own experiences should yield useful insights into the issues of place-ment instability, movement, problems of contact and temporary housing. Though bringing its challenges, we believe that the problems of team-working are easily outweighed by the benefits of collaboration and a multi-disciplinary perspective. The field of child welfare is a complex one and there may be risks in too narrow a stance. Our approach combined sociology, social policy, developmental and educational psychology, and social care economics, while our professional interests spanned looked after children and special education. These complementary perspectives were used to develop a child-centred approach rather than one that reflected traditional academic, professional and administrative boundaries. We also wanted to try to bring together the best of current thinking from related fields to address the problem of educating difficult and disadvantaged adolescents. The groups of children also share some common problems as we have already seen.

Our theoretical framework is consistent with that of Layder (1993, 1998), who has advocated the benefits in applied social research of what he terms 'disciplined eclecticism'. If we wish to understand the complexities of a social problem (and are more interested in theory-building rather than theory-testing) more than one perspective is often required. Thus, certain traditional disputes in the social sciences become rather sterile, between, for example, the respective merits of macro or micro, or quantitative or qualitative approaches. Instead, Layder highlights four dimensions for theory-generation in social research. First, there is the wider *context*, which includes macro-social forms such as social class, gender and ethnic relations. Second, is *setting* – the immediate environment of social activity – in this case the foster or children's home or residential school. Third, *situated activity*, which refers to the dynamics of face-to-face interaction. Finally there is *self*, which includes the individual's own biographical and social experience. All of this is enhanced by two further factors: *history* and *power*. It would be impossible fully to understand social behaviour unless there was some awareness of its precedents, such as the historical development of the care system and its associated stigma. There is also the fact that it is used by the poorest families in society (Frost and Stein 1989; Parker 1990), and the middle classes seek other solutions. Similar considerations influence the very political nature of special education and we need to understand the history of services for children variously deemed 'maladjusted', EBD and now BESD (Cole, Visser and Upton 1998).

Linked to this, we are concerned that child welfare studies into the schooling problems of looked after children have previously given insufficient attention to a significant body of educational research (Berridge 2007a). Taking this into account, a different perspective may emerge. For example, it is often claimed that the care system itself is an additional risk factor jeopardising children's educational achievements, but the situation is more complex than is usually assumed. Indeed, conceptually, we should be referring to *low achievement* rather than *underachievement*, as it is unclear with what, exactly, comparisons are being made. We should also be cautious in interpreting official statistics on educational outcomes for looked after pupils. Furthermore, the socio-economic risk factors associated with family breakdown and admission to care, such as social class, poverty and abuse, also predict low educational achievement. Evidence reveals that alternative welfare systems do not necessarily achieve better results with this group than England does (Weyts 2004). No doubt improvements in services can and should be made but we should not underestimate the difficulties. Otherwise we risk falling into the trap cogently identified by Sinclair (2000) when discussing outcome measures used by researchers:

> the criteria set may be too ambitious and out of proportion to the scale of the intervention. As a very rough rule of thumb, social work interventions seem capable of improving mood, morale and satisfaction with the service. They have great difficulty in changing the way people behave – e.g. whether they engage in delinquency or suicide attempts. This is particularly so if people have not asked for the service… By concentrating on ambitious and inappropriate targets, social work research may have given social work an undesirably bad name. Judged against over-ambitious and inappropriate criteria it is set up to fail. (Sinclair 2000, p.4)

We attempt to reflect these considerations in the chapters that follow. In addition, there is one final point for this Introduction. We have aimed to write this book for a general audience of researchers, policy-makers, managers and practitioners. Consequently, we have omitted some specialist, technical details, for example concerning statistical analysis. As a condition of DCSF funding, a previous version of this work was subjected to scientific scrutiny under peer review confirming the rigour with which these aspects were undertaken.

Summary points

- This study focuses on government objectives to improve educational experiences for children looked after by local authorities, in particular under *Quality Protects*. It concentrates mainly on achievement, attendance and exclusions for older, looked after pupils.

- GCSE results for looked after pupils are significantly worse than for the general school population. Though there has been some improvement, government targets have been missed.

- Previous explanations for this low achievement include: inadequate corporate parenting; failure to prioritise education for looked after children; low expectations; placement instability; and disrupted schooling.

- The study investigates in particular the contribution of placements to children's care and education – foster care, children's homes and residential special schools for pupils 'with behavioural, emotional and social difficulties' (BESD).

- The research was informed by a nine-month preparatory phase to clarify certain conceptual, methodological and practical issues as well as to negotiate access to study agencies.
- The research adopts a multi-disciplinary approach, combining perspectives from sociology, social policy, developmental and educational psychology, and social care economics. Our professional interests cover looked after children and special education. We also take account of other research on educational disadvantage.

Chapter 2

The Local Context

Our research was located in three local authority social services and education departments, which were included initially in our pilot study (Berridge *et al.* 2002). These were chosen to provide some variation in geographical location, ethnic population and local government structure. Certain details of the descriptions throughout this chapter have been amended to maintain anonymity. Thus, *County* is a large county in southern England in the London commuter belt with a population around one million. The minority ethnic population is about 5 per cent. It is growing in population and would generally be considered prosperous. *County* has no single major population centre but comprises several urban areas combined with pleasant rural scenery. There is much successful light industry.

Metro, in contrast, is a metropolitan borough located in the north with a population nearer a quarter of a million. Like *County*, the minority ethnic population is quite low. There is a strong local economy, including information technology (IT) and tourism. Yet *Metro* also contains pockets of extreme deprivation and has one of the most deprived wards nationally.

Our third authority, *Borough*, is an inner London borough, which once again demonstrates considerable variation – with some of the most expensive London housing juxtaposing another of the most deprived localities in England. Many small businesses, leisure, arts and media companies flourish. However, *Borough* has twice the average level of London unemployment. A great deal of inner city regeneration work is taking place there. More than 40 per cent of the population comprises minority ethnic groups, including 'other white', and this figure rises to 60 per cent of local children. But *Borough* has relatively fewer children overall than other London councils. Table 2.1 summarises some of the information, for the three authorities, on children in need and looked after children. This relates to 2003 when our study began.

Table 2.1 Statistical information on children in need and looked after children in the County, Metro and Borough authorities in 2003*

	Total children in need 'open cases'	Asylum-seeking children identified as children in need	Children looked after
County	7350 (3%)	35	1000 (0.4%)
Metro	1550 (2%)	85	350 (0.6%)
Borough	2650 (8%)	180	500 (1.4%)
England	388,200 (3%)	12,500	62,300 (0.6%)

Source: DfES (2004d).

*Figures refer to children in need and those looked after at any time during the survey week in February 2003. The latter are included in the former. Percentages relate to the whole authority child population. Figures have been rounded for anonymity.

Table 2.1 reveals that *County* faced the largest volume of child welfare work during the survey week: some 7350 children there were defined as 'in need' (Section 17 Children Act 1989), of whom 1000 were looked after. Proportionally, compared with the national average, *County* had slightly fewer looked after children, whereas *Metro* had a lower number of children in need than might have been expected. On the other hand, *Borough* had nearly three times the national rate of children in need and double the proportion who were looked after. *Borough* also had far more asylum-seeking children than the other two areas. Though no doubt linked to size and levels of social deprivation, there is much leeway in the definition and identification of children in need, and authorities differ in the level and type of services they provide (Aldgate and Tunstill 1995; Colton, Drury and Williams 1995).

Quality Protects and educational experience

Having provided some general background, we return specifically to educational issues. The previous chapter outlined the emergence of the *Quality Protects* initiative and explained that our focus was on educational achievement, unauthorised absences and permanent exclusion. We were particularly interested in adolescents. Detailed official statistics are produced annually for looked after children, and these include information about performance assessment framework (PAF) 'outcome indicators' (CSCI 2005). These indicators include, for example, health care, offending rates and educational performance (DfES 2006c).

Before we present relevant selected statistics we must first issue a strong note of caution as the nature and reliability of these various measures and indicators have been questioned. Munro (2004), for example, cast doubt on the growth of an 'audit culture' in 'new public management'. She argued that setting targets may have perverse effects, in that pursuing a target *per se* may override meeting the welfare needs of service users. Goodhart's Law, which has been applied to the field of economics, states that once a social or economic indicator (e.g. examination pass-rate statistics) is made a target to conduct social or economic policy, it will lose the information basis that would qualify it to play such a role (Chrystal and Mizen 2001). There may also be an inclination to measure what is measureable.

More prosaically, as we saw in Chapter 1, research into the education of looked after children has pointed out that comparisons of indicators over time and between authorities may be invalid as populations often differ; for example, the proportions of young people with special educational needs (SEN) or asylum-seekers (Berridge 2007a; Harker *et al.* 2004). Numbers in subgroups are sometimes small, which may lead to large fluctuations. Errors may be made in the local compilation and submission of statistics. There are also questions about how long it is necessary for children to have been looked after before a council may reasonably be expected to have had an impact on them: 38 per cent of care leavers over 16 years of age have been looked after for fewer than two years (DCSF 2007a). Educational statistics for looked after pupils are usually based on those who have been looked after for more than a year.

With these limitations in mind, analysing official statistics for the years 2000–2004 (when the *Quality Protects* initiative ended) reveals that the number of school-aged pupils who were looked after for more than a year in our three authorities ranged from 224 to 600. The proportion of looked after pupils with a Statement of Special Educational Needs (SEN) was slightly higher than the national average for the care population (27 per cent in 2004 (28 per cent in 2006; DCSF 2007b)) in *County* and *Metro*, but lower in *Borough*. The highest figure was 38 per cent in *County* in 2003 (Figure 2.1).

Missed schooling

Improving school attendance and parental responsibility have been general government priorities under the *Tackling It Together* initiative. Figure 2.2 concerns unallocation and absenteeism and sets out the proportion of pupils looked after for more than a year who missed 25 days of schooling during the 12-month period. Though the picture remained relatively stable in England, at around 12 per cent (13 per cent in 2006 (DCSF 2007b)), we may see fluctuations in each of the three authorities. *County* and *Metro* ended 2004 with slightly higher figures than four years earlier. Missed schooling fell notably over the period in *Borough*, but then rose sharply again.

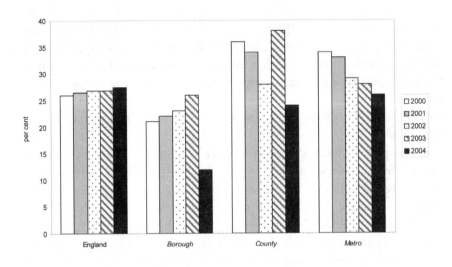

Source: DfES 2004b, 2005; DoH 2001, 2002, 2003.

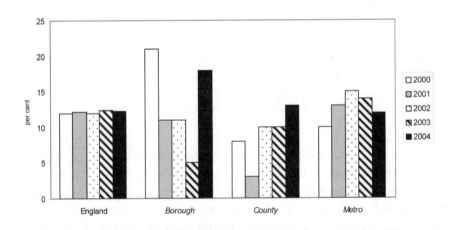

Source: DfES 2004b, 2005; DoH 2001, 2002, 2003.

Figure 2.2 Percentage of school-age pupils looked after for more than a year missing 25 days of schooling in the previous 12 months, 2000–2004

Permanent exclusion

Official statistics record that the percentage of school-age pupils, looked after for more than a year, who are permanently excluded from school declined from 1.5 per cent in 2000 to 0.9 per cent in 2004 (0.8 per cent in 2006 (DCSF 2007b)); this was still about nine times the rate for all English pupils (DfES 2004b). Because these statistics are small (in absolute if not relative terms) it is difficult to maintain anonymity. Indeed, the Department for Children, Schools and Families (DCSF) statistics withhold these figures for some councils for confidentiality reasons. However, in 15 sets of figures for our study authorities (three authorities, each with five years' data), at only three points were there any permanent exclusions of looked after pupils at all, and in the other 12 there were no permanent exclusions. Though there are complex definitional issues in exclusion from school, and looked after pupils have been prevented or deterred from attending school in other ways (Brodie 2001), nonetheless, this suggests an important accomplishment.

Key Stage 4 achievement

As our main interest is in adolescents, we concentrate especially on Key Stage 4 achievements (typically Year 11, 16 year olds). Indeed, the low educational achievement of looked after pupils generates much current debate and it is usually GCSE results that are closely scrutinised. But, once again, we need to be heedful owing to the low numbers in the three study authorities. In *Metro*, the total number of Key Stage 4 pupils who were looked after for more than a year between 2000 and 2004 was 20–30. This figure was higher in *County* and *Borough*, but still only between 45 and 80 looked after pupils. National aggregates tend to even things out but comparisons over time and between authorities may be unreliable and, therefore, unwise. This point is seldom made at a national level, yet the GCSE results (Figure 2.3) of looked after children have constituted a performance indicator which feeds into authorities' 'Star Ratings'. These ratings determine the degree of autonomy councils are allowed in using central government funding, as well as levels of inspection and monitoring, and requirements for planning information.

There is some overlap with the national statistics presented in Chapter 1, although the timescales are different. These figures show some gradual improvement overall, with the proportion of pupils achieving at least one GCSE rising from 49 to 56 per cent. This is steady progress but slower than the government intended. The position in the three authorities also shows some general improvement but progress was erratic. Nonetheless, each of the three was in a notably better position in 2004 than in 2000 and, in the final year, was also performing better on this indicator than the national average.

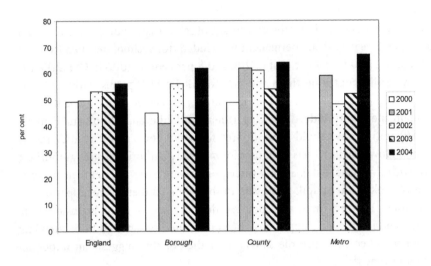

Source: DfES 2004b, 2005; DoH 2001, 2002, 2003.

Figure 2.3 Percentage of Key Stage 4 pupils looked after for more than a year obtaining at least one GCSE or GNVQ, 2000–2004

Many would question whether one GCSE pass is an adequate expectation, and most pupils are expected to achieve at least five. We next looked at five GCSE passes at grades A*–G (Figure 2.4).

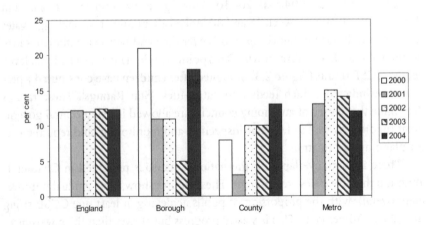

Source: DfES 2004b, 2005; DoH 2001, 2002, 2003.

Figure 2.4 Percentage of Key Stage 4 pupils looked after for more than a year obtaining at least five GCSEs grades A*–G, 2000–2004

These figures, again, show steady national improvement, but the picture in the three authorities is more mixed. Achievements were lower in *Borough* than in England as a whole, although its looked after children compared favourably with young people in care in inner London generally. Furthermore, GCSE passes for all *Borough* pupils (living with their families) tended to be lower than throughout inner London. So, from this relative perspective, *Borough*'s looked after children are not necessarily low achievers taking into account where they live. The situation was changeable year by year in *County* and *Metro*, too, but we should be reminded that, for example, for most years in *Metro*, the differences overall would be accounted for by the achievements of only *two* pupils, which in aggregate terms seems hardly worth mentioning.

Similar conclusions emerge if we consider five GCSE passes at grades A*–C (which many of us still recall as the equivalent of five 'O levels'). The national average for looked after pupils increased from just over 7 per cent to just above 9 per cent (about 12% at the time of writing). Compared with this, *County* had some relatively good years, rising to about 15 per cent. *Borough* nearly matched this for one year as well. However, most annual figures were very small and the official statistics withheld these for reasons of confidentiality.

Overall, therefore, as with our other research (Harker *et al.* 2004), we would urge strong caution in the interpretation of these statistics – something that is generally lacking. Official statistics may not reveal the full or even an accurate picture (Cicourel 1994), which is why the chapters which follow examine in detail the care and educational experiences and outcomes of a sample of looked after young people. However, over the five years studied, there was some gradual, national improvement in the educational experiences of looked after pupils. Permanent exclusions from school declined and, for most years, the three authorities studied had *none* whatsoever. Similarly, there had been a steady rise overall in GCSE achievements at Key Stage 4: patterns fluctuated in our study authorities but each ended the five-year period in a stronger position than when it began. Yet the problem of missed schooling seems to have been more entrenched and no real progress was indicated. Despite some general optimism, progress has generally been slower than the government anticipated.

National development of Quality Protects

Quality Protects was an important government initiative to modernise children's social services. It had specific objectives relating to educational experiences and here we consider its local implementation in some detail. We have seen that the government launched *Quality Protects* in 1998, with the announcement initially of £375 million of extra resources. It was described as a partnership between central and local government and, in order to receive the grant, authorities were required to submit for approval annual *Quality Protects* management action plans (MAPs). For the first three years, the local MAPs were analysed in detail by the Department of Health (DoH) and overview reports were produced (Robbins 1999, 2000, 2001). These MAPs were written to specific requirements and could be lengthy, repetitive documents (one that we examined ran to over 300 pages). Their overall analysis was an unenviable task.

There is space here to summarise only some of the main conclusions from the overviews as our main interest lies in the three authorities. In the first-year MAPs (Robbins 2000) authorities were required to provide baseline data to establish their starting point. Authorities often found this difficult, for example concerning the numbers of children in need and their ethnicity. Local *Quality Protects* responses to improving the education of looked after children were reported to have varied, and authorities often depended on isolated projects which were said to have lacked a strategic framework. Overall, both inspectors and authorities concluded that much effort was required. Some financial information was included in the appendix to the first-year report detailing how the *Quality Protects* grant was allocated. Services to enhance the life chances of looked after young people (reducing offending as well as promoting health and education) were combined with care-leaving, and the latter became a priority for grant expenditure. Of the total of £66 million allocated for the first year, almost half went to expanding placement choice – adoptive and foster families and residential placements. 'Care-leaving' received almost £9.5 million, and little went directly to promoting education, although general investment in infrastructure and areas such as management information, assessment and strengthening children's participation would have an indirect effect.

By the second year (Robbins 2000), authorities were reported to have a better grasp of local statistical information and to be more strategic in their approach. More joint working was evident, including education and social services departments, leading to some cases of data-sharing as well as joint research, development and planning. It was felt that educational considerations were becoming better integrated into overall services and care planning. Unfortunately, the first year of *Quality Protects* coincided with a dip in the GCSE achievements of looked after children, but these recovered strongly the following year, confirming the unpredictability of this indicator. Improving children's life chances – health, education, leisure and reducing offending – became a priority area for the *Quality Protects* grant in the second year, with planned expenditure of £8.3 million, 7 per cent of the total.

The third national overview report (Robbins 2001) concluded that services generally were improving for looked after children and therefore that 'Quality

Protects is working'. Education outcome indicators were moving in the right direction. Inter-agency working was reported to have strengthened. However, the report highlighted that the situation of children being placed out of area was often being overlooked. The education of children in need generally was included in the report, and this was said to have been a new area for most authorities to consider. Education and social services departments' partnerships were growing. Special projects were being developed, both to provide individual educational support and to monitor progress. Specific initiatives included using more educational psychologists for assessment or advice, as well as joint training between teachers, social workers and carers. In line with government guidance, designated teachers and personal education plans (PEPs) were being established (DfEE/DoH 2000).

In relation to *Quality Protects* educational objectives it was concluded that: 'The picture emerging from MAPs this year is of committed, energetic and focused activity, which is in many areas bearing fruit' (Robbins 2001, p.43). For the following year, the authorities proposed to spend some £15 million on improving the life chances of looked after children, 11 per cent of the total budget. Placement choice was again to receive the largest share: £54 million (35%), with £13 million of this earmarked for adoption. For the three years, 'life chances of looked after children' was generally ranked fourth out of the six priority areas, in terms of funding, with 'assessment' and 'management information and quality assurance', together with 'placement choice' usually receiving significantly more. (There was also an underspend of about 10% of the planned second year's expenditure.)

The general impression to emerge from these national overview MAPs is largely of advances in services for looked after children. Improved partnerships were perceived between education and social services departments, as well as better use of information and monitoring of progress. Educational performance indicators steadily improved but more slowly than central and local government had anticipated. This general picture from the overview reports is consistent with one of our authors' other evaluations of the education of looked after children (Harker *et al.* 2004).

The low educational achievement of children in public care has assumed a high political profile. But it is interesting to note that it was not made a higher specific financial priority within the *Quality Protects* initiative. It seems that little funding was allocated in the first year specifically for the education of looked after children, and if the grant had been allocated evenly across services and authorities, given the breadth of the *Quality Protects* initiative, it would have generated, on average for each council, about £14,000 in Year 2 and £25,000 in Year 3. Though no doubt welcome, this is barely sufficient to fund one post. Of course, change does not necessarily require targeted funding and *Quality Protects* was said to be concerned with bringing about *cultural change* in local government as well as specific initiatives. Moreover, as we shall see, the *Quality Protects* initiative was not the only source of funding in working with low educational achievers and vulnerable youngsters. However, when evaluating the impact of *Quality Protects* on education services, this funding distribution should be borne in mind.

Policy and practice development in the study authorities
County
Because of (or possibly despite) their size and level of detail, the local *Quality Protects* MAPs were potentially a rich source of information. Yet, with one exception, it proved very difficult to track down copies of our three authorities' MAPs. Admittedly our research began some four years after the first one would have been written, but not too long after the third. Nor were they obtainable from central government. We show in the methodological appendix how there had been considerable turnover of managers in the three authorities in the period leading up to our work, which exacerbated access problems. But the complications in obtaining the MAPs suggested, certainly by the time the research took place, that they were not the strategic working documents that they may once have been. That said, we were able to obtain other documentation related to strategic planning and policy development for looked after children.

County's documents demonstrated a strong degree of inter-professional commitment to formulating the MAPs (and previous children's services plans), including education, social services departments and health authorities. MAPs were constructed in association with Early Years Development and Child Care Plan, the Education Development Plan and Behaviour Support Plan and the Health Improvement Programme. There was also a parallel review of the child and adolescent mental health service (CAMHS) and joint assessment projects for disabled children. Clearly, there was much overlap. Other policy influences at the time included implementation of the national fostering standards, guidance on the education of looked after children, care leavers' legislation and development of a local advocacy service for looked after children. Additional multi-agency teams included, for example, community safety partnerships as well as a drugs action team. There was formal recognition of voluntary sector representation and a number of block agreements with independent sector child care providers, for example the NSPCC as well as with services for homeless people. There were considerations for combining, rather ahead of time, the education and social services departments into a single entity.

Concerning education in particular, the *County* MAP described a multi-agency panel that considered individual cases referred for specialist out-of-county provision: this panel made decisions about joint funding and both explored and initiated alternatives, for example local provision for pupils with behavioural, emotional and social difficulties (BESD) and learning disabled children who presented challenging behaviours. 'Children Out of School' groups met in local areas, and comprised education, social services and youth service representatives.

The *County* MAP stated that these wider, inter-professional initiatives would help to address *Quality Protects* educational objectives by: identifying and supporting pupils at risk of disaffection with or exclusion from school; by promoting learning opportunities out of school hours; by improving inter-professional working in the assessment and provision of services for pupils with SEN; by ensuring that carers valued the importance of education, as well as regularly attending and communicating with schools; maintaining a database on the whereabouts and educational attainments of looked after children; and ensuring that looked after pupils were provided urgently with alternative schooling as required. *County Quality Protects* efforts concerning placement choice were also expected to benefit children's education.

County already had in existence a group of five, dedicated, specialist, advisory teachers – funded by the social services department – who would provide individual educational support to looked after pupils without a school place (the educational support team). A joint protocol had also been agreed with the education department. In terms of future aspirations, *County* intended to extend this collaboration and establish a corporate parenting officer to lead this strategy. Attention would focus, too, on pupils in transition and on developing positive partnerships with schools. Work would continue on developing a joint education/social services database: *County* had been unable to provide baseline information for 1998 on the GCSE achievements of looked after pupils, but its 1999 figure had been 10 per cent better than planned. (Previously submitted data on other key stages had subsequently been found to be unreliable.) *County's* own analysis of its statistics at this early stage revealed that two-thirds of its looked after pupils had Statements of Special Educational Needs (SEN), three in every four of which were for BESD. Those placed out of county had the lowest educational achievements, and work was proposed to ensure that academic attainment was not overlooked alongside broader therapeutic goals.

In reviewing its *Quality Protects* plans, *County's* social services and education departments jointly funded an educational psychologist post to work specifically with pupils at Key Stages 3 and 4 as well as to provide specialist support to advisory teachers, foster and residential carers. The five advisory teachers would refocus their work on younger looked after pupils to maximise their accomplishments. It was reported that much progress had been made at senior and middle management levels but this now needed to be transferred to front-line practitioners. There were over 500 schools in *County* and increased contacts with head teachers' associations had been established. Concerning funding, £40,000 was to be allocated from the Standards Fund to support the advisory teacher service, and £15,000 for inter-professional training. Some £50,000 was to be used from the Learning Gateway Partnership to support care leavers and children in need to access further education and training. Interestingly, resources from the *Quality Protects* initiative grant were not requested specifically for these educational initiatives owing to existing council investment and alternative sources of funding. In contrast, over £500,000 was earmarked for increasing the range of adoptive, foster and residential placements for children.

The final-year MAP (2001–2002) reaffirmed the problems in achieving the GCSE targets and the high number of looked after pupils with SEN. The education support team continued and the Corporate Parenting Officer had been appointed. Permanent exclusions and schooling absence had been reduced. An authority policy on the education of looked after pupils had been formulated, most PEPs had been completed and designated teachers had been identified, most of whom had received specialist training. Young people had participated in a number of these initiatives.

Subsequent plans included sustaining progress on preventing exclusion and missed schooling, including transition projects for pupils in Years 6 and 7, and professional intervention to combat disruption and disaffection. In addition, there would be a termly newsletter for looked after pupils; implementation of education policies for children's homes; PEPs would be in place for all pupils, including those placed out-of-county; all staff would receive training and a dedicated website would be set up; a children's version of the joint guidance (DfEE/DoH 2000) would be produced; and focus groups of designated teachers, social workers, carers and young people would be organised to provide feedback on progress. Further specific initiatives included: introducing motivational schemes to encourage sixth-form study and celebration of achievement award ceremonies (subsequently to be extended to sport and leisure pursuits); foster carer and residential staff home-reading schemes; provision of computers in foster and residential homes; and education-focused summer schools for care leavers and school-aged pupils. In 2001–2002, only £25,000 of *Quality Protects* grant was earmarked across health, education, offending and leisure, in contrast to some £750,000 for services for disabled children and the same for placement choice.

Metro

It was much more difficult to obtain the *Quality Protects* MAPs in *Metro* than in *County* and, in fact, managers were able to locate only one, for 2002. However, there were other reports relating to developments with the looked after population, especially their education. As elsewhere, there was a tendency for managers to perceive the *Quality Protects* MAPs as historical documents that were produced mainly for government in order that they received the special grant, and which had since been replaced by up to date, more useful, strategic plans. It was recorded that in 2001–2002 *Metro* had budgeted only £20,000 of *Quality Protects* grant for the whole 'improving the life chances of looked after children' (including education) category. Placement choice was the largest area – £200,000. The 'life chances' bid was planned to double for the following year. Funding was accessed from a range of other sources, including the Standards Fund, Social Inclusion Grant, Vulnerable Children Grant, Choice Protects and European Social Funding.

As in *County*, *Metro* had established an education support team and this took the lead in promoting the education of looked after children. Its annual reports gave useful insight into how it approached the *Quality Protects* objectives as well as background information. Nearly two in every five *Metro* looked after children were placed and being educated outside the town, reducing its direct influence over their educational experience and progress. For example, authorities and schools elsewhere did not always give sufficient priority to PEPs and educational planning. Some independent residential providers were said to be reluctant to complete PEPs, insisting that they accepted referrals from several authorities and the plans adopted different formats. It was *Metro* policy to reduce the number of children placed elsewhere. One in three children were living either at home on care orders or being fostered with a relative; though possibly desirable in terms of their overall welfare and reunification (Farmer and Moyers 2008), this posed educational problems if parents or carers did not encourage school attendance and attainment.

Two-thirds of *Metro*'s looked after pupils were at various stages of the SEN code of practice. Half of those had Statements that were attributed to BESD and three-quarters of Statements were for boys. Accessing special educational support for pupils educated out of the *Metro* authority was often a problem, in particular for those in the process of SEN assessment; authorities might be reluctant to continue the assessment without reassurance about how long the placement would last. Nearly half of Key Stage 4 pupils were being educated outside mainstream schools in day or residential special schools, pupil referral units (PRUs) or specific educational projects. Seven pupils with SENs had significant learning disabilities, preventing them from taking exams. It was also stated that few residential special schools entered pupils for SATs or GCSE exams and there were concerns over the extent to which they followed the national curriculum. Year 11 pupils were particularly vulnerable to placement instability, potentially jeopardising their schooling and learning. It was also reported that the prospect of independent living could heighten anxiety in the lead-up to exams.

The *Metro* education support team was housed alongside referral and assessment social work teams, facilitating contact. Its staffing complement comprised a head of service, one part-time and four full-time teachers, three part-time education support workers and two part-time administrative posts. The team undertook a range of activities, including direct work with looked after pupils in school, indirect work – accessing provision, supporting and advising teachers and so on, and monitoring the educational progress of every looked after pupil, study support in care placements and database management for the authority. Importantly, the service's work embraced *Metro* children placed out of the town, as well as children from other authorities placed there. For historical, geographical and housing stock reasons, *Metro* is a popular location for independent fostering and residential care providers.

All the schools and social workers in *Metro* were offered multi-agency training on raising the educational achievements of children in public care. Every new teacher and social worker was offered an individual session with a teacher from the service as part of their induction. Apart from general oversight, more than half of the looked after pupils received a specific service from the team. About 30 children a year living in foster care experienced weekly home visits from support teachers. The team aimed to produce a same-day response to looked after young people who were excluded from school or waiting for a place to be allocated. Residential units mainly used this service. Although it was a school responsibility, the team also drew up temporary home study timetables for pupils out of school and produced a range of study packs as an interim, emergency measure. Workers contributed to attempts to prevent placement disruption but, when unavoidable, would seek to keep schooling unaffected.

The *Metro* education support team offered a carers' resource centre, where social workers, foster and residential carers and young people could borrow learning resources or obtain advice. In the weeks preceding GCSEs, the resource centre offered support to Year 11 pupils and their carers where help was needed with exams. This included advice on completing coursework, revision strategies, exam skills and dealing with 'exam stress'. Feedback from young people was said to be positive. Young people were provided with access to computers in their care placements, and the support team offered hardware and software advice and back-up. Targeted training was provided for *Metro* foster carers and workers in the borough's residential units. An annual 'celebration event' was held at the local football club and 70 young people received awards, presented by a *Coronation Street* celebrity, to recognise their hard work, participation and achievement in educationally related activities. Members of the team represented the department on a range of inter-professional groups.

Future plans included extending an incentive scheme (cash reward or vouchers), for Year 11 pupils in their final two terms who were at risk of becoming disengaged with school. This was felt to be very successful, with 27 of the 30 pupils completing the year: there had previously been a 50 per cent drop-out rate. GCSE results had improved. The incentive scheme was due to be extended to Year 10 pupils. Links with Connexions would extend alternative cur- riculum and vocational incentives (college, modern apprenticeships, Prince's Trust projects and so forth). In addition, more attention would focus on providing educational support for pre-school, looked after children.

Borough

Our efforts eventually yielded two MAPs in the *Borough* authority. The initial *Quality Protects* plan requested by the Department of Health (1999–2000) was produced by a multi-agency group comprising social services, education and health departments and the voluntary sector. The context was one in which the number of children living in *Borough* was steadily growing. Two in every five children lived in lone-parent households and three-quarters of them were in rented accommodation, much higher than the inner London norm. Over half of all children in *Borough* schools received free school meals, high for inner London, and much above the national average. The most recent statistics showed a quarter of *Borough* pupils gaining five GCSEs at grades A*–C – comparable with the overall inner London figure but significantly less than the national figure of 45 per cent. We would, therefore, expect there to be a strong inner London dimen- sion to the education of *Borough*'s looked after pupils.

Borough was seeking to reduce the overall number of looked after children and to strengthen family support services. It also intended to increase its pool of foster carers. Very significantly, some three-quarters of looked after pupils were placed outside of the *Borough* authority and therefore not attending local schools. A third of those eligible had achieved at least one GCSE pass. Placement instabil- ity was lower than the national average. Educational issues for looked after children were not a high priority in this initial MAP so baseline information was limited.

The third MAP described a substantial increase in the looked after popula- tion, partially accounted for by asylum-seeking children, who constituted 15 per cent of the total. Data collection had improved. Recruitment of foster carers and adopters had grown. None of *Borough's* looked after children had been excluded permanently from school. Funding had been used from *Quality Protects* and the Standards Fund to provide a project worker, a teacher and a part-time educational psychologist to help implement the joint guidance (DfEE/DoH 2000). Their initial steps had been to arrange a conference on corporate parenting, to draft a joint protocol for education and social services departments, to develop study units in the residential centres, establish designated teachers, create the system for PEPs and begin training for carers and newly appointed teachers as well as provide individual support, initially to young people in residential care and asylum-seekers.

Future plans included appointing a further project worker and developing a more strategic and targeted approach towards pupil support. This would include homework support and monitoring, access to Saturday schools, use of summer educational schemes, completion of PEPs, classroom and tutorial support and so on. It was proposed to spend £200,000 of the *Quality Protects* grant in 2001–2002 for looked after children across health care, CAMHS, teenage pregnancy, leisure, offending and education.

Interviews with managers

Semi-structured interviews were held with managers in the three authorities in early 2005, about half-way through the research. Contact had been established with several of them at the outset, as part of negotiating access. However, we wished to defer interviews until we had a grasp of some of the local structures and issues, and could make our questions more focused. These managers were busy people, yet they were generous with their time, informative and frank with their comments. We aimed to interview those lead managers from social services and education in the authorities, who would be best-placed to inform us about local development of policy and practice concerning the education of looked after children and the main outstanding challenges. Interestingly, it eventually transpired that we interviewed mainly service managers for children and families and heads of the education support teams. These were interviewed jointly; they were given the option of individual interviews but none said they would feel inhibited in what they said. In the *Metro* authority, the opportunity also arose during the visit to interview a social work team leader and education officer responsible for SEN. Hence, there were eight management interviews in total.

We were careful to emphasise ethical considerations, especially anonymity; the specific points and quotations that follow, therefore, are not attributable. It was possible to tape-record most interviews, and selective transcription occurred; otherwise handwritten notes were taken and subsequently written up. These management interviews were mainly to provide the context and to help interpret our other findings, and the main issues to emerge are described below.

Quality Protects

Managers were asked about their general perceptions of the *Quality Protects* education objectives and whether or not they thought *Quality Protects* was a positive development. Responses were overwhelmingly positive. One manager observed:

> (*Interviewer:* 'Has *Quality Protects* had a positive influence?') Oh absolutely! I think it's focused attention on the big gap between what all children achieve and what children with the local authority as a corporate parent were experiencing. There's a much greater acknowledgement of where they could do better.

Another interviewee made a similar point:

> It really forced social services to look more systematically at the needs of children... I think it was certainly needed... If they were in stable placements you concentrated on the caring.

The interviewee added that *Quality Protects* helped to promote inter-professional working.

An education manager described *Quality Protects* as 'a catalyst for bigger things'. Another education colleague made the important point that *Quality Protects* was complementary to education initiatives at the time, in particular the Standards Fund, the focus of which included school improvement, social inclusion and the development of learning support units. The same schools, teachers and pupils were often involved in both. Indeed, the positive assessment of *Quality Protects* was not particularly because of any additional funding that the initiative delivered: the education support teams in the authorities had been initiated prior to *Quality Protects* and were funded by social services. But *Quality Protects* did allow the teams to consolidate and to establish partnerships with education.

Managers had mixed views about the targets and performance indicators associated with *Quality Protects* and other recent policy developments. One common view was:

> I think the targets are very challenging and there's a problem for us with the year-on-year progression. But in terms of their aspirational quality, I think they're very healthy.

The drawbacks included:

> The objectives can bring about some game-playing. It can leave some casualties. It can dominate sometimes. They don't measure the softer data and other areas of success. It creates various statistical anomalies.

And elsewhere:

> Targets take you down a narrow path. The closer the link with how you are to be judged as an LA [local authority], the more focus you end up giving it. So I have lots of reservations. But being able to look at the crude reality does motivate. It's better to have a target than not.

One manager felt that a common approach was, first, to set out to achieve your target, which then freed you up to pursue the policies that you felt were the most suitable. Another admitted to frequent 'panic attacks' when looking at her current low achievement in Key Stage 3, which would soon filter through to the authority's very public GCSE results. Another anomaly existed in one authority, which had identified a group of 15 young people suitable for special guardianship. These were mainly living in long-term stable placements and were high educational achievers. If this change of status occurred, the youngsters would be lost for the next year's looked after pupils' educational results. If it was felt to be in the young people's best interests, special guardianship would certainly proceed but this would have important consequences for the authority. It was agreed in each of the three authorities that data collection and management information systems had generally improved, linked to *Quality Protects*. However, one manager considered that that their quality of information was now so good that they might be adversely affected on the performance indicators because they were able to offer a too authoritative and, therefore, too honest an opinion.

Practitioners' response

So, overall, there was now much more management commitment to promoting the education of looked after children and inter-agency working at a senior level. But we wanted to know if this commitment also applied to practitioners. The picture here was more patchy: we were informed that there were clear improvements in some teams, where there was also strong leadership and stability. But, elsewhere, it was felt that progress was probably due more to management scrutiny of social workers, for example when completing PEPs or identifying and targeting young people who were probably low achievers. But, social work practice in this regard was gradually changing, too:

> It's not as integrated into social workers' thinking as I would like it to be, that is a disappointment. It's going to be a continual 'drip-feed' process.

Two additional points were of interest. The first was that two of our authorities had problems with social work vacancies and had recruited social workers from overseas – who were not always familiar with the English education system. A second point was that one pair of managers who were interviewed argued that qualifying courses in social work should give young people's educational problems a higher priority, so that when new recruits joined they would already be familiar with the issues.

The perspective from managers was that schools are also generally now making more progress with looked after pupils. This was mainly attributed to progress with the designated teacher role. One manager was particularly upbeat:

> The designated teacher, that's working now, isn't it? We had 50 new designated teachers trained last week and they were very positive... I think schools have shifted over time. We have more problems in accessing SEN.

The manager pinpointed changes in the Ofsted regime, as school inspectors were now enquiring more about looked after children. School improvement partnerships had also helped.

Managers in another authority were slightly less positive but reported that initial resistance to the designated teacher role had now decreased. There was the problem of the designated teacher having adequate time: one local school had 20 looked after pupils. The designated teacher in primary schools was often the head teacher. There was still said to be a large cultural difference between schools and social services. The main issue was deterring schools from permanent exclusion of pupils. In the third authority, the main schooling issues were felt to concern the adequacy of information and planning ('Two years ago they would have said telephone the child if you want to know something!'). Broader educational issues were thought to affect looked after pupils in particular, such as the transition from Year 6 to Year 7 and the problems affecting pupils who changed schools mid-way through the school year. When asked directly how many schools he felt were genuinely cooperative, one social work manager responded 'About 50–50.'

Education support teams

We have seen that each of our three authorities had developed specialist educational support services for looked after pupils. These had preceded the government's *Quality Protects* initiative and were mainly funded from other sources. The number of such teams nationally is not known, although it appears that most local authorities have them (Harker *et al.* 2004). It would be useful for research to confirm the national picture, including the teams' structure, organisation and priorities. The management interviews gave useful insight into how education support teams functioned in our three authorities.

Teams concentrated on looked after pupils, although one team also included children who were not looked after with BESD. We discuss 'out-of-borough' issues below but teams generally supported children living elsewhere, too, although the extent of direct work offered tended to be limited. Ironically, those who probably need the most support were least likely to receive it. Interviewees were very complimentary about the contribution of these education support services; however, one interviewee pointed out the danger that other staff might not assume responsibility for a problem if too strong a specialist team existed. The education support teams were usually multi-disciplinary and could be quite substantial. One comprised 25 staff. Another consisted of nine staff with five other associates: these included teachers, education welfare officers, Connexions advisers, educational psychologists, an unaccompanied refugee worker and a play or youth worker.

Although no doubt useful, there are interesting questions about the balance of funding and resources, given the relatively limited number of looked after pupils in local populations, especially if teams focus disproportionately on Key Stage 4. A national problem concerning the link between the low academic achievement of looked after pupils and social exclusion may have different local manifestations. Schools have sometimes pointed out that the educational problems of children in care are not necessarily dissimilar from those of many of their peers and, therefore, they can be reluctant to give them special attention (Berridge et al. 1997). Teachers have also been alerted by past research to the dangers of labelling categories of pupils (Hargreaves 1967; Lacey 1970).

Education support teams prioritised a range of activities. There was often a strong corporate training function; for example, with social workers, teachers and carers to highlight the importance of looked after pupils' schooling, the requirements of PEPs and the responsibilities of designated teachers. They established links with social work teams and other professionals. The teams also played an important role in providing management information. One team gathered predicted grades and considered likely outcomes for SATs and GCSEs, as well as linking with the care leavers' service to facilitate post-16 education and training. The '25 days rule' was another priority (the target for the maximum amount of missed schooling in a year). One team used a national call centre to telephone schools around the country each day to check that the looked after pupils had arrived. If not, they immediately contacted the placement to discover the reason. If explanations were unsatisfactory, the education support team would be alerted by the call centre.

Interestingly, the teams could organise individual tutoring and intensive coaching for pupils. One manager explained that this was similar to what many middle class parents would provide. She said they could get looked after pupils through GCSE maths with 10–12 weeks of intensive coaching ('We had some tearful, joyous scenes last year from young people who had been so angry, but they managed to get their one or two...'). A different authority used a private college to help pupils obtain a GCSE pass in information and communication technology (ICT). It achieved very successful results within nine months: 'It was mainly about these young people being on a level playing field with others and the way they were being taught. Their work was extremely good.'

Other issues

We do not have the space here to discuss in detail further content of management interviews or points about the operation of education support teams. However, some additional themes struck us as interesting and to have important implications. The two main ones are listed below, and concern children living at home or fostered with relatives and those living out of borough. The two groups could be connected.

There was consensus that some of the major outstanding problems with the education of looked after children affect groups over which councils have rather less control, for example those placed at home while on care orders or being fostered with relatives. Councils had promoted fostering with relatives in recent years, as this had been felt to be an unexploited resource; it was a way of increasing the number of family placements – another performance indicator – and outcomes were generally felt to be positive. Recent research suggests that the results may be more mixed (Farmer and Moyers 2008). One manager cogently observed:

A lot of children in kinship placements are falling foul of the 25-day indicator. We've really promoted the kinship agenda… The parenting in that family may be good enough but that may not be what we're aiming for.

Interestingly, half of children in this authority lived with relatives outside the area.

Managers raised other issues concerning pupils who were placed out of borough. This applied, for example, to 70 per cent of *Borough* children. This group has been indicated recently by the government as being at particular risk of low educational attainment. As we have seen, these young people could be limited in their access to help from education support teams. One interviewee remarked that young people living out of area would often be placed in residential units run by independent sector organisations, which were frequently children's homes with education. The authority may not actually have wanted the educational component but would have to pay for it nevertheless if it wanted to use the placement. The quality of education was felt to vary and may not actually help the young person.

Another issue was that residential schools for children with BESD often did not follow the national curriculum or enter pupils for SATs and GCSEs. (We return to this topic later.) This could disadvantage young people who may have been eligible for these exams if they had continued to live locally, particularly if they experienced the intensive coaching programmes described above. We were informed that one authority now aimed for pupils to leave BESD schools at Year 9, at the SEN transition review. Whatever other advantages, doing this introduced considerable problems of transition in the run up to GCSEs. It also did not coincide with the transfer of responsibilities to leaving care teams, which occurred at age 16 years. Indeed, one manager stressed that young people in the midst of preparation for GCSEs might be faced with the prospect of, or actual, change of social worker as well as moving to independent accommodation. This could generate enormous anxiety at the worst time for the young person's education. The subsequent chapters return to several of these points for our sample of young people.

An interesting development was the emergence of regional consortia, which collaborated on certain care and educational arrangements, including out-of-borough issues. Two of our authorities were especially affected. Education support teams might offer certain services to resident children from other authorities, which would be reciprocated. This would not overcome all the problems but could prove valuable. It would be useful to know more about the extent and nature of these common arrangements.

Summary points

- The research was located in three contrasting local authority social services and education departments, which we termed *County*, *Metro* and *Borough*.

- We need to be cautious about the analysis of official statistics – over time and between authorities – on the education of looked after children. This is needed because, for example, populations differ and groups may be small. With this in mind, over the five years studied (2000–2004), indicators in the three authorities fluctuated on two measures: the proportion of pupils who were looked after for more than a year, with a Statement of Special Educational Needs, and those missing more than 25 days of schooling.

- On most occasions, for the three authorities over the five years, there were *no* permanent school exclusions recorded for looked after pupils, an encouraging achievement.

- As this study focuses specifically on adolescents, there was some general improvement nationally as well as in the three authorities on the proportions of pupils who were looked after for more than a year who achieved at least one GCSE or GNVQ. However, progress was not as rapid as the government intended. National rates also improved slightly for higher levels of GCSE achievement, but the position in the authorities studied was more mixed.

- Analysis of all local authorities' responses to government educational objectives for looked after pupils showed that, in the early stages, efforts varied considerably and were largely unco-ordinated. Generally speaking, over the duration of the initiative, authorities received relatively little *Quality Protects* grant income specifically related to their education objectives.

- Detailed analysis of local documentation for the *County*, *Metro* and *Borough* authorities demonstrated a noticeable increase in inter-professional working, and each had established forms of education support teams for looked after pupils.

- Interviews with eight managers in the three authorities who had lead responsibility in this area revealed that they were overwhelmingly positive about the influence of the *Quality Protects* initiative on improving children's education.

Chapter 3

Young People's Background Experiences

We begin our presentation of the findings from this part of the study by looking at the background experiences of the 150 young people included in the sample. We are primarily interested, at this point, to explore the similarities and differences of experience according to the route by which young people became part of the sample – we mean whether the young person was referred by *County, Metro* or *Borough* (the local authority groups studied) or by one of the eight residential schools for children with behavioural, educational or social difficulties (BESD).

A variety of factors are associated with difficulties in growing up and we were interested to find out the extent to which these factors varied across the main sub-groups in our sample. Much is known about the background of young people who enter the care system (Sinclair *et al.* 2006; Ward, Munro and Dearden 2006) but there has been far less exploration of those living and educated in the residential BESD sector (Grimshaw with Berridge 1994). We therefore asked informants in the initial, background interviews to tell us about the young people's birth families and their upbringing. We sought information on the presence of parents in young people's lives as well as family histories, legal arrangements, reasons for being away from home and any previous experience of separation or boarding education. We also explored distance from home and levels of contact with families.

Our informants for these interviews were social workers for the local authority groups and key workers or unit managers for the residential BESD schools group. We found social workers much more able to respond to our questions about birth families and early experiences than were staff in residential schools. As a result there were a number of areas in which information was missing for the schools group.

Characteristics of the selected sample

Our sample of 150 young people comprised similar numbers of boys and girls whose ages were reasonably spread across the desired range (11 to 15 years of age). The majority of young people were White British. As may be seen from Table 3.1 young people of a minority ethnic background were disproportionately represented across our sources of referral when the 'mixed ethnicity' and 'any other ethnic background' groups are combined. The inner London *Borough* group was ethnically more diverse.

Table 3.1 Sample characteristics

	County (n= 42)	Metro (n = 35)	Borough (n = 32)	Schools (n = 41)
Gender (%)				
Boys	64	51	53	75
Girls	36	49	47	25
Age groups (%)				
11.5–<14 years	40	29	25	42
14–<15.5 years	60	71	75	58
Ethnicity (%)				
White British	71	94	66	80
Mixed ethnicity	19	6	28	10
Any other background	10	0	6	10

Birth parents

We began by examining the presence of parent figures in young people's lives. There were relatively few young people whose birth parents were still living together and, as might be expected, many had not lived with either parent for some time. Because of this we coded whether birth parents were still involved with their children. We found that, overall, for those for whom this data was available (90% of the whole sample) both parents were involved in young people's lives in only one-third of cases (31%). Two-fifths (43%) came from lone-parent families. A further 18 per cent were living in a stepfamily, usually containing a stepfather. In seven cases young people were reported to have no living birth parents – each of these young people was looked after. Collapsing this information to produce a three-category 'family type' variable ('both parents present', 'one parent and one long-term step parent' and 'lone parent') we found no significant differences between the local authority and the residential BESD schools groups (Table 3.2). Neither were there any differences with family structure in relation to young people's care status, age, gender or their type of placement.

Table 3.2 Family structure of young people, according to source of referral

	Local authority group (%) (n = 100)	Residential schools group (%) (n = 36)	All (%) (n = 136)
Lone mother	41	36	40
Lone father	2	5	3
Both birth parents	29	36	31
Mother and stepfather	15	16	15
Father and stepmother	4	0	3
No birth parents	7	0	5

Risks to psychosocial development from young people's experiences with their birth families

We explored the early parenting histories of our sample in two ways: the first was to look at the number of known risk factors to which young people had been exposed, and the second was to explore the reasons for their being away from home.

The risk factors that we included in our background interviews were a family history of substance misuse, mental health problems, criminality or domestic violence. We also asked whether parents were known to have learning difficulties. These are factors identified by previous research to be associated with increased risk of entry to care and would be likely to have implications for young people's psychosocial development (Cleaver, Unell and Aldgate 1999; Reder and Lucey 1995).

This information was based on respondents' professional judgements and we did not seek out independent corroboration, for example, of criminal convictions or clinical assessments. Therefore, it should not be taken as definitive. The exposure to risk was usually, but not always, a result of the difficulties of a biological parent who was also a social parent to the child. However, there were occasions of step parents or siblings with major problems; these were recorded when the presence of this individual was felt to be significant to the development of the young person concerned.

Once again, our primary interest in collecting this data was to learn whether such problems were more frequent within our local authority sample than in those recruited through schools. Later, we explore whether such experiences were associated with differential care or education trajectories or outcomes for young people.

Figure 3.1 illustrates the extent of each of these risks among the young people in the two referral groups. While all types of adversity are represented in both groups, each tends to be more common among the local authority group. These adolescents looked after by councils had experienced very high levels of adversities: over two-thirds had parent(s) who had misused alcohol or drugs, and a similar proportion had witnessed the trauma of domestic violence (Hester and Pearson 1998). One heroin-addicted mother of a young woman living in a children's home was now cohabiting with, and carrying the child of, a much older partner who had learning difficulties. Furthermore, more than half of the local authority referrals had parents with histories of criminality and a similar proportion with known experience of mental health difficulties. With the exception of parental learning difficulties, the differences between the groups are statistically significant.

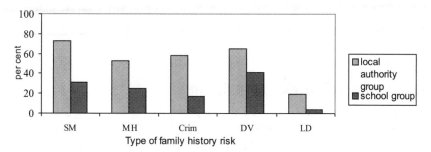

Figure 3.1 Incidence of family history risks for local authority and residential BESD schools groups

Numbers vary between 109 and 120 because elements of family history were not always known to our respondents. SM, substance misuse; MH, mental health problems; Crim, criminality; DV, domestic violence; LD, learning difficulties.

Boys and girls were equally likely to have experienced these family adversities and there were no age-related patterns.

It will be evident that with so many young people represented in each of these columns, there was a multiplicity of risk for many. By coding an experience as present or not and summing across categories, we were able to arrive at a broad indicator of the level of exposure to potentially adverse care-giving in the young people's earlier years. Through this, we were able to establish that although only 2 per cent of young people had been exposed to all five risks, only 13 per cent of young people had not been exposed to any. The majority of the sample was evenly spread across one to four risks. When we looked at these scores across our local authority and schools groups, we found that the local authority group scored a mean of 2.4 (out of 5), as opposed to 1.1 for the BESD schools group – more than twice as many.

Research has found that, generally speaking, many individuals can deal with the effects of one type of stress, but that multiple stresses may result in increasing difficulties (Caprara and Rutter 1995). We grouped our young people according to whether the level of risk was 'low' (either no known family history risk or just one) or 'higher' (two or more of these risks in their background). This was possible for approximately 80 per cent of the sample, and two-thirds of these young people (78/118) were identified as having a higher level of risk. Three-quarters of the local authority group (78%), compared with 31 per cent of the residential schools group, were rated as having a high level of background risk. The 40 young people with lower levels of risk were evenly divided between the residential schools sample and the local authority group. The *Metro* and *Borough* authorities had about 90 per cent of young people whom we judged to have a higher level of background risk, but for the *County* authority it was lower at 60 per cent.

Reasons for being away from home

We employed the criteria used by the Department for Children, Schools and Families (DCSF) (2007a) in order to categorise the reasons for being away from home (Figure 3.2). However, unlike the formal recording of a single reason for a period of care, we recognised that it is often a combination of factors that will coalesce over time and lead to the decision to place a child away from home. In addition to the DCSF categories, we added 'the existence of problems with education' as a potential reason for being away from home, along with 'young person's choice' to allow for the possibility that young people chose to be away from home. We included under parental illness the misuse of substances and parental mental health problems. Therefore, we asked respondents to rate how relevant each factor was to the young person's entry to care or residential education.

Again there were marked differences between the local authority and schools groups – many of these are unsurprising and some may be an artefact of the different focus of our professional respondents in the different groups. For example, social workers may be more likely to be aware of, and be involved in, the wider

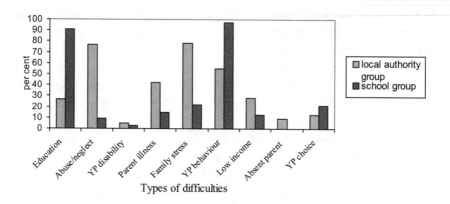

Figure 3.2 Factors influencing the decision to place or educate young people away from home

circumstances of the family than are professionals based in residential schools. That said, it is clear that these contrasts emphasise the differences between our groups, as observed in the previous analysis.

Figure 3.2 shows that concerns about education prompted the entry to residential BESD schools in 91 per cent of schools cases but were relevant in only 26 per cent for the local authority group. Conversely, abuse or neglect was a feature of young people's experience in 77 per cent of the local authority group, but this was true for only 9 per cent of the schools' referrals. Further differences were seen in relation to family stress, parent illness and child's behaviour as reasons for living away from home. Each of these differences was statistically significant (X^2 test values ranged from 7.8 to 46.5; $p <.05$).[1]

Even when we controlled for the age at which young people began living away from home (the care or residential education period), we found that problems of abuse, family stress and parental illness were less common among the BESD schools group, for whom education and behaviour were, unsurprisingly, almost always primary concerns.

Within the local authority group we found no differences in reasons for entry to care between boys and girls, or between young people of white, mixed or other ethnic background. One possible exception was a (non-significant) tendency for education problems to be more apparent for boys than girls. Young people for whom abuse or neglect were highly relevant to their entry to care or residential education were more likely to have begun living away from home earlier (X^2 test $= 10.5$; $df = 4$; $p <.05$).

Looking across our three participating local authorities, we found that the patterns of reasons for entry to care were similar, with one exception: behavioural problems were cited as relevant to the entry to care of over 70 per cent of young people in *County*, compared with 50 per cent in *Metro* and 33 per cent in *Borough*. Exploring this difference in more detail, we found that much was accounted for by a large proportion of *County* boys who entered with behavioural difficulties. Although not the sole reason, behavioural problems were relevant to the entry to care of 82 per cent of the boys entering care in the *County* authority, while proportions were far lower for all girls and for boys in the other two authorities. We did not find any other obvious differences for this group of boys, for example they were not significantly older as a group, and there was not a lower incidence of other factors. This, combined with the higher proportion of *County* cases that had relatively low levels of background risk, suggests that the *County* authority may have been operating in a somewhat different manner with regard to the support of families in the community and admission of young people to care, but this is a question that requires further investigation.

In order to simplify this data for later analyses, we created groupings of young people according to whether their reasons for being away from home were: 'child-related' – to do with their own education, behaviour or disability problems; 'family-related' – concerning the levels of stress, illness, poverty or parental absence in their families; or were 'abuse or neglect' (Table 3.3). This procedure was limited to some extent by missing data but it proved possible to group 88 per cent of the sample with a reasonable degree of confidence. The result was a three-category variable indicating that young people had been placed away from home primarily because of their own difficulties with education or behaviour, concerns about their parent's difficulties (with or without worries about their behaviour or education) or concerns about abuse or neglect, or both (with or without accompanying problems).

The categories and the distribution of frequencies across our sources of referral are listed in Table 3.3. For nearly half of young people recruited through BESD schools, the reasons for entry were described as mainly child-related with a further third being family-related. Less than 10 per cent of the BESD schools' population were known to have been separated from family primarily because of abuse or neglect. Of the young people recruited through local authorities, 70 per cent were described as living away from home mainly because of concerns over abuse or neglect.

Of course, these reasons for entry to care were pertinent at the point of separation but were they still relevant for the young person continuing to live or being educated away from home? For the most part we found that circumstances continued to prevail; thus where there had been parental illness or risk of abuse, very often these concerns persisted. However, there were some cases in each category where problems had reduced and for other young people new problems had arisen. Most notable among the changes that we recorded were 24 cases in which

Table 3.3 Primary reasons for entry to care or residential education

	County	Metro	Borough	Schools	All
Young person's behaviour or education	2	2	1	18	23 (15%)
Family-related ± young person's problems	9	6	3	13	31 (21%)
Abuse or neglect ± young person's or family problems	27	27	21	3	78 (52%)
Not known	4	0	7	7	18 (12%)
Total	42	35	32	41	150 (100%)

educational needs had become more relevant to the requirement for placement away, and the fact that 30 of the 106 young people for whom data was available were thought to want to remain away from home.

Legal arrangements for young people's accommodation away from home

Given the levels of family difficulties noted above, it is unsurprising that nearly seven in every ten children of our local authority sample were looked after under care orders. Proportions were broadly similar across the three local authorities, although, again, *County* stands out with a slightly lower proportion of care orders. Some of the residential schools group were also looked after by other local authorities, although the proportions were much smaller (see Table 3.4).

Table 3.4 Legal arrangements under which young people were placed away from home

	County	Metro	Borough	Schools	All
Not looked after	0	0	0	27	27 (18%)
Voluntary accommodation	16	10	8	4	38 (25%)
Care order	26	25	24	10	85 (57%)
Total	42	35	32	41	150 (100%)

It was interesting to observe that four of the young people in the BESD schools sample were adopted and returned to their adoptive families at weekends and between terms. Seven across the whole sample had been adopted but returned to care and a further five were known to have been previously placed for adoption but placements had been disrupted before an adoption order had been made. Therefore, for one in seven of our overall sample of 'difficult' adolescents, adoption had a part to play in their lives.

Duration away from home

Although it is relevant to know about the longer-term histories of the study sample, we were particularly interested in how long young people had been living away from home 'in this period' (i.e. the current separation or boarding experience).

With the residential BESD schools group, although most of the young people returned to family care for weekends and holidays, we took the date at which they were last enrolled in residential education as the starting point. For the local authority group we used the date that the most recent period of care began.

The duration that young people had been away from home in this period varied greatly across the sample as a whole with a range from just three months to 15 years and 6 months – in other words, since birth. However, this data was very skewed: thus the mean time away from home was 51 months but the median (i.e. half-way point) was just 38 months. That said, young people recruited through local authorities, generally, were likely to have been away from home longer than those recruited through schools. As illustrated in Table 3.5, of the local authorities, *Borough* in particular had a higher proportion of young people who had been in care for long periods.

Table 3.5 Duration away from home, according to source of referral

Time away from home this period (years)	County	Metro	Borough	Schools	All
<2	11	7	6	20	44 (30%)
2–<4	12	11	10	12	45 (30%)
4–<5	6	4	1	3	14 (10%)
5 +	13	13	12	6	44 (30%)
Total	42	35	29	41	147 (100%)

Note: Data unavailable for three cases.

We found differences in terms of the mean duration living away from home according to young people's care status (not looked after – away 28 months; Sect 20 (voluntary accommodation) – 41 months; Sect 31 (care order) – 61months). There were no differences in length of current separation or boarding according to young people's ethnic background or gender. As we might anticipate, those with experiences of abuse or neglect had been away from home for significantly longer than their more fortunate peers.

We were also interested to explore whether our sample had experienced previous episodes of care or education away from home. Where full data was available (125/150 cases), we grouped our young people to reflect the patterns of their separation or boarding experience. This process resulted in the groupings illustrated in Table 3.6. One in five of the young people had previously been reunited with their family. Of those who had remained away, just under one-third left the family home before their fifth birthday; for a further 11 per cent it occurred between the ages of five and ten years, and nearly four in ten children began living away from home when they were between 11 and 15 years old.

Table 3.6 Patterns of separation or boarding for local authority and residential BESD schools groups

	Local authority	Schools	All
Entry before five years of age, no returns	32	7	39
Entry aged 5–10, no returns	13	1	14
Entry aged 11–15, no returns	25	22	47
Entry at any age but previously reunited with family	25	0	25
Total	95	30	125

Thus, almost three-quarters of the BESD schools group had entered residential education (or occasionally care) after the age of 11 years and none had experienced returns to mainstream or day provision in the meantime (Table 3.6). In contrast, less than a quarter of those looked after by the local authorities had entered after age 11, and 26 per cent had experienced returns home. The maximum number of returns home we recorded was five. The residential schools group appears not to oscillate as does the care population. Indeed, there are interesting questions about how the 'BESD' 'label' may be reversed (Grimshaw with Berridge 1994). On the other hand, concerns have been expressed over how child–family reunions from care are too often poorly planned and supported (Farmer, Sturgess and O'Neill forthcoming).

Differences were also found between the local authority and the residential schools groups in relation to the number of previous placements away from home (Table 3.7). For over three-quarters of the schools group, this placement away from home was their first. In stark contrast, the same was true for only 9 per cent of the local authority group. The average (median) number of previous placements was four. (Exceptionally, the maximum we recorded was no fewer than 21 placements prior to our study beginning for a distraught 15-year-old young woman, who had first entered care as a baby and withstood two failed adoption attempts, the second of which lasted more than a year.) There were no statistically significant differences between individual local authorities in terms of the numbers of placements that young people had experienced.

Table 3.7 Frequency of previous placements away from home for local authority and residential BESD schools groups

	Local authority	Schools	All (%)
No previous placement away	9	28	37 (27)
One previous placement	11	6	17 (12)
Two to four placements	34	3	37 (27)
More than five placements	44	1	45 (33)
Total	98	38	136 (100)

Young people's perceptions of birth families

At interview, we asked the professionals where, or with whom, they thought young people would consider to be their home-base. Overall, it was believed that the birth family would be the home-base for 63 per cent of young people. However, this was much more commonly the case for young people sampled through schools. Almost 90 per cent of young people in the schools sample were thought to identify their birth family as 'home' and, for the remainder, a current carer occupied this role. For those sampled through local authorities, the birth family was thought to be the home-base for only half the young people (53%). About a quarter (26%) were thought to identify with a foster carer and a further 9 per cent associated themselves far more with extended family members. The remaining 12 per cent of young people were described either as not having a home-base or to be experiencing conflicting loyalties.

For the local authority group, identification with the birth family was seen to decline slightly, although not significantly, with time away from home and higher family risk rating. Those looked after subject to a care order were significantly more likely to identify with a current carer.

Distance from home

There has been much debate, both in the education and social care fields, about the use of placements which are either away from the geographical area or are provided by the private or voluntary sector (agency placements) (DfES 2006a). Here we consider the issue of distance from 'home': home being defined as the place of residence of young people's birth families. For the most part, young people's birth families lived in the local authority area that was responsible for the care or education of the young person. Thus, in the majority of cases, this discussion of distance concerns not only the physical displacement of the young person and the potential to affect opportunities for contact with their families or home environment, but also the ease, or otherwise, with which social workers and educational psychologists might monitor children's welfare and safety, the adequacy of placements and provide support.

The frequencies of 'in-' or 'out-of-area' placements according to our sources of referral are shown in Table 3.8. Predictably, because of its geographical concentration, *Borough* was far more likely than the other local authorities studied to have to place young people outside its borders. Less than a quarter of young people were placed physically within *Borough*, compared with over 60 per cent for the other two authorities. Members of the schools group also were highly likely to be placed outside of their own local authority, with over three-quarters of young people living in a different area.

Table 3.8 Frequency of in- and out-of-area care or educational placements, according to source of referral

	County	Metro	Borough	Schools	All (%)
Within local authority or local educational authority area	27	21	6	10	64 (44)
Out of area	15	14	20	31	80 (56)
Total	42	35	26	41	144 (100)

Of course, being placed outside an area does not necessarily mean being very far away, this is especially true in relation to a London borough. We endeavoured to examine how far away young people were placed but there was substantial missing data which limits our ability to draw firm conclusions. With that in mind, in Table 3.9, we have presented estimated distances between young people's birth families and their place of residence at the start of the study, according to the source of referral. The figures suggest that residents of BESD schools were less likely to be close to their families, but the proportions placed more than 50 miles away were similar across all groups.

Table 3.9 Distance of care or educational placement from birth family, according to source of referral

	County	Metro	Borough	Schools	All (%)
Placed within 20 miles of birth family	15	14	10	4	43 (29)
20 to 50 miles away	5	5	3	9	22 (15)
50+ miles away	13	9	8	10	40 (27)
Distance not known	9	7	11	18	45 (30)
Total	42	35	32	41	150 (100)

Contact

The final area that we examined in relation to young people's experiences with their birth families was contact. We might expect that levels of contact would be related to a number of the factors that already have been considered in this chapter, such as the reason for being away from home, care status and distance.

Young people recruited through residential BESD schools were much more likely to be described by informants as having regular and open contact with their families (75% versus 30% in our local authority group). The father of one young woman attending a residential BESD school telephoned her each evening to read a bedtime story. The only exception to this was the small group of young people who were looked after by other authorities and placed in our participating schools. Within the local authority groups there were some restrictions on contact in nearly 70 per cent of cases. In only a minority of cases was this choice made by the young person (7%) – or the birth family (14%). Rather, a professional had usually instigated the restrictions and, in 17 per cent of cases, this was sanctioned by court order. Predictably, restrictions tended to be in place where there had been incidents of abuse or neglect, or where parents' behaviours continued to pose risks to young people, such as those who misused drugs or alcohol.

We recorded enhanced categories of contact according to the following format: none, indirect (phone or letter), supervised, or unsupervised visits and overnight stays. Young people in the residential schools group were far more likely to have the opportunity for overnight stays at home (unsurprisingly, as several of the schools only offered termly accommodation). This was available to three-quarters of the schools group and around one in five of the local authority group (see Table 3.10). In comparison with those subject to a care order, young people accommodated voluntarily (under Section 20 of the Children Act) were rather more likely to spend extended periods with their families (33% as opposed to 11%) and it was less likely that their visits were supervised (11% versus 40%). There were no significant differences in levels of contact according to whether young people were placed in or out of area, or in terms of how far away they were placed. Interestingly, this held even when the residential schools group was excluded from the analysis. From this analysis, distance does not seem to be the overriding factor in determining contact. Although cell numbers were too small for detailed analysis, the level of contact did vary according to whom young people identified as their home-base. Thus, around 96 per cent of those identifying with birth family were in visiting contact with them, mostly (56%) with overnight stays.

Table 3.10 Level of contact with birth family, according to source of referral

	County	Metro	Borough	Schools	All (%)
None	8	9	5	6	28 (22)
Indirect (telephone or letter)	0	4	2	0	6 (5)
Visits supervised	7	13	10	2	32 (25)
Visits unsupervised	11	5	2	1	19 (15)
Overnight stays +	11	1	6	27	45 (35)
Total	37	32	25	36	130 (100)

It was interesting to note that only one young person in the *Metro* authority experienced overnight stays, in comparison to over a quarter of young people in the other two authorities. We could find no obvious reason for this.

Summary points

- There was a relatively high level of step and lone parenting of the young people in our sample. This was similar across both the local authority and schools groups.

- The local authority group was significantly more likely to have been exposed to a number of background risk factors (parental criminality, alcohol or drug misuse, or mental health problems). The incidence of parental learning difficulties was relatively low for both groups.

- Three-quarters of the local authority group and one-third of the schools group were rated as having a high level of background risk (exposure to two or more of the factors mentioned in the previous bullet point).

- Exploration of the reasons for living or being educated away from home recorded marked differences in the rates of abuse or neglect between the local authority and schools groups. The predominant reason for being away from home for the latter group was difficulties with behaviour or education, or both.

- The local authority group was more likely to have been away from home for longer and to have experienced more placements away than the schools group. Within the local authority group, those who had experienced abuse or neglect tended to have been away from home longer than those entering care for other reasons.

- The use of out-of-area placements was common in all three local authorities but was particularly marked in *Borough*. Over three-quarters of the schools group were attending residential schools outside their own areas.

- Young people in the local authorities group were somewhat less likely than those in the schools group to identify with their birth family as their 'home-base'.

- Levels of contact with family were much higher in the schools group than the local authority group. Within the local authority group, contact arrangements varied with the reason for entry to care and the degree of 'risk' posed by parental behaviour and characteristics. There were no significant differences in levels of contact according to whether young people were placed in or out of area.

Note

1   This statistic 'X^2' is known as 'chi-squared test'. Throughout this study we used statistical analysis to see the extent to which our research findings could have arisen by chance or

be statistically 'significant'. This is measured using the probability (p) value: $p<.05$ means this finding would have arisen by chance on fewer than 1 in 20 occasions; $p<.01$ would mean by fewer than 1 in 100 occasions and so on. We have omitted reporting X^2 test (and other) results too frequently for this more general readership but statistical analysis of our data was used throughout to test whether our findings were likely to be meaningful ('significant') or not.

Chapter 4

Placements and Stability

Types of placement and grouping the sample

As explained in earlier chapters, our major aim for this research was to explore the experiences, costs and outcomes for a group of difficult-to-manage adolescents placed in one of three settings: foster care, children's homes or residential BESD schools. We had identified the groups of looked after young people that we wished to 'screen' by asking local authorities to provide anonymised data on the numbers of young people in our age range who were placed in foster (including relative and friends) care or children's homes (see Appendix). We also asked these authorities each to identify three residential BESD schools that they used the most frequently.

On examination of this information, one of our first discoveries was that the placement options were less clear-cut than anticipated and a sizeable proportion of looked after young people were placed in dual-registered facilities; that is, registered children's homes which were also registered as schools. Initial discussions with representatives from some of these establishments and with those who identified placements for young people suggested that this type of facility provided an important service for this group.

We therefore decided to include young people placed in this type of establishment and re-define our major grouping variable accordingly. Hence, our eventual sample was divided between the resulting *four* placement categories, as illustrated in Table 4.1.

Table 4.1 Numbers of young people, according to type of placement at Stage 1

Foster care	Children's homes without education	Dual-registered establishments	Residential BESD schools	Total
51	39	29	31	150

A further complication was that we found some of the residents in BESD schools were, in fact, looked after by *other* local authorities. These young people would return to their local areas to foster carers for weekends and holidays. Thus, while the majority of the BESD school group were not looked after this is not true for all. Our approach to the categorisation was to focus on the *type of service* rather than the care status of the young people.

With the exception of dual-registered facilities, in each of the placement categories there were examples of both local authority and independent provision. When we first selected our samples, around 41 per cent were placed within local authority-provided placements, 45 per cent of placements were from private provision and 13 per cent by voluntary organisations. However, where we had limited contact with placement providers, we were not entirely confident that respondents were always fully aware of whether independent providers were operating as private companies or charitable organisations. Therefore we prefer, at this stage, to use a local authority versus 'agency' categorisation: 'agency' referring to both private and voluntary organisations.

There was substantial reliance on the private and voluntary sector for our group of adolescents (Table 4.2). This was most marked in the provision of residential special education placements but was also very evident in both of the non-educational categories. Predictably perhaps, of our participating local authorities it was *Borough* that made the most use of agency provision.

Table 4.2 Type of placement provider, according to category of care or boarding placement

	Foster care (including family)	Children's home (no education)	Dual-registered home/school	Residential BESD schools	All (%)
Local authority	33	18	0	9	60 (40)
Private or voluntary provision	18	21	29	22	90 (60)
Total	51	39	29	31	150 (100)

Almost all of the agency provision was physically located some distance from young people's local areas, but there were a few examples of agency-run facilities within a local authority area, as well as local authority-managed establishments outside the council's boundaries.

Characteristics of the placements

As might be expected there was a good deal of variation in the characteristics of the foster care placements – especially since we included placements made with family and friends. However, the characteristics of both types of foster placement have been described in detail before (Farmer and Moyers 2008; Sinclair, Wilson and Gibbs 2004) so we shall not repeat this here. There has been less written recently about the current range of provision in terms of residential homes and schools, so it seems worthwhile to outline the establishments that participated in our study.

Overall we encountered some 45 different residential establishments (children's homes, dual-registered establishments and BESD schools) at Stage 1 of the study. The children's homes which did not provide education generally catered for four to eight residents, although we came across some which took only two at a time. The majority of those in the private and voluntary sector were operated in fairly large residential properties, which provided each resident with their own room with shared access to living spaces and other facilities. The children's homes generally catered for boys and girls, some focused on specific age groups (e.g. 7–12-year-olds or 11–18-year-olds); others took children over a wide age-range, creating a very diverse grouping. Children's homes operated by local authorities tended to cater for the older age group (over 11) and were more often housed in purpose-built accommodation but, like their private counterparts, tended to be in residential areas of substantial towns.

Some of the dual-registered facilities that we came across resembled the children's homes in that they catered for relatively few young people (between eight and ten), and provided both care and education in converted houses. Most, however, were somewhat larger and frequently had separate living and classroom accommodation, and some provided education on a different site. The residential BESD schools tended to be larger, catering for perhaps 50 young people; most were housed in substantial buildings in large grounds, some distance from local communities. Several of these schools catered only for boys.

We found that there was much variety across the establishments that we visited. The majority, in both the public and private sectors, came across as committed to the young people they cared for, concerned with providing a pleasant, welcoming and caring environment. Some, thankfully only a small minority, felt rather uncared for and not well managed. Here is a brief picture of each main type of residential resource that we encountered. These are for illustration only, they are not necessarily 'typical' and some features have been changed to preserve anonymity.

Box 4.1 A local authority children's home without education

This facility was a modern building based in a residential area just outside a large town centre. The facility was divided into two sections: a unit for younger residents and a unit for those who were older, which was intended to promote independence. Each unit could house up to eight residents. The experience of one of the researchers attending the unit for younger residents was that the staff members were very welcoming towards children and visitors. The interior and furnishings were modern and looked newly decorated. The atmosphere was friendly and homely.

Young people were encouraged to express their emotions through art and poetry, and examples of these were displayed on walls. There was a computer room that was very popular with the young residents, which was decorated with educational materials and posters on the walls.

One visit coincided with Halloween and the researcher found all the staff and young people preparing for a 'Ghost Hunt' to be followed by a special dinner that evening. The young people were involved in the preparation of this meal alongside the staff.

The decoration of the unit for older residents was not quite as modern and the unit did not have the same 'homely feel'. There was a group of young people standing outside smoking and talking when the researcher arrived. Staff and residents did not appear to get along as well as in the unit for younger residents, and the boundaries between staff and young people in this unit appeared unclear at times.

Box 4.2 A private dual-registered establishment

This resource was a small, dual-registered facility, set on the outskirts of a small, well-presented town. It was entirely independent and run as a limited company. The school was housed in two substantial residential dwellings, set in two acres of grounds. There was a small, separate house within the grounds used for older residents as a 'semi-independent' living resource.

The home offered long-term care for boys and girls aged between 8 and 19 years of age. It described itself as a therapeutic community. Overall, the building was well-decorated with a 'homely feel'. There were examples of pupils' work displayed on the walls in the main hallway.

All of the residents of this establishment were looked after by their local authorities, and the majority of places were secured with three-way, joint-funding from education, health and social services departments. Despite the small numbers and the disparate age-range, the school offered a full range of subjects and almost all were taught by subject specialists.

There appeared to be much commitment to community relationships, with the school belonging to the local business consortium. There were also links with the local college to provide opportunities for older residents in work-based learning and vocational training, although staff recognised that this needed further development.

Box 4.3 A residential BESD school operated by a voluntary organisation

This was a mixed school, housing and educating both boys and girls. It was located on the outskirts of a medium-sized town in a rural setting. The facility consisted of a large main building used for classrooms and administration, and a series of purpose-built, modern residential units situated apart in the very substantial grounds. The school could accommodate 50 residential pupils but also took additional day pupils. The individual houses were decorated in a comfortable country style with modern facilities on site. Although the units physically were very much alike, each had a slightly different feel as the residents and staff had chosen the furnishings and decoration. There was sufficient space in each unit for private meetings to be held.

All members of staff that we met were friendly and helpful to our research team, and they appeared to have developed good relationships with young people. Doors to the staff offices were rarely closed. The majority of the residents of this school were not 'in care'; their residential education being funded entirely by their local education authorities. The school offered term-time provision only and most of the residents returned home at weekends.

The characteristics of young people resident in different settings

It seemed important to explore at the outset not only how many of our sample attended which settings, but also their respective characteristics. We were particularly interested here in whether there are differences in relation to age, gender, ethnicity, levels of family history problems (background risk), experiences of abuse or neglect and earlier care experience.

Table 4.3 presents the results of these analyses and reveals substantial differences between young people in different types of setting in each of these areas apart from ethnicity. (We did, of course, carefully select our residential BESD schools so as to provide some girls as well as pupils from minority ethnic groups;

see Chapter 1). The majority of the difference is accounted for by the group sampled through residential BESD schools. But, even if this group is excluded, differences remain across types of setting in terms of age, length of time away from home and levels of difficulty at Stage 1. Residents of children's homes tended to be older (χ^2 test $=7.8$; df $= 2$; $p<.05$); there was a greater proportion of more recent entrants to care among those placed in dual-registered accommodation (χ^2 test $=16.7$; df $= 6$; $p <.05$); and the foster care group tended to have fewer behavioural difficulties (χ^2 test $=13.7$; df $= 4$; $p <.01$).

Table 4.3 Characteristics of young people resident in different settings

	Foster care (n = 51)	Children's homes without education (n = 39)	Dual-registered homes/schools (n = 29)	Residential BESD schools (n =31)
Gender (%)				
Boys	61	46	76	71
Girls	39	54	24	29
Age (%)				
From 11–<14	41	15	41	42
From 14–<16	59	85	59	58
Ethnicity (%)				
White British	77	74	76	87
Mixed ethnicity	18	18	14	10
Any other ethnicity	6	7	10	3
Background history[a] (%)				
Low-risk	14	33	36	70
High-risk	86	67	64	30
Reasons for being away from home[a] (%)				
Young person's behaviour or educational needs	2	6	21	52
Family problems	15	23	21	41
Abuse or neglect	83	71	58	7

Table 4.3 cont.

	Foster care (n = 51)	Children's homes without education (n = 39)	Dual-registered homes/schools (n = 29)	Residential BESD schools (n =31)
Time away from home[a] (%)				
0–<2 years this period	20	23	41	52
2–<4 years this period	8	26	10	20
4–<5 years this period	39	10	14	22
5+ years	33	41	35	6
Prior placements away from home[a] (%)				
No prior placement	8	9	18	86
One prior placement	13	12	18	7
2–4 prior placements	49	19	25	3
5+ prior placements	30	59	39	3
Number of behavioural problems at screening (%)				
0–2	59	5	31	52
3–4	35	56	55	45
5–6	6	39	14	3

[a] Data is missing for 32 young people.

Overall, children's homes' residents were more likely to be female and substantially more likely to be in our older age group. Most had been admitted to care because of abuse, neglect or wider family problems and had stayed a relatively long time in care. The majority had experienced several different placements in care and a large proportion displayed multiple behaviour problems.

Young people in foster care resembled children's homes' residents in their care histories and their reasons for being away from home; indeed, 83 per cent had experienced abuse or neglect and nearly 90 per cent were recorded as having a high number of background risk factors. They tended, however, to have been away from home for longer than children's homes residents and very few were recorded as showing the higher level of difficult behaviours (see Table 4.3). The gender- and age-distributions were fairly even across this group.

In the dual-registered placements there tended to be more boys, the age-spread was fairly even, there was a moderately high level of background risk, most had experienced abuse or neglect (but not all) and several were fairly recent entrants to care or residential education. Although only one-third appeared in the low category for behavioural difficulties, relatively few were in the highest category.

We have to be cautious in interpreting the information about the BESD schools group because some data about their previous experiences was missing. That said, as far as it was possible to tell, like the dual-registered establishments the group sampled from residential BESD schools comprised more males and their ages were relatively similar. Unlike the dual-registered group, the majority had a low level of background risk and most entered care relatively recently, primarily because of their own problems with behaviour or education, or both. For the great majority, this placement away or boarding experience was their first. Somewhat surprisingly, comparatively few young people in this setting showed multiple behaviour problems.

Time in existing (Stage 1) placement

Figure 4.1 reveals how long young people had been living in their existing (Stage 1) placement. It demonstrates marked variation both within and across the types of settings. This type of chart displays, for each category, the range of values (here indicating months in placement) by the short horizontal marks displayed at the top and the bottom of each vertical bar. The boxes on each bar indicate the range in which 50 per cent of values fall and the thick black line denotes the median value. As may be seen, within each category there were some very long-, and some very short-duration placements. In general children's home placements were found to have been significantly more recent.

Age was not associated with the length of the current placement but, interestingly, boys' placements tended to have lasted longer and this finding held even when the children's home residents (with a predominance of older girls) were excluded. There were no significant differences according to the source of referral (participating local authorities or schools), nor according to whether placements were within or outside young people's own local authority areas. The length of time that young people had already been living in their Stage 1 placement was found to be unrelated to the number of different behavioural problems that young people presented. The extent of previous placements was, however, linked to the level of behavioural problems and this finding also held when examining the local authority group separately.

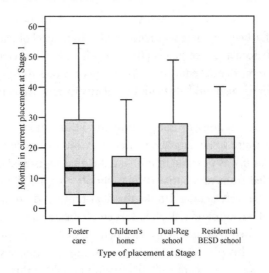

Figure 4.1 Duration of current placement at Stage 1

Of course, how long a placement lasts is subject to a number of influences: the plan may always have been that the placement be short term with a view to more appropriate longer-term accommodation or a return to family or mainstream education. Alternatively, a placement may prove inappropriate for a young person for a variety of reasons. Moreover, older adolescents especially may act to achieve their own preferences – whether trying to contrive an alternative placement or initiating a return to their family (Sinclair, Garnett and Berridge 1995). There is a suggestion above that levels of behavioural problems were associated with a higher number of prior placements but, as we shall see, when we move on to consider stability of placement during the study period, this is far from straightforward.

Thus, we have observed that the characteristics of groups of young people in different placements at Stage 1 vary in important ways. In particular, we need to bear in mind the influence of gender disparities, pre-care or pre-residential education experiences and the level of behavioural difficulties.

The pattern of placement change between Stages 1 and 2

Stability of care and educational placements for looked after young people were primary objectives of the *Quality Protects* initiative. Generally speaking, stability is important in maximising the opportunities for later life chances for young people (Berridge 2000; Sinclair *et al.* 2006).

As discussed in our methodology sections (see Appendix), where we explore the representativeness of participating young people and factors associated with attrition, young people who were very mobile were less likely to participate in the study and more likely to be lost to the sample at Stage 2. We had elected to study a group of young people who were at particularly high risk for instability in their care and education because of the challenges they presented. We were not surprised, therefore, to find a good deal of movement in our nine-month follow-up period.

We begin our analysis of placement change by examining the reports of informants at the follow-up stage. We elected to talk to the carer or professional who was best placed to comment on young people's progress over the period. For young people who declined to be interviewed, this information was usually obtained from their current social worker. Where young people were participating, we spoke as appropriate with their foster carers (or relative in the case of family and friends placement), residential key workers or heads of care. Information concerning whether young people had changed placement was available for 148 of the original 150 cases, although the group for whom we had full information about the reasons for and impact of changes at follow-up was slightly smaller.

Of those for whom data was available, 40 per cent of young people moved in the nine months between Stage 1 and Stage 2 (Table 4.4). One in nine changed more than once. The maximum we recorded was five different placements. Of course, that also means that six in every ten young people did not move, despite their levels of behavioural difficulty.

Table 4.4 Reason for placement change and number of changes

	No change	One change	More than one change	All (%)
No change	87	–	–	87 (60)
Age-related change	–	6	–	6 (4)
Move to long-term or permanent	–	6	1	7 (5)
Meet behavioural needs	–	20	12	32 (22)
Return to parents	–	9	–	9 (6)
Meet other needs	–	4	1	5 (3)
Total	87 (60)	45 (31)	14(10)	146 (100)

Excludes four cases where data is missing.

There were a host of reasons for young people moving placement and we have systematically recorded the primary 'reason' for the first move. There were very few occasions of young people having to move for 'administrative' reasons; for example, when a children's home closed down or a unit became a single-sex establishment. But, on the whole, moves took place in an attempt to meet young people's needs more effectively, or to remove them from environments which either could not contain their behaviour or keep them safe (or both).

Table 4.4 presents the data concerning the reasons for placement changes set against the number of changes experienced in the follow-up period. Data is available for 146 of the original 150 cases. Of these, 87 (60%) remained in their original placement over the follow-up period. Of those who did move, the table shows how some of these were expected or planned changes either due to age-related transitions; for example, from residential schools or children's homes (6/61) or because the plan was a move to a long-term or permanent placement (7/61). There were also some situations (recorded under 'meeting other needs') where it was clear that the Stage 1 placement was not meeting specific needs for the young person (5/61). One young person, for example, was placed in a residential BESD school but proved to have specific learning difficulties that were not appropriate to that environment. In another case a young woman became pregnant and needed to move to a more suitable environment to raise her child.

Table 4.4 also reveals a group of nine cases where young people returned to live with their birth families. These were cases in which there was no 'reason' for the placement ending other than the social work plan becoming reunification, or that young people simply 'voted with their feet' and the plan subsequently changed. These young people were very often (9/17 cases) looked after under voluntary arrangements or not looked after at all.

But the most common reason for placement change, was to 'meet behavioural needs'; that is, the original placements broke down (32/61) because the placement was unable to contain the young person or to keep them safe. Comparing the reason for moves with the number of moves (Table 4.4), it is clear that the reason for the majority of multiple moves in the follow-up period was behavioural difficulties.

Which young people changed placement?

We examined the data to ascertain whether there were particular characteristics that were associated with placement changes. We found no differences according to personal circumstances, such as gender, age group or ethnic background. Nor did we find any differences associated with adverse family history, with reason for entry to care or education or length of time away from home. There was a tendency for those who did not move during follow-up to have had fewer prior placements but this was not statistically significant and was almost entirely accounted for by the residential schools group (many of whom had not experienced a prior placement away from home).

We did find significant associations between placement change and both the type of setting in which young people were living at Stage 1 and their level of behavioural problems at screening (see Figure 4.2). Thus, young people were less likely to leave residential schools and more likely to leave children's homes than would be expected by chance (χ^2 test = 8.3; df = 3; p <.05). Perhaps unsurprisingly, we also found that the greater the number of behavioural problems the higher the likelihood of young people moving placement (χ^2 test = 8.4; df = 2; p< .05). However, these two factors interact: we have seen previously that children's homes have a very high proportion of young people with multiple behavioural problems and that pupils at residential schools frequently showed fewer difficulties. Cell sizes become too small to take this analysis any further with this sample, but the data suggests that it is the multiplicity of behavioural problems, rather than differences in practice between settings, that led to the greater proportion of placement endings in the children's home group.

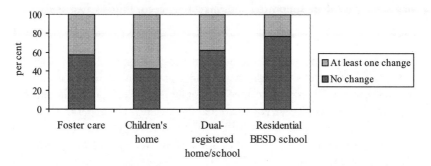

Figure 4.2 Patterns of placement change, according to type of placement at Stage 1

As may clearly be seen in Figure 4.2, overall residents of BESD schools experienced greater stability than young people recruited to the study through the three local authorities. The setting least likely to offer stability over the nine-month period was a children's home.

That said, we were struck by how much the residential special schools varied: several of them experienced no unanticipated change during the follow-up period, but we lost at least 50 per cent of our sample in two schools. Of the three local authorities represented, fewer young people in *County* experienced a change of placement (37% compared with 50% and 59% in *Metro* and *Borough*, respectively). Interestingly, only one young person in *Borough* moved more than once in the follow-up period, and a number of those moving once did so to return to birth parents. Conversely, more than a quarter of young people sampled through *Metro* had more than one move in the follow-up period. The circumstances of one young woman experiencing multiple placements between Stages 1 and 2 are conveyed below.

Case Study: Claire

Claire had been living in a local authority children's home for about six months at Stage 1 of the research. She was 15 years of age. At that time the social work plan had been for a move to foster care and mainstream schooling. She left this children's home some three months into our study period following an assault on staff. The plan for foster care was abandoned and she moved to another children's home which was designed to bridge to independence – that broke down rather dramatically after five months. She went to a hotel for the weekend and was then placed in supported lodgings but, according to her social worker, she would not stay there. Much time was spent trying to find her when she repeatedly went missing.

As we got in touch for the nine-month follow-up, we learned that Claire had just moved into unsupported B&B provision. By this time she was 16 years old. She was described as happier in the B&B provision but the social worker was very concerned that there were no boundaries. The social worker described her as 'very difficult to engage with – all our arrangements are very "last-minute". She is, however, staying there and wants to remain.'

According to the social worker, Claire had not engaged at all with education since she left the original children's home. Despite this she did gain five GCSEs, although her grades were much lower than they should have been. She has refused assistance from Connexions: 'she says she wants to do everything herself. I wonder where she gets her money from. She did get herself a part-time job but lost it because of continued lateness.'

Claire has been in trouble for shoplifting and was charged for the original assault. She is described as heavily involved in 'clubbing' and the drug and alcohol lifestyle of her group of friends.

The impact of changes of care placement

In the majority of cases where information was available from informants, the impact of a change of placement on young people was said to be positive. Here is one such example.

Case Study: Jack

Jack was 13 years old at Stage 1 of the research. He was placed in a local authority children's home at that point. He had originally entered care as a toddler, and had experienced a failed adoptive placement alongside five other different placements before this one. A children's home placement was not thought the appropriate placement for him and his name had been on the family-finding list for nearly four years. In the course of the study period, a foster family was identified through a private agency and he eventually moved as planned.

This move was described as having been very positive for Jack, early behaviour problems had settled down and his self-harming behaviour was improving. Although he was described as not 'academic' and that emotional problems still held him back in school, he was thought to be maturing and his school attainment was improving.

These improvements were thought to be a result of 'a stable placement, the carers' contribution and the one-to-one attention'. 'He is laying a lot of ghosts – working through difficult experiences with his carers.'

The following is a situation where the effects of the placement change were perceived to be less successful.

Case Study: Julie

Jennifer was in our older age group when we first met her. She was resident in a small private children's home, some distance from her local area. She told us that she had lived in 15 different placements, mostly residential units, since entering care four years previously.

When we met again for the follow-up, Jennifer told us her original placement had ended – she did not go into detail as to why. In the intervening period she had lived in another children's home, had a failed reunification attempt with her birth family and finally moved into 'homeless' accommodation.

Asked to sum up how the nine-month period had been for her, Jennifer replied, 'On the whole things haven't been great – up and down.' She spoke about a number of issues with a great deal of sadness and regret, especially her educational opportunities. She had been out of school for some time and had not entered for any GCSEs.

The staff at the unit felt that they had offered a great deal of support but that Jennifer was not always making the most of this. Indeed, she told us that she had twice been on 'seven days' notice' (of eviction from the unit) in her short time there. She clearly continued to have problems about dealing with her anger and she talked a lot about 'when she was feeling low'. She described how she had been charged with two further assaults since we had first met – although she wasn't unduly worried by this 'I've had loads of warnings and nothing ever happens – it is possible I'll have to go back to court' (she had already been to court several times for similar offences). She also mentioned her overdose attempt.

And another.

Case Study: Josh

Josh was 15 years old at the first meeting; at that time he was living in a residential setting and had been there for about two years. Josh was enthusiastic about his current college course (training to be a mechanic) and was preparing hard for the two GCSEs he was due to sit.

When we got in touch again for the follow-up interview, we learned that he had left this placement. His head of care told us that, shortly after our meeting with him, he had been allocated a new social worker in the leaving care team. The new social worker had mentioned to him that, if he wished, he could be supported in independent living accommodation in his home town. This appealed to Josh, though the unit didn't feel he was ready and was resisting it.

When we spoke with Josh the second time he told us 'I wanted to leave but they said no, so I did something to make sure that I left.' When back in his home town he rapidly found himself in trouble. He had been through a series of placements, mostly 'homeless' hostels, had received one custodial sentence and was facing two court appearances. He was offered a place at an education centre but didn't really attend 'they did get me a job in a shop but I never went because they found out about the ASBO and then I couldn't go'. He sat his GCSEs – 'I failed, got Fs, I could have done better if I wasn't doing the drugs – cannabis, LSD, I did all of them.' When asked how he felt about what had happened he replied 'stupid, but glad. It [the custodial experience] taught me a lesson.'

Type of setting at Stage 2

The experience of a move will potentially have a major impact in a variety of ways on the individuals involved but, with this research, we were particularly interested in the comparative effectiveness of different types of care and education services. For this reason, we concentrate in subsequent analyses on the extent to which the *type* of package offered to young people was consistent over the nine-month period. For this purpose, we paid less attention the number of moves that young people made but concentrated rather on the extent to which they moved between the different types of package.

Table 4.5 illustrates the degree of movement between types of setting and Table 4.6 lists the frequencies for our final 'consistency of care package' variable. We saw earlier that some 38 per cent of young people in dual-registered provision experienced a change in placement; however, Table 4.5 reveals that relatively few of these were moves away from this type of provision. In contrast there was a good deal of movement across categories for young people originally placed in children's homes or foster care. As the account proceeds, this is the variable that will be subjected to further analyses as we move on to examine care and educational experiences, costs and outcomes over the nine-month period. The young people shown in Table 4.5 and Table 4.6 as having been placed with parents will be included in the 'changed' category for further analyses.

Table 4.5 Setting at Stage 2, according to setting at Stage 1

Setting at Stage 2	Type of setting at Stage 1					
	Foster care	Family and friends care	Children's home (no education)	Dual-registered home/ school	Residential BESD school	Total
Foster care	22	2	3		1	28
Family and friends care		8	1			9

Table 4.5 cont.

	Type of setting at Stage 1					
Setting at Stage 2	Foster care	Family and friends care	Children's home (no education)	Dual-registered home/ school	Residential BESD school	Total
Children's home no education	5		**18**	1		24
Dual-registered home/school				**22**		22
Residential BESD school		2			**25**	27
Placed with parents	4	2	5	1	5	17
Semi-independent accommodation	1		5			6
Secure or custodial	1		1	1		3
Not known	4		6	3	1	14
Total	37	14	39	28	32	**150**

Table 4.6 Consistency of care package type over the follow-up period

Placement	Frequency (%)
Foster care (including family and friends) throughout	34 (23)
Children's home no education throughout	19 (13)
Dual-registered establishment throughout	23 (15)
Residential BESD school throughout	25 (17)
Changed category (including change from family and friends to foster)	26 (17)
Placed with parents	16 (11)
Not known	7 (5)
Total	$n = 150$

Summary points

- We identified four major types of placement option for our group of 'difficult' adolescents: foster care, children's homes without education, dual-registered children's homes with formal educational provision, and residential BESD schools. There was significant variety regarding the types of residential provision.

- The characteristics of young people varied by setting. Variations were detected in relation to age and gender distributions, the extent of prior adversity and the range of types of behavioural difficulty.

- Residents in children's homes tended to be older and to exhibit a greater range of behavioural problems than those in foster care. Young people in residential BESD schools had experienced less prior adversity than any of the other three groups and also had fewer types of difficult behaviour.

- Across the whole sample, 40 per cent of young people moved placement in the course of the follow-up, including 6 per cent who returned to parents in line with a (revised) social work or educational plan. Residents of children's home were most likely to experience a move, and a move was least likely for those in residential BESD schools.

- Changes of placement were related to the range of behavioural problems at Stage 1, which was generally far greater for children's home residents than pupils at residential BESD schools.

- Exploring the consistency of 'type of facility' rather than specific placements, we found that a total of 28 per cent of young people moved between types of provision in the course of the follow-up period.

Chapter 5

Quality of Care

Social work research is increasingly concerned with seeking to assess outcomes –
the extent to which particular interventions produce desirable results. This is a
complex area and we should not underestimate the severity of some children and
families' problems and the likely limits of social work influence. Furthermore,
there are dangers of assuming too mechanistic an approach: the nature of child
welfare problems and their possible resolution are likely to be multifaceted (Webb
2001). Thus, our approach to outcome measurement is intentionally broad. The
overall theoretical framework outlined in Chapter 1 helps us to understand the
inter-relationship between these different components. This approach is also
consistent with the 'production of welfare' model (Knapp and Lowin 1998),
which underlies the costs analysis discussed in Chapter 8.

Researchers may approach 'outcomes' in a variety of ways (Parker *et al.*
1991); for example, in their effects on different audiences – children, families,
services or society at large and so on – or over varied time-periods. Most of our
concern is with 'final outcomes', that is, changes in children's welfare such as
well-being, behaviour and attainments. These are discussed in the next two
chapters. However, researchers are also often interested in 'intermediate outcomes'; that is, the quality of care and experience that children receive, such as
being looked after by caring, considerate adults. For children who come from
socially and emotionally deprived backgrounds, this is a positive 'outcome' in
itself. There is a moral, let alone a legal, obligation to provide good quality care to
children living away from home.

But identifying and analysing good quality care is also important as certain
intermediate factors are believed to be linked to improvements for children in the
longer term. These will be reflected in much of the professional and training literature. Later chapters look at the relationship between quality of care, costs and
outcomes for different groups of young people.

Our approach to assessing the quality of care experienced by our study sample was as follows. Information was derived mainly from the nine-month follow-up interviews with young people and carers. Therefore, we are able to analyse the quality of care offered in relation only to those 75 young people who agreed to be interviewed at Stage 2. Although much of the focus is on experiences in foster and residential (school) placements, the analysis concerns the overall 'care package' during the follow-up period, including, for example, social worker contribution and inter-professional working. Some young people moved between placements in any case. Specific educational issues, such as teaching, resources and access to the curriculum, were dealt with separately (Chapter 7). As our research had a particular focus on education, this required more detailed examination and is discussed in the subsequent chapters.

In defining what constitutes quality of care, we sought to identify a common set of experiences that would apply to young people across the settings of foster care, children's homes and residential BESD schools. Too much previous research has been constrained by legal and administrative boundaries, and we set out to develop a more child-centred approach. These rigid divisions have probably contributed in the past to (special) educational concerns being undervalued for looked after children, and insufficient acknowledgement of separation issues and the broader care experience for the residential special schools' population (Berridge et al. 2002).

We could find no existing research tool or scale to assess quality of care and so developed our own. This was a complex task; no doubt our analysis has its limitations but we hope to have taken some useful steps. Discussions with our advisory group were very useful. A number of sources were used to identify the common dimensions. In particular, for foster care, we consulted Sinclair et al. (2004), and Wilson et al. (2004). For children's homes there was again Sinclair and Gibbs (1998) and Berridge and Brodie (1998). In the residential BESD field we found Cole et al. (1998) helpful, as well as Grimshaw with Berridge (1994). More generally, there was our preparatory work and report for Department of Health (Berridge et al. 2002), and Gilligan (1997) and others on resilience. As our study focuses especially on adolescents, there were the Department of Health (1996) research overviews on teenagers and caring for children away from home (DoH 1998b). The *Report of the Special Schools Working Group* (DfES 2003c) helped to incorporate relevant thinking from the special education field.

'Quality of Care' Index

From these and other relevant sources, we identified nine key areas for our 'Quality of Care' Index. These were:

- care and control
- stability and continuity
- safety
- inter-professional working
- family links
- close relationship with at least one adult
- ethnicity and culture
- friendships
- planning and aftercare.

There are no doubt others but these were felt to be the most significant. Appropriate care and control are at the core of effective parenting and there is evidence of the importance of supportive professional relationships *per se*, irrespective of their instrumental value (Jordan 2006). All children require some stability and predictability in their lives in order to make sense of the world and develop trusting relationships (Howe, Brandon and Schofield 1999). Safety is a key consideration and something that services have not always guaranteed. Government policy under *Every Child Matters* (DfES 2003b) increasingly emphasises inter-professional working, and it is essential in promoting the education of looked after children. Careful nurturing of family relationships is generally considered valuable but exposure to possible harm from birth parents is not. Research emphasises the benefit of a positive, close relationship with at least one adult who provides either unconditional love or, at least, stands up for the child (DoH 1998a). Ethnicity and culture are important for us all but especially for minority ethnic groups, whose role, identity and acceptance in society may be problematic (Thoburn, Chand and Procter 2005). Friends may be a mixed blessing, depending who they are, and the youth crime area highlights the importance of encouraging *pro-social* friends (Nacro 2005). Good assessment and planning are essential preconditions (Cleaver and Walker 2004).

Each of the nine dimensions of the Index was divided into a number of subcategories, as set out in Figure 5.1. There is not space to discuss the subcategories here and it is hoped that they are self-explanatory. There was no attempt to 'weight' sections, which would be difficult, although the first and third probably feel particularly important. (In the *safety* section, young people were not asked themselves if they had made an allegation against their carers of maltreatment but, if we became aware that they had, this seemed a relevant consideration.)

Care and control

- Addressing children's needs, child-oriented
- Warm and caring, responsive
- Quality of physical environment
- Praise and responsibility, positive expectations
- Opportunities for success, improvement of self-image
- Clear boundaries, behavioural management
- Opportunities for inclusion

Stability and continuity

- Placement changes
- Pressure to move prematurely, opportunity to remain
- Changes in caregivers, predictability in daily care

Safety

- Child protection issues
- Management of risk, e.g. lifestyle
- Peer violence
- Allegation(s)

Inter-professional working

- Support for identified problems, particularly liaison between placement and school
- Help with behavioural, emotional and social problems
- A coherent approach

Family links

- Encourage contact in a discriminatory way (including siblings)
- Consider young person's views
- Attempt to obtain support of parents
- Consider transport issues

Close relationship with at least one adult

- Champion, advocate, someone to stand up for young person (including professional)
- Support, time to spend with young person
- Reliability
- Effectiveness of social worker or educational psychologist role
- Encouragement of appropriate contact with key adult(s) from the past

Ethnicity and culture

- Culture, language and religion
- Context or location
- Consideration to ethnic matching, staff mix or role models
- Daily care

Friendships

- Encouragement of *pro-social* friends

Planning and aftercare

- High-quality assessment and planning, follow processes
- Desired placements; choice, matching
- Young person's involvement, listen to young person

Figure 5.1 The 'Quality of Care' Index

These different dimensions were then converted into a number of questions, which the young people were asked in a follow-up interview at Stage 2. These are listed in Table 5.1, together with a summary of interviewees' answers.

An additional four questions were asked about stability and continuity. However, most of the young people we were able to meet with at Stage 2 had not changed placements in the follow-up period. Although three of the questions were still relevant for those who remained, we felt that there was some confusion in young people's answers and therefore decided to omit them from the analysis.

Table 5.1 shows that most young people were very positive about the care they received. One pupil said of his BESD school: 'It's like my second home. I love this school more than anything.' This, of course, raises questions about reliability and whether the youngsters were being truthful in their responses (the same obviously applies to adults). It may be difficult to encourage those receiving services to be critical of the care provided: despite our efforts at explanation, including producing written leaflets, young people may be unclear about our status and the implications of expressing disapproval. Assessing the caring qualities of professionals also depends on expectations and young people's previous experience of adults with parenting responsibilities. We were particularly aware of the context in which interviews were conducted with those living in foster homes: we usually sat in the lounge, generally a confined area, and foster carers (mainly female carers) often sat in or were within audible range of what was being said. This was appropriate, caring behaviour and provided support for young people meeting an unfamiliar adult, at least during the initial contact. But it would have been difficult for some young people to express critical opinions without foster carers being aware so they may have felt constrained. We wonder if other research on foster care has taken this into account. Similar considerations may apply in residential care, but the public space is quite different and the environments are more emotionally neutral.

Our responses are generally consistent with findings from other relevant studies in foster care (Wilson et al. 2004) and children's homes (Berridge and Brodie 1998; Sinclair and Gibbs 1998) – young people are mostly positive about the care they receive. Hence, the perhaps surprisingly high figure of nine in every ten responding that, overall, they had been well looked after. A large majority of respondents also felt that people looking after them had been caring and interested in their welfare. Four in every five said they were praised when they did something well and the same proportion felt that carers had tried to help keep them out of trouble. Encouragingly, 80 per cent also thought that there was an adult in their placement(s) who, when required, would stand up for them and really help them out. However, responses were not indiscriminate and one in

Table 5.1 Young people's responses to 'Quality of Care' questions at Stage 2 (n =75)

Question	No (%)	Not really (%)	Sort of (%)	Yes (%)	Don't know/no answer (%)
Care and control					
Overall, do you think the people here have looked after you well?	1	1	7	91	0
Have the people looking after you been caring and interested in what happened to you?	3	0	9	85	3
Would you say the building(s) and rooms are nice and comfortable here (or not)?	13	0	19	68	0
When you've done well at something, have the people looking after you given you praise?	5	3	8	84	0
Have the people looking after you trusted you to do things (like around the house, with things that are expensive or to go and buy things from the shops…)?	13	0	3	84	0
Have you been given chances to do things that you might be good at and that might make you feel good about yourself?	15	0	4	81	0
Do you think that the rules here are clear that you are expected to follow?	8	3	1	87	1
Have the people looking after you tried to help you to keep out of trouble?	4	3	7	80	6

Table 5.1 cont.

Question	No (%)	Not really (%)	Sort of (%)	Yes (%)	Don't know/no answer (%)
Safety					
Have you felt safe where you have been living over these last few months?	1	4	11	82	1
If you didn't feel safe, is there someone you have been able to talk to who would do something about it?	4	3	4	88	1
Do you think the people looking after you would help if young people were drinking too much, taking drugs or putting themselves at risk?	5	0	3	81	11
Has there been much bullying here between people or name-calling that's meant to hurt?	45	1	20	29	4
Do you think the people looking after you have tried to stop people being bullied or called names?	7	3	8	69	13
Inter-professional working					
Do you think the people looking after you have been good in getting outside help for young people to deal with their problems, like if they were using drugs or thinking of harming themselves?	12	0	1	68	19
Would someone have been given outside help if their behaviour was getting out of control, such as stealing things or being violent?	12	0	1	68	19
Do you think the people looking after you and your teachers have been good at keeping in touch with each other about how you are getting on or any problems you might be having?	9	3	3	79	7

Question					
Does it feel like the different people (carer/teacher/social worker and so on) know what they are all doing – or does it all get mixed up sometimes like 'communication problems'?	21	4	9	59	7

Family links

Have the people looking after you been good in helping young people's relationships with their families?	7	3	7	81	3
Do you think the people looking after you would try to do something if contact with a family member was not helping a young person?	11	0	11	72	7
Have the people who make decisions taken into account your views about the contact you want with your family?	8	1	3	80	8
Have the people looking after you been good at getting on with your family?	8	1	5	79	7
Have the people who make decisions asked your family about how you should be looked after and taught at school?	23	4	3	45	25
Has travelling to your home and back been difficult for you?	33	3	4	48	12
Do you think the people looking after you make young people's families or friends welcome when they visit?	7	3	8	75	8

Close relationship with at least one adult

Has there been an adult where you have lived who will stand up for you and really help you out?	11	0	5	80	4
Has that person given you as much time and support as you need?	9	1	3	79	8
Has that person been reliable – do what they say they'll do?	8	1	16	67	8
Have people encouraged you to keep in touch with people who have been important to you in the past, like a teacher or social worker?	16	4	7	59	15

Table 5.1 cont.

Question	No (%)	Not really (%)	Sort of (%)	Yes (%)	Don't know/no answer (%)
Ethnicity and culture					
Do people understand your way of life here or has it felt different? I'm thinking about things such as the food you like to eat, the music you like to listen to, the clothes you wear or how you look after your hair and so on?	16	3	7	52	23
Are there enough staff or teachers here from your own background?	20	10	4	51	15
What about the area where this home or school is – does it feel the same as where your family lives or where you come from?	40	5	4	36	15
Friendships					
What have the people looking after you been like at helping you keep in touch with friends who are important to you?	23	4	5	61	7
Would your carers or the staff say something if they felt a friend was a bad influence on you, like they might get you into trouble?	8	3	5	79	5
Have you been given chances to mix and meet different people away from here?	21	3	3	71	3
Planning and aftercare					
Do you think the people who make decisions have been good at planning what's going to happen to you in the future?	15	3	11	71	4
Do you think this is the right home or school for you (or should you be at a different one)?	12	0	12	73	1
Have you been given a say in what happens to you?	13	0	16	68	3

three respondents were more equivocal about the quality of their physical environment.

About four in every five young people indicated that they had generally felt safe where they were living over the follow-up period. Nearer 90 per cent replied that, if they did not feel safe, there was someone to whom they could talk and who could do something about it. Interestingly though, half felt that they had encountered some bullying or name-calling in placements and carers had not always intervened. Perceptions of care planning and inter-professional working were mainly positive but tended to be more mixed: around two-thirds felt that future planning had been good and the same proportion answered that outside specialist help would be sought where necessary for specific problems, such as drug misuse or self-harm. One in three respondents thought that communication problems sometimes occurred between different professionals.

Responses signalled that services had been mainly sensitive concerning relationships with young people's families. Only one in eight young people felt that their own views about the contact they wanted with their family were not taken into account. Interestingly, as many as half the sample commented that the journey was difficult between home and placement. Responses for cultivating friendships were mainly encouraging.

About a fifth of the young people providing information for the 'Quality of Care' Index questions were from minority ethnic groups. Though numbers were small, those from minorities did not give particularly different answers to the ethnicity and culture questions. Thus, white and minority ethnic young people were equally likely to feel that their way of life was not understood where they lived; that there were insufficient carers or teachers from the same background; or that the area where they were based felt the same as their own neighbourhood or locality. This suggests that neighbourhood or locality, class and upbringing are important alongside ethnicity in the cultural differences experienced by looked after children.

Young people's summary responses to the 'Quality of Care' questions

Summary responses to questions in the eight subsections of the 'Quality of Care' Index are presented in Table 5.2. For easier interpretation, categories have been retitled 'very good' ('yes'), 'good' ('sort of'), 'fair' ('not really') and 'poor' ('no'). The overall positive nature of findings is again evident. Eighty-eight per cent of responses were 'very good' for the 'care and control' issues. There were nearer four-fifths of 'very good' responses for the 'safety', 'family links' and 'close relationship with at least one adult' sections. Some young people were unaware of inter-professional links and so were unable to respond. Young people's friendships received a more mixed response.

Table 5.2 Summary of young people's responses at Stage 2 to subsections of the 'Quality of Care' Index (n = 75)

Subsection	Very good (%)	Good (%)	Fair (%)	Poor (%)	No answer; missing (%)
Care and control	88	11	1	0	0
Safety	81	15	1	0	3
Inter-professional working	61	9	4	5	20
Family links	82	15	9	3	1
Close relationship with at least one adult	77	8	3	5	7
Ethnicity and culture	33	24	9	11	23
Friendships	59	24	13	3	1
Planning and aftercare	74	15	6	6	3

Researcher ratings

The next stage of the analysis was to apply researcher ratings to the 'Quality of Care' data. This is, no doubt, subjective to some degree, but it may be useful to attempt to begin to theorise by recognising patterns in the data and seeking to impose some order on complex social experiences and relationships. We did this in view of the caveats expressed earlier about developing the schedule, but there were also some inconsistencies in young people's responses. However, one of the main influences on our ratings was young people's responses to the Index questions listed in Table 5.1. Our researcher ratings also took account generally of Stage 2 interviews with young people as well as with carers or social workers. Stage 1 background and young people's interviews helped to provide a context, particularly for those living in long-term placements.

To reiterate, we were seeking to rate the quality of care offered during the nine-month, follow-up period, and this included the overall 'care package' as well as what specifically had occurred in placements. (For example, one young woman was very self-conscious about her appearance and had attempted to 'superglu' back her ears. Her social worker had organised corrective surgery to deal with the problem.) Ratings were therefore founded on the eight subcategories already discussed and excluded educational experiences and services, which are discussed later. (We appreciate that some in the boarding school world would question whether pedagogy may be separated from the overall residential experience and 'the 24-hour curriculum'.) One important factor was whether or not placements had broken down during the follow-up period. We took into account young people and carers' comments on the extent to which it was felt that needs were being met, if the young person was said to be settled, as well as social work and wider professional involvement.

Initially, two members of the research team independently rated the quality of care offered. One had undertaken the majority of the fieldwork interviews and was, therefore, well-positioned to do this, although it could be difficult not to bring in extraneous information, for example on education. We read detailed summaries that we had produced from interviews. As above, ratings were undertaken only for the 75 young people who agreed to be interviewed for Stage 2. A four-fold classification of the quality of care was used: 'very good', 'good', 'fair' and 'poor'. (For statisticians, inter-rater reliability [kappa] was 0.49, a moderate level of initial agreement.) This was a complex task and cases were discussed where different ratings were given and a final judgement was negotiated. Overall ratings are presented in Table 5.3.

Table 5.3 'Quality of Care' researcher ratings (%) (n = 75)

Very good	36
Good	45
Fair	17
Poor	1
Total	100

Our research ratings were, in part, derived from the interviews with young people so we would expect some similarities between the two measures. Table 5.3 shows that the researcher ratings found the quality of care to be mainly positive, a finding that is consistent with young people's own general views but less optimistic.

There were few significant differences in researcher ratings for children with different characteristics. The quality of care provided was very similar for males and females alike. It appeared slightly better for minority ethnic than white children but numbers were small and differences not statistically significant. The same applied to younger members of our sample (aged 11–13 years at the outset) compared with those who were older (aged 14–16 years). There was no evidence that either the *County*, *Metro* or *Borough* authorities stood out from the others in the quality of what was offered.

The one area where there was a difference was according to placement at Stage 1. For 12 of the 18 young people living in foster care, the overall quality of care provided was judged to be 'very good'. Only one of the residential BESD school experiences was judged to be less than good. In contrast, 5 of the 17 children's homes' (without education) residents were considered to have been provided with care that was only 'fair'. This still meant, though, that 10 of the 17 children's homes group had been provided with 'good' care. Nonetheless, if we contrast the quality of care provided to those resident at Stage 1 in children's homes with the other categories combined, we find that the care offered to the latter was significantly better (χ^2 test; df = 1; $p <.01$). This is an important and complex issue to which we return in Chapter 8, alongside other findings on the use of services, care outcomes and costs. We also incorporate this rating in our analysis of outcomes in the next two chapters.

Summary points

- Quality of care was assessed for the 75 young people who agreed to participate in the nine-month follow-up interview.

- We developed our own 'Quality of Care' Index based on up-to-date knowledge in child welfare and (residential) special education.

- Young people were mainly very positive about the quality of service they received. They perceived it to be particularly good in relation to providing overall care and control, as well as safety – two very important elements. We need to be cautious in how these findings are interpreted, especially perhaps for those in foster care.

- Researcher ratings confirmed these generally positive results but were less optimistic. The only main variable that distinguished the quality of care offered was placement at Stage 1. Three in every five residents in children's homes (without education) had been provided with care that was 'good' but the quality of care was significantly better for those who had been living in foster care or residential BESD schools.

Chapter 6

Outcomes

Patterns of behavioural, emotional and social difficulties (BESD) and outcomes

In relation both to patterns of current difficulties and outcome, we were interested to explore behavioural and educational progress separately. Here, we focus on changes in young people's behavioural, emotional and social problems and we turn to educational progress in the next chapter.

Since our sample of young people was selected on the basis of the behavioural management challenge that they presented, we expected high levels of difficulty across the sample. Evidence of this is included in Chapters 3 and 4, and in the Appendix. Here, we look in more detail at the sorts of difficulties presented, the level of agreement between different informants and the change in difficulties over time.

We measured the behavioural problems that young people presented initially for the purposes of screening (see the Appendix) and then again at Stage 1 and Stage 2. At Stage 1, information about behaviour was sought from social workers or heads of care and young people. For the adult perspective, we asked young people's social workers whether particular types of behaviour were typical of each young person and we applied a rating to indicate the frequency and the severity with which the behaviour was evident. Young people were asked to indicate the extent to which each of these behaviours applied to them on a tick-box questionnaire.

At Stage 2, the intention was that the adult perspective would be provided by the person who best knew the young person: for those young people who participated in the research, this was usually a carer, a residential key worker or a unit manager. For non-participating young people, social workers fulfilled this role. We refer to these informants as providing 'carer or professional' viewpoints. At Stage 2, adults were asked not only whether the behaviours still applied but whether they detected changes in the frequency or severity of the five key problem behaviours mentioned previously.

Several carers and professionals, in particular those in the residential BESD schools, described how noticeable changes in young people's behaviour were to be seen in their first few months in placement, which frequently pre-dated our contact with them by some time. These improvements were rarely a complete cessation of a given behaviour but rather a reduction in its intensity or frequency. Moreover, there were fluctuations; thus, young people might be relatively well-behaved for long periods but both predictable and unpredictable events in young people's lives might be associated with a re-emergence of difficult behaviour. An example of the former might be the prospect of returning home for holidays for some of those in residential school settings, and for all young people a variety of events such as a young person joining or leaving a placement (Barter *et al.* 2004) or experiences with birth family members could upset their equilibrium. Whitaker, Archer and Hicks (1998) have highlighted the tendency for cyclical turbulence in residential care.

Thus, trying to identify quantifiable 'outcomes' is certainly complex. The subtlety of such fluctuations is not easily captured by standard instruments (Parker *et al.* 1991). It is also the case that the group of troubled young people in our study had not been exposed to circumscribed conditions or a standard period of either risk or intervention. Nevertheless, we anticipated that it would be possible to assess whether or not young people's problems were showing signs of improvement over this period.

For the purposes of this chapter we focus largely on the information provided *about* young people by carers and professionals at the follow-up interview. This is because the information is available for a far larger proportion of the sample than if we relied solely on the young people's reports. That said, we will present some information from young people themselves and explore the extent of agreement between the reports from young people and those from the adult carers or professionals.

Representativeness of the sample

As already noted, it did not prove possible to meet with all of the young people selected for the first interview and further cases inevitably were lost between Stages 1 and 2. Difficulties were sometimes encountered in obtaining follow-up information from carers or professionals as well. The sample sizes for the analyses included in this and the next chapter on educational outcomes are: 130 professionals and 99 young people at Stage 1; 139 carers or professionals and 75 young people at Stage 2.

As we have also discussed, we compared the young people who took part with those who declined the second or both interviews. We found that there were no differences in their age, gender or ethnicity and there was no systematic difference according to level of behaviour problems as measured on the Strengths and Difficulties Questionnaire completed by professionals or carers (see below). We were more likely to maintain contact with young people in the residential BESD schools and to a lesser extent, dual-registered establishments, than those in children's homes or foster care. However, the factor bearing the strongest association with young people's participation, perhaps unsurprisingly, was their mobility. Young people who moved placement in the course of our study period were significantly less likely to participate in Stage 1 and were very much over-represented in the group that could not be interviewed at Stage 2.

Measures used in assessing BESD and outcomes

In order to assess change over time, we employed at Stages 1 and 2 both the self-completion and the informant (parent) versions of the Strengths and Difficulties Questionnaire (SDQ) (Goodman 1997). This validated instrument is commonly used by child welfare researchers. However, our view was that this instrument might not be sensitive to subtle changes in the frequency or intensity of behaviours and we did not necessarily expect to see dramatic changes in young people's scores over the nine months.

For this reason, we also questioned both young people and carers or professionals about their perceptions of changes in behaviour over time. The specific areas we focused on that are relevant to this chapter were: behaviour in the home and community environment (in particular, aggressive and violent outbursts); peer relationships; adult relationships; misuse of alcohol or drugs; self-harm; and police contact. These areas of difficulty are broadly consistent with those discussed in relation to the screening process (see the Appendix), although we added questions about difficulties in relationships.

We had always been interested in exploring more general outcomes for young people: their own perceptions of how life was treating them. The young people who agreed to take part in an interview were therefore also asked to rate themselves, using a visual scale (a ladder with ten rungs), on six areas of general well-being at Stages 1 and 2. The areas we selected were: schooling, general happiness, relationships with family, staying out of trouble, achieving their own set goals and relationships with friends.

The nature of young people's behavioural, emotional and social problems

We have noted that the most common problems for the young people initially selected for our sample were reported, at screening, as being violent or displaying aggressive outbursts, or both, in the previous three months, which applied to 80 per cent of the sample (these are referred to as general 'behaviour' difficulties). One young man we met at a residential BESD school explained it well:

> Do you want to know what 'EBD' is [emotional and behavioural difficulties]? Well EBD is where you're on the garage roof and you throw a brick from it and it hits a window and when the teacher tells you off you say 'fuck off'. With EBD you get stressed and act younger than your age.

Around half the sample had run into problems significant enough to earn them police cautions or convictions; about one-third were reported as having worrying problems with drugs or alcohol misuse; and a quarter were described as self-harming. Our interviews broadened this out to cover a wider range of issues, including peer and adult relationships. Figure 6.1 illustrates the professionals' views of the severity of these problems for the young people concerned at Stage 1.

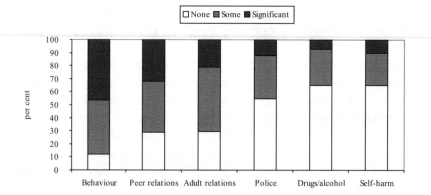

Figure 6.1 Frequency and severity of specific problems at Stage 1

The general behaviour problems illustrated in the first column of Figure 6.1 refer primarily to the angry outbursts mentioned above. Problems with police contact, alcohol or drug consumption and self-harm were much less frequent than difficulties with controlling anger and managing relationships with other people.

All the young people experienced problems in more than one domain, although their severity varied. A simple summing of the number of difficulties showed that just short of a quarter of the sample (23%) were described as having difficulties in two areas. Slightly more than a half the sample (58%) had three or four problems; the remaining 19 per cent were showing multiple difficulties; that is, five or more types of problem. We found significant positive correlations between behavioural problems and relationships with adults, and between relationships with adults and interaction with peers.[1] There was a very weak association between behaviour and problems with the police but the stronger relationship was between police contact and alcohol or drug misuse.[2]

We were interested in whether the characteristics of young people were associated with the sorts of behavioural difficulties they presented. Unfortunately, the number of young people in some categories (e.g. when identifying whether the young person had 'some' or 'significant' problems in a particular domain) became quite low. We elected to simplify this categorisation to indicate the presence of any level of difficulty in a given domain. We then explored whether particular problems were more common given the young people's gender, age, ethnicity, the level of background 'risk', reason for being away, length of time away from home, time in current placement, type of current placement, and the route by which young people became part of the study.

The results of these analyses are presented in Table 6.1. There were no differences in levels of general behaviour problems according to any of the characteristics: this is because behaviour problems were so common within the sample. Peer and adult relationship problems showed a fairly similar pattern: both tended to be less common where young people were in foster care, had been away from home for more than four years, had higher levels background risk or had experienced abuse or neglect.

Alcohol or drug misuse were more common among girls and, more to the point, among older girls. Although age was not related to alcohol or drug misuse for boys (26% of 11–13-year-olds against 31% 14–16-year-olds), there was a dramatic increase in use among older girls (10% in the younger group rising to 56% of the older group) despite the fact that the girls in our sample tended to be older than the boys. When the schools group was excluded some difference remained but its magnitude was reduced and was no longer statistically significant.

We were unable to record systematically the types of substances that young people were using. Our contemporaneous research notes suggest that several of the older girls were experiencing problems with alcohol, in particular binge drinking, which was increasing their risk both of health and personal safety problems. Alcohol consumption is a wider problem among young women and girls than males (Advisory Council on the Misuse of Drugs 2006). The other relevant finding for alcohol and drug misuse concerned the particular difficulties

Table 6.1 Frequency of specific types of behaviour problems at Stage 1, according to young people's characteristics

	Behaviour problems (%)	Peer problems (%)	Adult relationship problems (%)	Substance misuse problems (%)	Self-harm problems (%)	Police contact problems (%)
Gender						
male (n = 73)	88	75	70	29	26	45
female (n = 45)	86	64	71	44	49	44
Age (at start of study)						
11–<14 years (n = 43)	93	65	67	21	37	37
14–<16 years (n = 76)	84	74	73	42	34	49
Ethnicity						
white (n = 94)	85	75	70	35	37	40
any black or other minority background (n = 25)	96	56	75	36	28	63
Type of placement – Stage 1						
dual-registered children's home (n = 24)	96	79	78	29	46	50
children's home, no education (n = 31)	80	70	80	67	43	70
foster care (n = 39)	82	55	53	26	21	31
residential BESD school (n = 24)	96	89	81	13	36	32

Table 6.1 cont.

	Behaviour problems (%)	Peer problems (%)	Adult relationship problems (%)	Substance misuse problems (%)	Self-harm problems (%)	Police contact problems (%)
Duration away from home (at start of study)						
<2 years ($n = 36$)	94	75	86	44	40	54
2–<4 years ($n = 21$)	76	90	71	35	43	42
4–<5 years ($n = 30$)	93	58	58	29	30	31
Over 5 years ($n = 32$)	81	66	66	30	28	49
Duration current placement (at start)						
<6 months ($n = 31$)	94	74	87	43	37	55
6–<12 months ($n = 23$)	91	54	71	50	37	58
over 12 months ($n = 65$)	83	75	63	25	33	35
History 'risk' group						
low ($n = 32$)	88	84	81	29	38	61
high ($n = 68$)	88	64	66	40	38	42
Reason for being away from home						
behaviour or education ($n = 19$)	90	84	89	22	36	42
family difficulties ($n = 23$)	96	83	74	35	34	52
abuse or neglect ($n = 68$)	84	61	62	49	34	47

experienced in children's homes (without education). Some residents who were unoccupied during the day, posed problems with cannabis use.

Case Study: Andy

Andy's difficulties with drugs were more severe than the majority of our sample. According to his social worker Andy began smoking cannabis when 11 years old. At Stage 1 of the research, aged 13, he was described as smoking large amounts of 'skunk'. He was thought to be quite involved in the drugs scene in his local town and spent a good deal of time with older males. He had recently been caught in possession of heroin, which he was holding for others. He was described as 'a real tough character' who liked to be 'top dog'. He had been in and out of care, primarily because of his unmanageable behaviour, and he had a string of at least 40 offences, including street robbery, mostly committed, according to his social worker, to fund his drug habit. He had previously spent time in a secure unit and at follow-up he had just been returned there for the second time. The social worker believed that the secure unit had helped while it lasted but, as soon as he was released, his difficulties with drugs and the offences needed to keep him supplied, re-emerged.

Although not presented in Table 6.1 we did find that misuse of alcohol or drugs was more common in our London Borough than either of the other two authorities. It was also much less evident among our schools group. It is tempting to assume that young people have easier access to alcohol or drugs in the capital; however, as a greater proportion of the *Borough* sample lived out of area this may not be a valid assumption. But, despite the small numbers it did appear that even when comparing children's home residents across the three authorities, there were higher rates of misuse within *Borough*.

In relation to the relatively low alcohol and drug misuse among the schools group, two factors may be at work. It is possible that our professionals' reports were an underestimate. Residents of several of these schools returned home for at least some weekends or holiday periods and the school-based staff admitted that they may not have been aware of alcohol or drug use outside the school. These schools generally provided a protected environment for young people where their ability to access substances while on-site or in the immediate vicinity would be severely limited. They are no longer (if ever) 'total institutions' in Goffman's (1961) parlance. The degree of social protection they offer should count in their favour, so long as residents' separation from home does not jeopardise their re-integration and adjustment. The penultimate column in Table 6.1 is for self-harming behaviour. The only significant association here was with gender, with self-harm being more common among girls. Proportions were otherwise similar across age, ethnicity and type of placement.

Case Study: Julie

Julie, aged 15, lived in a small children's home when we first encountered her. There were only two residents and before this she had experienced 15 different placements. Julie missed much of her education and would not take any GCSEs. By Stage 2 she had moved again to a hostel for homeless young people. She was very unhappy there and had two trips to the 'emergency room', one for smashing glass and injuring herself and another for taking an overdose. Julie felt very low about her family life and the limited opportunities open to her because of her lack of education. She was taking anti-depressants and attending sessions with a psychiatrist. She had been charged with two assaults and one count of criminal damage since the Stage 1 interview.

Julie wanted to study hairdressing but was unable to do so without GCSEs so she enrolled on a college course for basic skills. She was to attend four hours each week but her attendance was poor most of the time due to 'feeling low'.

Our final area of interest in behavioural problems was police contact. We tried to include all arrests that led to cautions and/or convictions; that said, it was often unclear whether cautions were informal or formal warnings, so the numbers may be rather higher than they might have been. Again, problems were relatively frequent for this sample. In relation to the characteristics of young people, we found a slight increase (not significant) for police contact to be more common among young people from minority ethnic backgrounds. This of course is consistent with other evidence, which suggests a tendency for African-Caribbean young people to be more likely to come into contact with the police (Pitts 2001). We had only a small number of young people from minority backgrounds so it was not possible to investigate this issue in more detail.

Police contact was less common for young people who were either looked after in foster care or who were not looked after but placed in residential BESD schools, slightly under one-third of young people in each case. Half of looked after young people who were attending dual-registered establishments had experienced problems with the police but by far the most frequent difficulties were to be found, again, among those who were placed in (non-educational) children's homes, where 70 per cent of young people had experienced police contact.

One factor that should be borne in mind when examining the high levels of police contact for residents of children's homes is that many of these contacts arose from difficulties within the residential home. We did not systematically record the detail of the misdemeanours but anecdotally we are aware that assaults on staff or damage to property within children's homes may routinely be reported to the police. Some of the incidents we heard about were serious but there were others that might have been handled by other means in a different setting. One young woman told us that she was waiting for a date to appear at court following her arrest for 'affray'. This would be her fourth visit to court. 'I was drunk and swearing at the police woman and I pushed staff here'. 'It's very scary – I've been to court before for the same thing – I wasn't always drunk though.' Nacro (2005) has highlighted how children's homes can 'criminalise' young people by the way they respond to their different behaviours. This may account for quite a lot of the apparent difference between authorities in offending rates of looked after young people.

Some commentators suggest that the over-representation of difficulties for looked after teenagers may, in part, be concerned with the fairly recent entrants to the care system or those entering care with pre-existing problems. Of course our study design cannot fully address this question since we deliberately omitted young people without problems. However, there was surprisingly little association between any of the problem areas we identified and the young people's time away from home. Therefore, while we cannot say whether those who stay long in care are less likely to be problematic, we can say that the looked after population who present behaviour management challenges are by no means all recent entrants to care.

Correspondence between carer or professionals' and young people's views of their behavioural, emotional and social problems at Stage 1

We have discussed the patterns of behaviour problems as identified by carers or professionals, but did the young people's reports agree with these findings? We did not manage to speak directly to all of the young people but there were sufficient numbers to make the exercise worthwhile. While there was a reasonable degree of agreement in the majority of cases, there was a minority of young people who seemed to view things quite differently from carers or professionals. In many ways this is perhaps understandable since, ethically, we needed to be careful about the phrasing of our questions when interviewing young people. For example, we asked carers or professionals directly about the extent of young people's behavioural problems, but we asked young people whether they got into trouble because of their behaviour. The two questions not only draw on individual perceptions but do so in ways that are conceptually different.

Though numbers were small, young people sometimes declared themselves as having been in more contact with the police than carers or professionals had reported; and, on occasion, denied any contact with the police when, according to adults, they had received unofficial or official warnings. Similar patterns emerged when it came to looking at alcohol or drug misuse and self-harm. That is, while the answers of most adult and young respondents showed some agreement, there was a minority where views diverged. However, it was rare for young people and carers or professionals' responses to disagree across several different domains, and neither was there an obvious pattern in reporting higher or lower frequency or severity by either type of respondent.

Changes in outcomes over time

Both carers or professionals and the young people themselves reported considerable behaviour management challenges at Stage 1, but the main focus of this study was to examine 'outcomes' for young people. To this end, bearing in mind the limitations outlined at the beginning of the chapter, we now consider the degree to which changes for better or worse could be identified for young people over the nine-month follow-up period. Most of what follows uses reports from carers or professionals. We found a reasonable amount of agreement between adults' and young people's perceptions of progress but, as with the Stage 1 data, there were some areas of difference.

Figure 6.2 illustrates the direction of change over the follow-up period in each problem area, showing five discrete categories of outcome for each domain: deteriorating, continuing, improving, resolved, or never been a problem. The relative size of the 'improving' categories, particularly in the area of general behaviour and relationship problems, is encouraging. Although the numbers are relatively small, the fact that some young people have managed to resolve their problems in one or more domains is certainly to be welcomed. Yet it is also the case that problems continue without change for many and some young people have developed new problems (included with those marked 'deteriorating' on the chart).

Clearly, given our sample size, more detailed analysis on a five-category outcome variable was not feasible so we created two new variables by combining the 'improving' and 'resolved' categories, and combining the 'continuing' with 'deteriorating' categories.

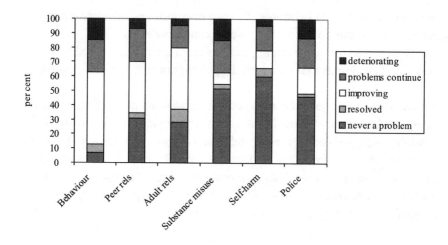

Figure 6.2 Change in young people's problems over the follow-up period

Factors associated with change in levels of behavioural, emotional and social problems

There were very few significant associations between these outcome ratings and the young people's characteristics. Gender, ethnicity, family history (level of risk and reason for entry) or factors such as time away from home or length of placement were unrelated to changes in young people's behaviour. Whether placed in or out of area was similarly unrelated. The type of placement experienced over the nine months (described in Chapter 4) had little influence, although there were signs that self-harming was less likely to improve for those who remained in the residential BESD schools or those who changed type of package over the follow-up period, but there were too few for statistical tests. Those who had any placement change were more likely to be described as improving with regard to their use of drugs or alcohol. Overall, whilst there was a good deal of change for the better, no clear patterns emerged to suggest any particular course of action may be more likely to bring these outcomes about. Other explanations, therefore, must be sought.

We have not yet considered the association between age and changes in types of problems. Interestingly, we found that difficulties with *general behaviour* (our shorthand for behaviour characterised by violent or aggressive outbursts) were significantly more likely to improve for the older group – the 14–16 rather than 11–<14-year-olds (χ^2 test = 4.8; df = 1; p <.05). There was a tendency for greater improvement in this type of behaviour among girls but this was not significant and may well be accounted for by the fact that girls were slightly older than boys. Age was not, however, associated with any of the other difficulties we have been exploring.

The finding that aggressive outbursts tend to reduce with increasing age does merit further discussion in so far as it might, at first, appear counterintuitive. We asked the carers and professionals how they understood the changes in young people's behaviour to have come about. There were a variety of responses but, broadly speaking, carers talked about simply growing-up; about the role of boundaries and structure within the home or unit; about their response as carers in how they dealt with issues; and about increases in young people's self-esteem and self-confidence, which enabled them to deal with disappointment and frustration without 'kicking off'. The following are a series of responses which illustrate these themes.

A typical response was 'Maturing, he is now one of the older boys in the home'. Further discussion suggested that, in the carer's view, this young man now saw himself as something of a role model for the younger boys and had grown into the responsibilities implied by that position. However, one young man reported how these circumstances could lead to too much unwanted pressure:

> There was no one in my age group – well, there was one but we didn't get on. [My friend] had left and I missed him. They [younger residents] all started looking up to me – like a big brother – I didn't like it.

A key worker saw one young person's adaptation as more of a pragmatic response:

> She has reached adolescence, she sees herself as an adult and is demanding rights and respect as an adult. Previously she couldn't express herself in a way that was reasonable, she made demands and ran straight into a head-on collision course – especially at home. Her main attributes and skills now are that she understands the 'rules of engagement' – that makes it sound like a battlefield but it feels that way sometimes – but she understands now that in order to get where you want to go, you have to abide by the rules, which allow that to happen. Last year she was really struggling with this.

One foster carer, who had cared long term for a young man who had just left school at the time of the Stage 2 interview, also acknowledged the impact of intensive efforts to plan appropriately for the young person in her care. She stated:

> In the last year his attitude has changed completely… I couldn't say anybody could have done any more… It's the work they [the social worker and the education team] have done and that he has grown-up.

Others recognised growing-up but also emphasised that the way boundaries were set and conflicts dealt with were important:

> It is how you treat them. Where she came from was a strict regime and you can't be strict with a tearaway. We gave parameters and we made a deal and she has stuck to it – she's broken it occasionally but not on the whole.

Another foster carer introduced the idea of the young person coming to accept the way things were:

> Time and growing-up, [she said] accepting the way life has been. That his friends might have the perfect family but he doesn't. He also knows that whatever happens here we confront it and we deal with it then carry on.

The final area that carers touched on when discussing positive changes in young people's behaviour was that of consistency of care and trust of adults. One young woman's head of care described her thus:

> She appreciates that we care consistently. She's tested and we are still here, this is true of all of them [residents in the unit] but especially this young person.

Concerning another form of behavioural control, of the 75 young people we talked with at Stage 2, 71 were able to say whether or not they were prescribed medication for attention deficit hyperactivity disorder (ADHD) symptoms. Of these, one-quarter – 18 of the 71 – confirmed that they were taking stimulant drugs such as Concerta® or Ritalin®, which are designed to alleviate ADHD. Although these drugs are reported to have produced positive results in terms of changes in the behaviour of individual young people (Jensen *et al.* 2001), their use remains controversial and attracts criticism (Timimi and Taylor 2004). We found, perhaps unsurprisingly, that the use of these drugs was disproportionately represented within the residential BESD schools group. Twelve of the 23 young people in residential BESD schools were using ADHD medication, compared with just 1 of the 15 residents of dual-registered establishments, 2 of the 18 living with foster carers, and 3 of 14 residents of children's homes. Comparing the residential BESD schools with all other types of placement, the difference is statistically significant (χ^2 test $=12.9$; df $= 1$; $p < .001$).

ADHD medication use was more common for boys and somewhat more common among the younger age groups. However, numbers were relatively small and it seems likely that these observed differences may be a reflection of the characteristics of the schools population, rather than different group practices. This use of prescribed drugs in the residential BESD schools strikes us as high and merits more detailed examination.

In terms of difficulties with *peer and adult relationships*, we found no significant differences in the levels of change according to the overall characteristics we included in the analysis. *Misuse of alcohol or drugs* was less likely to show an improvement over time when young people were in either type of residential education setting. And finally, although numbers were small, significantly more young people of minority ethnic background were reported to be in the improving category for *police contact* $(\chi^2$ test = 6.2; df = 2; p <.05).

We looked at one further measure: whether change in young people's problems varied with their reports of the quality of care they received. Quality of care, as measured by our index (described in Chapter 5) was not systematically associated with changes in any of the problem areas we examined.

Constructing a single BESD outcome measure

We wanted to develop a single variable to indicate an overall picture of the level of young people's behavioural change, which incorporated the direction and extent of change in all problem areas (general behaviour, relationships with peers and adults, alcohol and drug misuse, self-harm and police contact). Obviously, young people varied in the changes they made over time: a few young people appeared to resolve their main problems, while some were developing additional areas of difficulty.

To develop this composite variable, two of the authors independently examined the direction of change in each problem area for each young person. Each case was then allocated to one of four groups: 'much improvement', 'some improvement', a mixed picture or little change or 'worsening problems'.

These independent ratings were then compared. The initial level of agreement was acceptable (explained statistically, kappa = .83) and the disputed cases were discussed and a joint rating agreed.

What was encouraging about this approach was that over half of the young people in the sample were grouped into one of the 'improving' categories, although problems were worsening for one in five young people.

We did not find any significant associations between this overall outcome measure and any of the personal characteristics or other factors that we have included in these analyses so far. This is not particularly surprising. The individual domain ratings were rarely associated with these measures, and, as shown previously, some young people showed improvements in some areas but worsening problems in others. Thus attempts to amalgamate such scores may mask any change that may exist.

The 'Strengths and Difficulties Questionnaire'

The 'Strengths and Difficulties Questionnaire' (SDQ) focuses on four types of problematic behaviour: conduct, hyperactivity, emotional difficulties and peer relationship problems. Each of these may be seen to bear some relationship to the first three of the types of difficulty discussed in the preceding section, namely, *general behaviour problems, peer relationships* and *adult relationships*.

Regrettably, we had much missing data. Completed SDQs from carers or professionals were available for 97/150 young people at Stage 1 and 115/150 at Stage 2. However, there were only 80 cases where they were available at both time-points. Moreover, in the majority of cases, the carer or professional completing the SDQ at Stage 1 was not the same person who completed it at Stage 2. In general, a social worker was responsible for completing the Stage 1 forms, whereas a carer or key worker participated more frequently at Stage 2. It is perhaps worth noting that, even had our aim been to obtain these measures from the same adult at both time-points, we would very often have been frustrated. There were high levels of staff turnover among social workers and almost half of young people reported at least one change of social worker in the follow-up period and a similar proportion changed key workers. The findings discussed below should be read with this caveat in mind.

In common with most studies that explore SDQ scores for looked after children, we found rates of difficulties that were far higher than general population norms and, of course, this is entirely to be expected given our sampling frame of 'difficult adolescents'. Table 6.2 shows the proportions of the sample scoring 'normal', 'borderline' or 'abnormal' (as defined by the SDQ's authors) for each of the five subscales and the total scale at both Stages 1 and 2.

The table makes it very clear that substantial proportions of the sample were experiencing difficulties in a variety of domains – at least according to carer or professionals. The reports of young people tell a rather different story, with much-reduced proportions of young people identifying themselves as having problems. Of course some variation is due to the inclusion of slightly different samples of young people but even when we look at only those for whom we have both adults' and young people's reports, we find quite an interesting pattern of agreements and disagreements. Table 6.3 presents the correlations between the carer or professional and the young people's scores across time-periods. While, for the most part, there is substantial consistency *over time* for young people's scores and for carers or professionals' scores separately, there is little correspondence *between* adults and young people at any given time-point.

As is clear, the correlations between the reports of young people over time are quite marked and all are highly significant with the exception of young people's reports of peer problems and pro-social behaviour. We might reason that these two dimensions are ones that may well be easily influenced – for the better or worse – by relatively fluid features of young people's environments, such as who is resident in a home or what peer group options are available. Examination of the

Table 6.2 Frequencies for SDQ subscales and total scales for Stage 1 and Stage 2

	Stage 1 Carer or professional (n = 97)	Stage 1 Young person (n = 86)	Stage 2 Carer or professional (n = 115)	Stage 2 Young person (n = 75)
Emotional scale (%)				
'normal'	73	79	72	80
'borderline'	9	7	10	4
'abnormal'	18	14	18	16
Conduct scale (%)				
'normal'	25	39	35	52
'borderline'	9	27	14	17
'abnormal'	66	34	51	31
Hyperactive scale (%)				
'normal'	42	60	50	64
'borderline'	14	14	17	11
'abnormal'	43	26	33	25
Peer problem scale (%)				
'normal'	45	67	50	80
'borderline'	28	20	23	4
'abnormal'	27	13	27	16
Pro-social scale (%)				
'normal'	43	76	60	75
'borderline'	23	15	11	14
'abnormal'	34	9	28	11
Total score (%)				
'normal'	30	49	37	59
'borderline'	23	25	22	28
'abnormal'	47	26	41	13

SDQ, Strengths and Difficulties Questionnaire.

carer or professional ratings between Stages 1 and 2 shows a good deal of agreement across most of the subscales, although not for the total score or the hyperactivity subscale.

Looking at the correspondence between adult and young person reports at each individual time-point, we find an almost complete lack of strong correlations between the reports of carers or professionals and those of young people.

Table 6.3 Correlations between young people's and carers' scores within each scale of the SDQ at Stages 1 and 2

	Total scores	Conduct scales	Hyperactive scales	Emotional scales	Peer problem scale	Pro-social scale
YP1–YP2 (n = S 59)	.704	.468	.592	.773	–	–
Carer 1–Carer 2 (n = 81)	–	.526	–	.428	.552	458
Carer 1–YP1 (n = 61)	–	–	–	.412	–	–
Carer 2–YP2 (n = 69)	–	–	–	–	–	–

All listed correlations are significant at the 5 per cent level unless otherwise stated.
'–' = correlation <.4.
SDQ, Strengths and Difficulties Questionnaire.

The lack of correspondence does raise some questions. Other research, most notably a publication by Goodman, Meltzer and Bailey (2003), has noted quite substantial correlations across parent- and self-report SDQs in both clinical and community samples. We can only surmise that carers and professionals do not perceive and reflect on young people's difficulties in the same way as do parents.

Looking at the total SDQ scores from carers or professionals in relation to the characteristics and other factors identified earlier, we found no systematic differences at any point in time in relation to gender or ethnicity. The tendency for behaviour to improve with age that was observed from our interview data was supported by the carers' SDQ reports, in so far as age was not related to Stage 1 SDQ scores but the Stage 2 scores were significantly lower for our older age group. Young people's reports on the SDQs tended to reflect higher scores for the younger age group at both research stages.

There were no systematic differences in SDQ scores with regard to either the reason for being away from home or the number of family 'risk' factors to which young people had been exposed. In thinking about the type of environment in which young people were living, we found that those living in foster care had lower total SDQ scores on both adult and young person reports but the differences were not significant.

Young people's SDQ scores showed lower group averages (means) for those who had been away from home for four years or more. This tendency was evident in the carer or professional reports also, but not to the point of significance. There was, however, no relationship between SDQ score and the length of time spent in the current placement.

Young people's SDQ total scores at both time-points were associated with our ratings of the overall quality of care reported by young people (see Chapter 5). The mean SDQ scores of young people who received very good quality of care were significantly lower than those we classified as receiving just good or reasonable quality of care. Carers or professionals' SDQs were unrelated to the quality of care measure.

To summarise, this examination of the SDQ scores at each time-point has confirmed the association observed in data from our interviews concerning a reduction of behavioural difficulties with increasing age. There was a tendency, although not always statistically significant, for the scores for young people in foster care to be somewhat lower when compared with scores for those resident in other settings. Lower scores were also more likely for young people who had been away from home for longer. Again, these findings may be seen to reflect, to some extent, the tendency for foster care and longer periods away from home to be associated with better relationships with others (as reported in Table 6.1). We have also seen that the SDQ reports from young people, but not from adults, were inversely associated with their ratings of the quality of care that they received.

Changes in SDQ scores over time

Rather than absolute scores on this measure, we were primarily interested in indicators of change over time. Because different people completed the SDQ at Stage 1 and Stage 2, we chose to explore change over time by using *young people's* reports on their own behaviour, even though this meant using a smaller group of young people. The first analysis looked at changes in the total score, over time for all of the young people who had provided SDQs at Stages 1 and 2. This showed a significant, if modest, reduction (improvement) in the average score for the whole group (statistically, – student's t test=3.0; df = 65; p <.005).

As well as providing a 'score' for the total number of problems, the instrument provides 'cut-offs', which allow allocation of cases to one of three groups: problems within the 'normal' range, 'borderline' and an 'abnormal' level of problems (see Table 6.2). The results of a simple cross-tabulation are presented in Table 6.4. This reveals that just over half of the sample responded in such a way as to score within the 'normal' range at Stage 1, and the majority remained in this group at Stage 2. Fourteen young people scored in the 'borderline' range at Stage 1, and most of them (8/14) showed an improvement by Stage 2 and scored within the normal range. Ten of the 18 young people who had initially rated themselves so that they were placed in the 'abnormal' group also showed improvements over the follow-up period; eight were in the 'borderline' group at Stage 2, and two were in the 'normal' group. These are encouraging results.

Table 6.4 Patterns of consistency and change in SDQ groups between Stage 1 and Stage 2, according to young people's reports

SDQ group at Stage 1	SDQ group at Stage 2			
	Normal (0–15)	Borderline (16–19)	Abnormal (20–40)	Total
Normal (0–15)	29	5	0	34
Borderline (16–19)	8	6	0	14
Abnormal (20–40)	2	8	8	18
Total	39	19	8	66

SDQ, Strengths and Difficulties Questionnaire.

Of course, using a 'cut-off' means that movement between categories may occur by virtue of quite a small change in absolute score; equally, quite marked changes might not be reflected as a change of category. To explore this in more detail we undertook a simple comparison of Stage 1 and Stage 2 scores by subtracting the former from the latter. This resulted in what might be termed a 'change' score. These scores ranged from '–13' (i.e. a reduction over time of 13 points) to '+7' (an increase in the difficulties score). The median (mid-point) for this score was a reduction of one point and the standard deviation (SD) (a measure of dispersal) was 4.5. This process allowed us to identify young people for whom there had been major changes – according to their own reports – in both directions, in their behaviour over time. There were ten young people for whom these SDQ change scores suggested major improvements and just four who indicated a sharp rise in difficulties.

Drawing on the findings presented so far in this chapter, the analysis of the interview material and the SDQ responses both from professional or carer reports and the young people's reports has allowed us to identify small groups of young people whose difficulties had either improved markedly or shown some deterioration over time. On closer examination of the qualitative material from the study, we note that the circumstances surrounding these changes in behaviour vary. We have chosen, completely at random, one young person from each of these groups to illustrate the sorts of scenarios we came across.

These case studies illustrate how different aspects of life interact for young people and how they are subject to a wide range of experiences. We hope that they highlight the complexity of trying to understand the volatile and often uncertain worlds they inhabit.

Case Study: Sam

Sam entered care shortly before his tenth birthday. His parents had separated and repartnered, and neither could manage his behaviour. There was physical violence. He was 14 when he joined our sample. We learned about his earlier experiences from talking to a social worker who had known him for about a year. At the first interview Sam was in a 52-week placement in an 'out-of-area' independent sector dual-registered establishment. Apart from a short spell with one foster carer and a few months in a Council-run children's home, Sam had been at this school since coming into care. The social worker described the objectives of the placement as being, first, to provide education but also to provide therapeutic intervention to help him manage his behaviour and anger. She felt these objectives were being met very well and that Sam was making progress. There were some issues in that the school catered only for boys and Sam found peer relationships difficult. The social worker said 'He does mix, but they don't respect each others' property.' Sam did have plenty of female friends whom he had met outside the school.

Reports on Sam's progress at follow-up were less optimistic. He had been getting into more trouble, his attendance in the school-room and the extent to which he was felt to be 'accessing' educational opportunities were diminishing. The head of care, whom we spoke to about Sam, felt that this may have something to do with an increase in the amount of contact he had with his family, but, equally, his interest in sex, alcohol and drugs was increasing as he grew older.

The dilemma faced by those charged with managing the young people we were studying is well illustrated by the words of Sam's social worker when we spoke to her at follow-up.

> Sam has had a really hard time this last couple of months, he has been absconding with a vengeance. He has been close to being given notice to leave on numerous occasions but we are putting sticking plasters all over this placement. This placement is very good at holding on to their young people but there comes a time when they have to think of the impact on the other young people there. We think it is to do with other young people he has been mixing with outside of the unit. He is on cannabis and getting into lots of trouble. He was sat down a week ago and given seven days to turn around, he has been better but whether he can stick with it… He desperately wants a family, there are no plans for this.

('*Is this placement meeting its objectives?*') Yes, but it is very difficult if he's not accessing therapy or anything. We finally got him to CAMHS [the Child and Adolescent Mental Health Service], he went to the first appointment but then refused all subsequent ones.

It will probably not come as a surprise to learn that we didn't get to talk with Sam when we returned for the follow-up. At the first interview he seemed to enjoy meeting with us and told us that, although he still got bored with a lot of subjects, he thought his school work had improved since he had been there. He did not have particular complaints about the placement, although he did echo what others had said about not having friends within the unit.

Case Study: Anthony

Anthony was 13 when we first met him at home at his aunt's house. He had entered care at 11½ when his mother's drug habit caused her health and her ability to care to deteriorate. Anthony had several brothers and sisters but they all lived with their respective fathers. He was placed initially with foster carers but then moved to live with his aunt a few months later. His aunt loved him but was struggling to manage him. Anthony had faced a lot of setbacks, which culminated in his mother's death shortly after he moved in with his aunt. Within a few of weeks of this happening he was permanently excluded from school. The exclusion put even more strain on his aunt. Respite carers were found to look after Anthony at the weekends but this brought its own difficulties in that the respite carers' approach to caring for teenagers was different to that of his aunt. Eventually a PRU placement was found for him but, according to his social worker, this was quite a negative experience for him. His peers did a lot of 'hanging around' and there was considerable use of drugs.

At follow-up Anthony had made huge strides in positive directions. He had moved to live full time with foster carers. Initially, after the move, he had a complex but highly effective individual education package put together for him which included one-to-one tuition at an education centre every morning, two evenings at college plus extra home tuition some afternoons. He was doing very well and was reintroduced to mainstream school. He had also been diagnosed as having ADHD and medication was felt to be improving his behaviour and he was having weekly therapy. He had become involved in more constructive leisure activities. His social worker thought he still used cannabis but much less than before. He had less contact with the police and relationships with adults and peers were much improved, although she thought he could still be frightening to other young people when he 'got wound up'.

Anthony himself had some quite interesting comments about his experiences at school when things were difficult for him:

> I tried hard and [then] couldn't be bothered. All the bad things got reported. All the good things didn't get reported. They put me in all the lower sets and I knew it all – it was too easy. Then they put me in the higher sets and it was too hard. This is because I moved school at the end of Year 7, they didn't know about me so they put me in lower set.
>
> At first I was brilliant then I went to that school and got messed up. [School was] Terrible – I hated it – I didn't understand it so I messed around. The teachers didn't understand me…I ended up being bad.

These comments of Anthony's highlight the importance of the school experience on young people's day-to-day lives. He is clearly an intelligent and articulate young man, who explained that he was experiencing frustration because he was being asked to study to inappropriate levels; he felt misunderstood, misrepresented and ended up thinking of himself as 'bad'. At follow-up, in a new placement and a new school, although he had mixed views about his schooling, he knew he was at a 'good school'. He acknowledged that his carers 'kept him on the straight and narrow' and was talking about going to university and becoming a teacher.

Young people's sense of well-being as indicated by the ladders

The final way that we elected to obtain information from young people about their views and experiences, was to ask them to complete a series of six 'ladders'. These were developed from the ideas behind Cantril's (1965) approach and asked young people to reflect on aspects of their lives concerning school, friendships, relationships with family, happiness in general, staying out of trouble and achieving their self-set goals. We were aiming here to obtain a sense of young people's feelings of more general 'well-being'. In each area young people were asked to indicate their view on a visual scale (a ladder), with the lowest rung suggesting things were about 'as bad as could be' and the top rung 'as good as it could be'. Young people completed these at both the Stage 1 and Stage 2 interviews.

This group of teenagers seemed genuinely to enjoy the opportunity to make their mark on the ladders and some of them went to great lengths to ensure that their mark accurately reflected exactly how they felt about that aspect of their life. We had intended that the positions on the ladders would broadly correspond to a rating of between zero and ten. However, a small minority of young people were very keen to ensure that we recognised that, for them, a certain aspect of life was 'worse' or 'better' than this. That is, they deliberately drew in more negative or positive positions and wrote alongside '12' or '–5'.

Regrettably, the strictures of science made it impossible to retain these in the analysis and we recoded their responses to zero or ten as originally intended. But these experiences do serve to underline that young people – even when they may not have the vocabulary or the confidence to articulate their feelings in a face-to-face interview with a stranger – nevertheless may hold strong views about various aspects of their lives.

Comparing young people's responses at the two time stages again shows a mixed picture with a reasonable degree of consistency in the reports of many young people but some revealed quite dramatic changes of view. Statistical tests of association revealed only weak correlations for each area between Stage 1 and Stage 2 responses. One young person, for example, rated herself as zero on happiness at Stage 1 and as ten at Stage 2. This rating is probably consistent with what she told us in the interviews and emphasises that the more general well-being, at least as expressed by this sort of indicator, is very susceptible to change according to circumstances.

Figure 6.3 provides a graphic representation of the ratings made by young people for each of the six areas at Stage 2. Most of the charts show a 'skew' towards greater satisfaction but within this there are some differences depending on which area of life is examined. Thus, a substantial number of young people expressed a good deal of satisfaction with their family relationships and their friendships, although a minority (15% and 10% respectively) was less satisfied in each case. Schooling, achievement of own-set goals, staying out of trouble and general happiness showed a more mixed picture.

On detailed statistical analysis, young people's satisfaction with their schooling was associated with their educational progress, stability of the current care placement and their ratings on the quality of care they received. General happiness was associated with satisfaction with schooling and current quality of care.

Satisfaction with friendships was also associated with stability in the current placement.

The only factor that was associated with relationships with family was the presence of abuse or neglect in young people's backgrounds. Satisfaction with their ability to stay out of trouble tended to be higher among young people of a minority background. There were no associations between any of the factors that we tested and young people's perceptions of their self-set goal achievements.

This exploration of young people's broader sense of well-being confirms the findings of other research in this area, namely, that young people can and do find satisfaction in many areas of their lives, despite what has happened to them in the past. Not all of the factors in young people's lives may be influenced by carers or professionals but, in particular, we saw that satisfaction with schooling, general happiness and friendships – all very important parts of the lives of teenagers – were each negatively associated with changes in placements, whatever the reasons for those changes. Conversely, higher ratings on these scales were recorded where quality of care was rated as 'very good'. We hope this message can act as an encouragement to those who have been working hard to provide excellent quality of care.

In summary, we have seen that young people's general level of behavioural problems, that is their aggressive and sometimes violent responses, tended to decrease with age. Carer or professional views suggested a variety of reasons for this but, in the main, this was seen to be a result of 'growing-up', learning from experience and developing more socially acceptable strategies for dealing with disappointments or conflicts. Difficulties with social relationships (with both adults and peers) also tended to ease alongside the problems in anger management and general behaviour. Concerns about consumption of alcohol and drugs (mainly cannabis), however, tended to become more common as young people got older. This is probably related to the increased accessibility of such substances as young people mature and as their social groups begin to experiment with what they perceive to be more adult activities. Difficulties with police contact were often associated with problematic use of alcohol or drugs, but were also found to occur more frequently in children's homes (without education). One possible reason, aside from the level of difficulties of the residents, was that staff may have called for police support to settle disturbances within the homes. While this may be unavoidable at times, similar behaviour in a family environment would be less likely to attract a police response (Nacro 2005).

We also looked at more general measures of young people's well-being. We did not find that these varied by type of placement but there were clear indications that placement change was associated with less satisfaction with some areas of life, in particular schooling, friendships and general happiness. Moreover, the

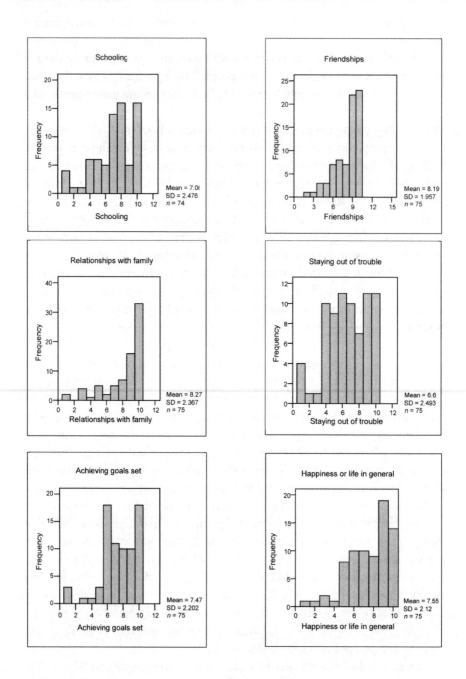

Figure 6.3 Ratings of satisfaction with six areas of life, according to young people at Stage 2 (n = 75)

more positively young people described the quality of care they received, the higher also was their satisfaction with schooling and levels of general happiness. Overall, it may be seen that there were few factors that could be described as 'determinants' of outcome for these adolescents. Young people's lives and problems are complex. But the finding that quality of care does relate to satisfaction with school and with happiness more generally, suggests a way ahead in helping young people in overcoming their problems.

Summary points

- Problems with anger management, violence and aggression were extremely common in the sample, with nearly nine in ten being so described. Some 70 per cent of the sample had problems with adult or peer relationships, or both.

- Between 35 and 45 per cent of the sample had difficulties with alcohol or drug misuse (mostly cannabis), police contact and/or self-harm. We found problems with substance misuse somewhat more frequent for girls and definitely more frequent for older adolescents; and they were more common among young people in care generally rather than the BESD schools, and among residents of children's homes without education.

- Problems with self-harm were more common among young women.

- Police contact was found to be more frequent in the *County* and *Borough* authorities than in our third local authority or residential schools. Again, this was more evident in children's homes and there was some evidence that it was more common for young people of minority ethnic background.

- Overall, it seems that residents of children's homes that do not provide education are more likely to present a variety of management difficulties than those from our other placement types.

- Our preliminary analysis was able to confirm that those presenting behavioural challenges were by no means all recent entrants to care.

- A quarter of those interviewed at Stage 2 told us that they were prescribed Concerta® or Ritalin®, medication for ADHD. This included *half* of the residential BESD group (12/23). This seems to us high and the use of such stimulants with children and young people is controversial. This issue merits further investigation.

- Using researcher ratings – based on carer or professionals' data – we concluded that the majority of the sample had shown some general improvement in behavioural, emotional and social difficulties over the follow-up period. Those who were older showed most improvement in general behaviour problems.

• Our standard measures of BESDs (SDQs) revealed high levels of problems as reported by carers or professionals. There was some incongruity and inconsistency in the description of problems provided by adults and young people. But, overall, these standard measures confirmed the improvement in behavioural problems as young people got older. Young people's SDQ responses were associated with their own ratings of the quality of care that they received.

• Young people's overall perceptions of their satisfaction with different areas of their lives, using the 'ladders', revealed interesting associations. These confirmed that changing placement was associated with lower levels of general happiness, with less satisfaction with the school experience and to some extent with friendships also. Happiness and satisfaction with schooling were also associated with young people's perceptions of the quality of care they received.

Notes

1   This means, for example, that a young person who has problems in their relationships with adults was also likely to have problems relating to their peers.

2   Correlations: behaviour and adult relationships $r = .54$; $p < .001$; adult and peer relationships $r = .52$; $p < .01$; behaviour and police contact $r = .23$; $p < .05$; police contact and substance misuse $r = .45$; $p < .01$. Please note that Spearman's r was used for all the correlations.

Chapter 7

Education

Educational issues were central to this research and so the schooling experiences of our sample of young people merit detailed discussion. We gathered a wide range of educational information in our interviews with professionals or carers and young people, both at the outset of the fieldwork (Stage 1) as well as at follow-up nine months later (Stage 2). The views of some observers are, no doubt, more accurate and insightful than others but they will all have important consequences. We approach the task thematically allowing us to avoid repetition and to contrast how different informants perceive events. The themes are consistent with the objectives for the research, outlined in Chapter 1. We are particularly interested in the relevance of care settings to educational experiences and progress.

Stage 1 interviews
Current schooling

To set the scene, the type of educational setting attended by our sample of 150 young people at the beginning of our fieldwork can be found in Table 7.1.

Table 7.1 reveals that the most common (39%) form of education received was residential schooling; of course, 50 of our sample of young people from residential special schools were selected specifically for this reason. Just over a quarter attended mainstream schools. Interestingly, 14 young people attended educational centres of various types: these included pupil referral units (PRUs) or other alternative, flexible educational settings for pupils requiring a more individualised educational package.

Eight of the 39 young people living in children's homes attended such centres and a further seven received less than five hours of education a week; another three did not receive schooling. As we see below, the children's homes group posed particular educational challenges. There were no gender or ethnic differences in the type of educational provision received.

Table 7.1 Type of education received at Stage 1

Type of school	Care setting				
	Foster care	Children's home (no education)	Dual-registered home/school	Residential BESD school	Total (%)
Mainstream	31	10	–	–	41 (27)
Day BESD	12	6	–	–	18 (12)
Full-time BESD or SEN boarding	2	–	24	32	58 (39)
Education centre	4	8	2	–	14 (9)
Full-time mixed provision – academic + vocational	1	2	–	–	3 (2)
5 hours education per week	–	7	2	–	9 (6)
None, out of school	1	3	–	–	4 (3)
Other	–	3	–	–	3 (2)
Total	51	39	28	32	$n = 150$

BESD, behavioural, educational and social difficulties; SEN, special educational needs.

Case Study: John

John was 14 years old and living in a local authority children's home. He was not committed to schooling and his attendance was sporadic. Therefore, he was enrolled at an education youth centre, which combined academic education with part-time attendance at college for vocational training in building and construction. John stated that he was happier since this change. His key worker informed us: 'His education is more hands-on and vocational and he enjoys that.' The plan was for him to take NVQ and GNVQ qualifications if he continued to make progress.

Educational history

Information about previous education was obtained from the 97 young people who agreed to be interviewed at Stage 1. Of these, three-fifths stated that they had not truanted in the past, but one-third had done so and seldom was this limited to post-registration or selective absenteeism. Young people living at children's homes or dual-registered establishments had truanted in the past much more often than others in the sample. Histories of fixed-term and permanent exclusions were more complex: the fostered group had experienced slightly fewer school exclusions than others but this was not statistically significant. (The fostered group includes family and friends care unless otherwise stated.) The residential behavioural, educational and social difficulties (BESD) school group was comparable with the children's homes and dual-registered groups and exclusions were, no doubt, a contributory factor to their referral to a special residential school.

To ascertain previous educational attainment, we asked the professionals about young people's SATs scores at Key Stage 3 (Year 9, usually 14-year-olds) and Key Stage 2 (Year 6, aged 11). Some pupils were too young to have taken Key Stage 3 tests but by excluding this group, the professionals did not know and could not discover the SATS results for a quarter of our study participants. Disconcertingly, Key Stage 3 results were much less likely to be known for the children's homes group – 16 of the 37 – than others. Numbers are small but where these Key Stage 3 results were known, more than four-fifths of our total sample achieved below-average scores, across all Stage 1 placement categories. The same picture applied to Key Stage 2.

Information was provided by 97 professionals interviewed at Stage 1 about the stability of young people's previous educational histories. From this we judged that 56 per cent had educational histories that were 'very' or 'reasonably' stable, and 44 per cent had been 'fairly' or 'very' unstable. There were some noticeable differences between groups and, once again, the fostered group had experienced much more continuity in schooling – for 31 of the 41 young people schooling had been reasonably stable or better.

Special educational needs

Professionals interviewed at Stage 1 informed us that four-fifths of the sample were considered to have special educational needs (SEN) (Table 7.2).

Almost two-thirds of the sample were said to have BESD. An additional eight young people were reported to have been assessed with attention deficit hyperactivity disorder (ADHD). Another five had SEN associated with Asperger Syndrome (AS). Only one of the pupils attending the two categories of residential schools were reported not to have SEN. Two-thirds of residents in foster homes

Table 7.2 Special educational needs at Stage 1

Type of SEN	Care/educational setting				
	Foster care	Children's home (no education)	Dual-registered home/school	Residential BESD school	Total (%)
BESD	28	23	21	22	94 (63)
BESD + ADHD type	–	–	3	5	8 (5)
BESD + moderate learning difficulty	3	–	1	1	5 (3)
BESD + AS type	–	1	1	3	5 (3)
Moderate learning difficulty	3	2	–	1	6 (4)
No SEN	16	14	1	–	31 (21)
Total	50	40	27	32	$n = 149$

BESD, behavioural, educational and social difficulties; ADHD, attention deficit hyperactivity disorder; AS, Asperger Syndrome; SEN, special educational needs.

or children's homes (without education) had been assessed with SEN, although a high proportion this is lower than for the two residential schools groups.

All residential BESD school pupils had a Statement of Special Educational Needs, as did almost all of those living at the dual-registered establishments (Table 7.3). Over a third of the fostered group had Statements and, interestingly, the proportion was slightly higher for the children's homes' residents (over two-fifths). In addition, 15 of the 50 young people living in foster homes were receiving specialist support for their SEN in school in other ways, mostly though School Action Plus.

School behaviour at Stage 1

Interviews with professionals at Stage 1 and a scrutiny of case records indicated that a number of our sample posed a range of behavioural problems at school (Table 7.4).

The children's homes group was the worst-behaved at school, with over a third of young people felt to behave 'very poorly'. In contrast, a quarter of the residential BESD pupils were considered to behave 'very well'. Merging categories, the children's homes residents were worse-behaved than the remainder of the

Table 7.3 Special educational needs by care setting at Stage 1

SEN register	Care setting				
	Foster care	Children's home (no education)	Dual-registered home/school	Residential BESD school	Total (%)
Statement of SEN	18	18	26	32	94 (63)
School action or equivalent	4	–	–	–	4 (3)
School action plus or equivalent	7	3	–	–	10 (7)
SEN assessment in progress	4	–	–	–	4 (3)
Never on SEN register	14	18	1	–	33 (22)
Other	4	1	–	–	5 (3)
Total	51	40	27	32	$n = 150$

BESD, behavioural, educational and social difficulties; SEN, special educational needs.

group (χ^2 test = 56.1; df = 4; $p < .001$). There was no difference in school behaviour by gender, nor by ethnicity.

Generally, our sample attended school regularly and, for most categories, approximately two-thirds of the young people were felt to attend 'very well'. Our expectation was confirmed that there would be less truancy from residential schools, where not attending classes is a more complex social act than truanting from a separate educational setting in the community. The exception, again, was with the children's homes group, for a third of whom attendance was rated as 'very poor'. Combining those who attended 'not very well' and 'very poorly', the children's homes group had much poorer attendance at Stage 1 of our study than others in the sample. Girls' attendance appears worse than boys' but this difference is not statistically significant and may be accounted for by the smaller number of girls in our residential BESD sample.

Young people's relationships with teachers were considered by professionals to be mostly positive, with half thought to be getting on 'very well' or 'fairly well', and another one in three 'mixed'. Continuing the previous pattern, the 18 pupils from children's homes for whom information was available had noticeably worse relationships with teachers than those from the other placement types combined.

Table 7.4 Current school experience, Stage 1

How does s/he currently behave at school?	Care or educational setting				
	Foster care	Children's home (no education)	Dual-registered home/school	Residential BESD school	Total (%)
Very well	4	1	2	8	15 (13)
Fairly well	10	6	13	7	36 (30)
Mixed	15	5	4	7	31 (26)
Not very well	10	4	1	3	18 (15)
Very poorly	4	9	3	4	20 (17)
Total	43	25	23	29	$n = 120$

BESD, behavioural, educational and social difficulties; SEN, special educational needs.

It was interesting to discover that pupils' relationships with each other appeared worse than with staff but this did not quite achieve statistical significance. But young people interviewed at Stage 1 told us that they had a variety of friends at school. Only 11 per cent stated that their social experiences at school were mainly negative. Just a quarter said that there was no bullying or teasing at school; one in five observed it more than monthly, and just over half less than monthly. Most felt that their schools made efforts to address bullying. There were no significant differences in these social experiences at school by care setting, gender or ethnicity.

Study support

As we were particularly interested in exploring the relationship between care settings and young people's educational experiences and achievements, we asked young people at Stage 1 whether a range of study supports were available to them. We repeated a schedule that one of us had used in a previous study with the National Children's Bureau (NCB) (Harker *et al.* 2004); later, we compare the results from these two studies. Table 7.5 shows the results by component item.

Certain caveats apply to this data. Young people who were not looked after would not have a personal education plan (PEP), for example. The exercise also reflects certain value judgements: enquiring about borrowing books from the

Table 7.5 Study support at Stage 1

Do you have (access to):	Yes (%)	No (%)
A quiet room or space to study in?	85	14
Enough good books and guides to help you with your studies?	82	16
A personal education plan (PEP)?	47	32
A computer and printer to do homework on?	77	21
The internet?	50	48
Newspapers and magazines to read?	85	11
Information about your education rights and educational procedures?	64	25
Money for leisure activities and facilities?	88	8
Interesting places to visit and learn from, e.g. museums, theatres?	74	22
Money to buy your own books?	70	24
A local library nearby?	71	8
Someone who takes an interest in your education?	86	9
Someone who attends school events – school concerts or parents' evenings?	77	6
Any friends who are doing well at school?	80	7
		Total ($n = 98$)

library aroused a degree of humour, or disbelief, in some of our study members. Nonetheless, we thought it valuable to repeat what had been done before.

Table 7.5 shows that the 98 young people interviewed at Stage 1 felt that a wide range of study supports were generally available. Almost all could access money to visit leisure facilities and nearly nine in every ten young people could identify someone whom they felt was interested in their education. Four-fifths had access to good books and study guides to help with their academic work. Of the lower responses, although three-quarters had access to a computer, only half stated that they had internet access. Later interviews with carers and professionals indicated that internet access was sometimes regulated for reasons of costs or when it needed to be shared across a family or between residents. No doubt, and like some of their peers, a few young people were mainly using the internet to access inappropriate websites and concerns were voiced over safety in social networking 'chat rooms'. Access to the internet was fairly strictly, and successfully, controlled in most environments. One interviewee had managed more than once to delete the entire contents of the hard disk of his foster carers' computer.

We have not presented results by care settings as numbers were sometimes small and could, therefore, be misleading. However, it was interesting to discover that the four categories of care settings were very alike in the high level of study support they offered. Generally speaking, therefore, the residential BESD schools did not offer more of these facilities and opportunities than did foster homes or local children's homes. There were only two exceptions. The first was that foster homes offered slightly better access to computers than did other settings. Second, children's homes residents reported fewer interesting places to visit, which may have reflected the localities in which they were based or the preferred pastimes of their occupants.

Comparing these results with those from the NCB study mentioned earlier (Harker *et al.* 2004) is complex, as residential BESD schools were not included in that work. It was a study of three local authorities, which had been specially targeted to receive significant added investment and development work funded by a charitable trust; the aim was to see if the educational experiences and achievements of looked after children could be improved in 'optimum' circumstances. Some progress was observed over a follow-up period (see Chapter 1). The figures reported in Stage 1 of the current study are higher in all but two of the categories than at the *beginning* of the NCB study in 2001. This suggests that there has been some general improvement in access to educational supports. Furthermore, comparing the situation with NCB authorities *after* the significant financial investment and development work (in 2003), the average (mean) difference in the proportion responding positively to each of the questions is just seven percentage points lower. This difference does not strike us as large and suggests, again, that there may have been some general improvement since the increasing government emphasis on this topic.

Our Stage 1 interviews with young people included questions about help with homework and responses were generally similar across settings. A quarter of the total sample commented that no homework was set. One in eight young people were given homework but usually ignored it! A fifth did not receive help with homework but did not want any but virtually all those who said they were prepared to accept help with homework received it (37%).

Achievement and effort

Half of the young people interviewed in the initial round informed us that they were not due to sit exams in the foreseeable future. Most of the remainder, across care settings, expected to do 'average'. We wondered how they felt about taking exams and a minority – only two-fifths – said they ever worried about exams 'a little' or 'a lot'. This apparent lack of concern seemed to us a combination of complacency and bravado. Two-thirds felt they were doing 'quite well' at school and a further 17 per cent 'very well'; in contrast to 15 per cent who thought 'quite badly' or 'very badly' (Figure 7.1).

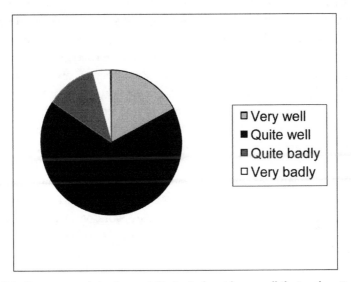

Figure 7.1 Young people's views at Stage 1 about how well their education is going

Half of our young interviewees responded that they were making 'a fair effort' in their education, the remainder were quite evenly divided between 'not much effort' and 'much effort'. They were also asked what teachers felt about their efforts at school. Responses were broadly equal between 'good', 'fair or moderate' and 'little'. There was no noticeable difference between groups, except that half of those living in foster care replied that they thought their teachers would consider them lazy. Reasons for this were unclear but might include a lack of self-confidence, greater ambition or openness. More males than females admitted to lethargy. Most young people, across settings, felt that the overall education services they received were appropriate but a fifth did not.

Statistical analysis based on professionals' interviews at Stage 1 showed that current behaviour in school, attendance or achievement were unrelated to the range of characteristics and other social background factors (see Chapter 6), including the constitution of the young person's 'home base', separation history or the number of different family risk factors on leaving home. In addition, a history of child abuse or neglect was not associated with patterns of attendance or attainment but it *was* significantly associated with greater current behaviour problems in school (χ^2 test = 12.3; df = 4; p <.005).

Other interests

Though educational achievement is a main route to social mobility in the UK, those with different talents may succeed in other ways. In our preparatory report, for example, we encountered one young man who had been taken on by a premier division football club and a young woman had appeared on television in *Coronation Street* – positive outcomes for both of them (Berridge *et al.* 2002).

Young people were asked about their leisure interests and the usual wide range of teenage activities emerged, across placements. A fifth of the sample was interested mainly in physical sport. One in six spent most of their spare time engaged in solitary activity, such as watching television or computer games. One in ten preferred internet chat rooms; and only 3 per cent mainly read, browsed the internet or undertook further study. A third spread their time over several activities. As might be expected, boys were more likely to prefer mainly sports (31%) and girls liked chat rooms (26%). Though many would have been too young, one in eight young people did either some voluntary work or a part-time weekend job. Numbers interviewed at Stage 1 are low, but interestingly all the 13 young people who did part-time or voluntary work were white (two others were undergoing planned work experience), whereas none of the 16 who were working were from minority ethnic groups. We are unclear why this might be; it was not age-related.

Professional liaison

We know that inter-agency and inter-professional collaboration are important for looked after children living away from home, not only to ensure adequate protection but also to promote their educational achievement and more general well-being (DoH 1998b). We therefore asked, in our Stage 1 interviews with professionals, a range of questions about the degree of liaison with schools for our sample of young people. We did not ask this for young people attending residential schools, where the informant was a school employee, nor where young people were out of school.

Where information was available (n = 88), we were told that there was 'considerable' liaison with schools for three-fifths of young people; 'some' liaison for about a quarter; and 'none or little' for the rest (16%). We questioned informants at Stage 1 about their experience of working with the local authority education department in relation to the particular case. General liaison between social services and education departments was felt to be 'easy' for half, 'reasonable' for a fifth and 'difficult' or 'no or little liaison' for another fifth ($n = 85$). Some of this latter group of responses would include cases where educational progress was unproblematic and so not much liaison was required. Where liaison occurred, it was thought to be 'very effective' in 44 per cent of cases, 'reasonably' effective for a third and 'not effective' for only a fifth. The degree and effectiveness of inter-agency or inter-professional liaison was similar for fostered and residential care groups.

Educational planning

There is a requirement that all looked after children should have a PEP, which is developed in association with the school and is reviewed alongside the child's care plan. As all of our looked after group had been accommodated for at least three months, they should all have had PEPs. Ninety per cent of them did and the ten young people who did not have a PEP came equally from foster care, children's homes and dual-registered establishments.

We asked young people in our Stage 1 interviews about the extent to which they participated in PEP meetings and educational planning more generally. The vast majority across different types of placements said they were involved: around two-fifths of replies were coded to indicate that there was 'substantial involvement' and about the same had 'some' involvement. Some were encouraged to be involved but declined, and very few were involuntarily excluded from educational planning meetings.

In addition, all pupils who have reached the school action stage of the special educational needs assessment are entitled to an individual education plan (IEP), which focuses on their individual circumstances and learning objectives. Where information was available, nearly a quarter of those eligible did not have an IEP, although schools often used other versions of planning documentation.

Future aspirations

Young people were also asked if they intended to continue with their education at college or university after leaving school ($n = 92$). Two-fifths said they definitely wanted to; for a third it was a possibility, and only 15 per cent at this stage completely ruled it out. Girls were more committed to continuing with their education than boys. There was no difference by ethnicity or separation history. The foster care group appeared more educationally ambitious but sample sizes were too small for reliable analysis.

Well over half the young people had definite career plans and another 30 per cent wanted a career but were undecided exactly which; only 7 per cent said they were uninterested in a career. Career plans could change and might be unrealistic: one young man told us 'I want to go to college or university to be a lawyer or bricklayer like my brother.' It is no doubt better to have ambitions than not.

Summary of Stage 1

From the first round of interviews with professionals and young people, we found that our sample attended a range of educational provision. Many had posed educational challenges. Approaching half of the young people were felt to have had unstable educational careers and a third had truanted. Indeed, professionals considered that four-fifths of our sample had special educational needs; for two-thirds of the total, including most of those who were looked after, this concerned BESD. Disconcertingly, professionals were often unaware of Key Stages 2 and 3 results.

However, most young people were attending school or other educational provision and they mainly reported good relationships with teachers. Our sample generally conveyed that their schooling was a positive social experience; most said that bullying existed but that schools were addressing it.

An impressive range of study supports was available to these pupils. This compared favourably with findings from a previous study of the education of looked after children and suggests that there are likely to have been some recent general improvements. Professionals' assessments were that inter-agency and inter-professional working between social services departments, schools and education departments were mainly good. Ninety per cent of the looked after group had PEPs, although all should have had them, and most young people said they were involved in educational planning meetings.

Depending on expectations and motivation, and other things considered, most young people considered that they doing reasonably well at school and were making an effort.

Many of these findings applied to young people across our four categories of care settings and there were few differences by personal characteristics, such as gender or ethnicity. But there was evidence that the group living in children's homes at the outset of our study posed particular challenges with their education. They had previously truanted more; currently, they were worse attenders, they were worst behaved at school and they had more problematic relationships with teachers.

The question arises as to whether young people were referred to children's homes because of their extreme difficulties, or did the homes themselves contribute to, or even cause, these problems. We return to this later but our evidence indicated that the educational support for the children's homes group, within the placements as well as through outside professionals, was generally not inferior to that available for those living elsewhere. The extent and quality of inter-agency and inter-professional liaison was also similar between placement types.

Stage 2 interviews

We explained in Chapter 4 how we dealt with the analysis of placements during the follow-up period. We were interested in overall care and educational experiences, outcomes and costs, and whether these were related to particular placement experiences. As about a quarter of the sample whom we were able to follow up moved placement types between the Stage 1 and Stage 2 interviews, we present the findings for young people who remained within the four original placement categories (e.g. foster care) but included also a fifth, where young people moved across categories (e.g. from children's homes to dual-registered establishments).

Changes in schooling

In revisiting our study sample after nine months, we were particularly interested in whether their educational circumstances had changed, and whether the young people were making progress. We saw in Chapter 4 that 40 per cent of young people moved placement between Stage 1 and Stage 2, including returns home, but changes also occurred in their educational arrangements as well (Table 7.6).

Table 7.6 Changes in schooling or educational package during the follow-up period, by care setting(s)

Change of schooling or educational package	Care or educational setting(s) during follow-up					
	Foster care	Children's home (no education)	Dual-registered home/ school	Residential BESD school	Changed category	Total (%)
No change	18	3	14	25	10	70 (59)
One change	7	11	4	–	10	32 (27)
More than one change	1	2	1	–	6	10 (8)
Other or not known	–	1	2	–	4	7 (6)
Total	26	17	21	25	30	$n = 119$

Merging categories where one or more changes in educational arrangements occurred, there were very significant differences depending on where young people lived (χ^2 test = 36.0; df = 4; p <.001). Twenty-five of the original 31 residential BESD schools group remained at the same school throughout. In contrast, only three of those living in children's homes throughout the follow-up maintained the same educational arrangements and 13 changed. The foster care and dual-registered groups experienced more educational stability. In order to investigate this further we need to consider why these changes occurred. Carers or professionals informed us that approximately one in six of the education changes were age-related and thus unavoidable (Table 7.7). Over a quarter occurred where the school or other setting could not cope with the behavioural or emotional challenges posed, or, phrased more positively, that the young person's educational needs would be better met elsewhere. One in six moves were a consequence of a change in care setting. Three pupils changed school because their learning needs were not met adequately, and the same number because of refusals to attend the previous setting. More of the girls' schooling changes appeared to be age-related and the boys' were more commonly linked to their behaviour, but these gender differences did not quite reach statistical significance.

Given the antisocial behavioural problems these 'difficult' adolescents had posed in order to be eligible for inclusion in our study, it is unsurprising that some educational changes would be required over a nine-month period, but did these changes have a positive impact?

Nearly three in every five educational changes that occurred were perceived by professionals or carers to have had a positive impact, which is encouraging (Table 7.8). The effects were mixed for another quarter. A quarter of young people at follow-up were now considered to be 'very settled' at school, half were 'reasonably settled', a fifth 'not very settled' and only four pupils 'not at all' settled. Young people themselves when interviewed were slightly more optimistic than this. Only 4 of the 21 young people we interviewed at follow-up who had changed schools expressed dissatisfaction with the move. Indeed, most young people we interviewed for the second round felt that they had benefited from their past year's schooling: a third said they had got 'a lot' out of their education and half 'quite a lot'. The children's homes group were slightly more dissatisfied (not statistically significant). Three-quarters of young people told us that they felt they were at the right school and only 12 per cent thought they definitely were not.

Table 7.7 Reasons, given by carers or professionals, for changes in schooling or educational package during the follow-up period, by care setting(s)

Reason for change	Care or educational setting(s) during follow-up					
	Foster care	Children's home (no education)	Dual-registered home/ school	Residential BESD school	Changed category	Total (%)
No change	18	4	16	25	11	74 (62)
Age-related transition	2	2	–	–	4	8 (7)
Behavioural or emotional needs	1	5	–	–	7	13 (11)
Change of care setting	2	1	1	–	4	8 (7)
Learning needs	1	1	1	–	–	3 (3)
Young person refused previous education package	1	1	1	–	3	6 (5)
Other or more than one	1	3	2	–	2	8 (7)
Total	26	17	22	25	31	$n = 120$

Table 7.8 Carers' or professionals' views of the impact of educational changes during follow-up, by care setting(s)

Impact of education changes	Care or educational settings(s) during follow-up					
	Foster care	Children's home (no education)	Dual-registered home/ school	Residential BESD school	Changed category	Total (%)
Mainly positive	7	7	4	–	8	26 (22)
Mixed	–	3	–	–	8	11 (9)
Mainly negative	–	4	1	–	2	7 (6)
Not applicable, no changes	17	3	15	25	9	69 (58)
Not known	1	–	–	–	4	5 (4)
Total	25	17	20	25	31	$n = 118$

Behaviour

Of the 69 individuals who responded to the question at Stage 2, a quarter of young people said that they had been excluded from school during the nine-month follow-up period. But nearly half said that this was fewer exclusions than previously and two-fifths had said it was about the same. No particular care setting stood out as linked to the extent of school exclusions, nor did other individual characteristics.

Educational attainment

The overall assessment of changes in young people's educational attainment made by professionals or carers during the follow-up period is summarised in Table 7.9.

Table 7.9 Carers' or professionals' views of changes in young people's educational attainment during the nine-month follow-up, by care setting(s)

Changes in educational attainment	Care or educational setting(s) during follow-up					
	Foster care	Children's home (no education)	Dual-registered home/ school	Residential BESD school	Changed category	Total (%)
Never a problem	4	2	2	8	5	21 (19)
Resolved	2	1	–	1	–	4 (4)
Improving	11	4	10	6	10	41 (37)
No change	4	3	3	8	9	27 (24)
Fluctuating	1	1	2	1	1	6 (5)
Deteriorating	1	5	3	1	3	13 (12)
Total	23	16	20	25	28	$n = 112$

Nearly one-fifth of the young people were considered never to have posed educational problems and their progress was in line with their age group. Among young people who had difficulties, 4 per cent were thought by adults to have overcome their educational difficulties and, in total, half had made educational progress. Over a quarter had stayed about the same, 5 per cent were fluctuating and 12 per cent were deteriorating. Merging categories into those which were improving or not, differences in progress across care settings were not statistically significant. Indeed, perceived educational progress, the impact of educational changes or whether currently settled did not vary by care setting, gender or ethnicity.

Educational progress was very difficult to predict, even when, as the following case study reveals, it appeared that the right supports were in place.

Case Study: Chris (Stage 1)

At the Stage 1 interview Chris was in Year 11 (16 years old) and had been living in a foster home in northern England for two months. He liked it there and was living with experienced carers.

His social worker said that this was one of the worst cases of neglect the department had seen. There were scars all over Chris's back. There was domestic violence and his father sexually abused Chris's two sisters (and possibly others). The family moved frequently. Chris has eight siblings. He sees them occasionally but wants no contact with his parents. Previous fosterings had broken down because of his aggressive behaviour. He assaulted his foster mother and was charged for this. Chris shows an unhealthy interest in fire. His social worker commented that '...he tends to gravitate to younger ones.'

Chris attended the same school as he did prior to this foster placement, involving an hour's taxi journey each way at a cost of £100 a day. His social worker observed: 'School has been the main stable thing – it is an excellent school' and Chris commented: 'I've got used to the journey, I don't mind.' Chris was attending a learning support centre at school and shared a classroom assistant. An education advisory teacher from the authority also went into the school to work with him and chaired his reviews. At that time there were 28 pupils in his class. His social worker felt he should get the three Ds at GCSE that were required to stay on at school: 'He wouldn't succeed at college, he's too vulnerable.' The foster carers were supportive and attended parents' evenings. Chris said: 'I think they really want me to do well.' His favourite subject was resistant materials and he liked geography, science, art and maths. He felt 'English is boring' but read fiction, for example, he had read all the novels by one author (whom the interviewer didn't recognise).

Case Study: Chris (Stage 2)

At Stage 2 Chris was still with the same foster carers but was due to leave the day after our research interview. He had previously thrown a computer at the carers and they said he had been angrier recently. Departmental restructuring meant that Chris had a new social worker but he knew her from previous contacts with social services. Chris was moving to live in semi-independent accommodation supported by a private-sector organisation.

Chris had left school the previous summer. He didn't get the GCSE grades required for sixth form and was doing an NVQ in horticulture at the local college. His foster carers felt the social worker had been unrealistic in her expectations. They reported that Chris did not cope very well with the study leave given from May onwards as he could not organise himself adequately or structure his time. Unfortunately, Chris would not let his carers help him. The foster carers reported that they have had problems before with Year 11 children in the run-up to their exams.

Two-thirds of young people at Stage 2 were felt by carers or professionals 'definitely' to have the right educational package, as with Chris above. There was a higher number than would be expected of young people living in children's homes who were thought not to have the right educational arrangements at Stage 2, several of whom were not engaging with school. There was no clear link with gender, ethnicity or separation history. As at Stage 1, professionals or carers reported good links with schools with 'quite a lot' of contact for three-fifths of the young people. Encouragingly, for 82 per cent of the young people, schools were said to be 'very easy' to work with. This applied to over two-thirds even if the residential schools (where care–school relationships on a campus would be different) were excluded.

A quarter of the young people interviewed at follow-up told us that their education was progressing 'very well' and two-thirds 'quite well'. Only five of the 74 who responded said 'very badly' (Figure 7.2). Differences were not linked to care settings, gender, ethnicity or separation history. Four-fifths commented that they received enough extra help at school. Interestingly, 5 of the 15 whom we had initially met living in children's homes in Stage 1 reported that they did not get enough extra help at school, but this did not quite reach the required level of statistical significance. It was pleasing to discover that, of the ten young people interviewed who had said that their education was going badly at Stage 1, by

Stage 2, eight of them said that it was now progressing 'quite' (seven) or 'very' (one) well.

Figure 7.2 Young people's views at Stage 2 about how well their education is progressing

Most of those interviewed were clear that their education was 'very' (54%) or 'quite' (42%) important to them. Only three suggested that it was unimportant. Its significance was appreciated across all groups.

Out-of-area placements

Just above half of young people in our sample were placed out of area at both Stage 1 and Stage 2. The dual-registered and residential BESD schools were mainly run by independent-sector organisations and children placed there were living out of borough. There is currently much concern about out-of-area placements, with a perception of worse educational achievements. Paradoxically, greater use of boarding schools is being encouraged under government policies today.

There was a tendency for there to be more concern at Stage 2 over whether young people had the right educational package if they were living within the authority rather than placed away but the difference was not statistically significant. Some providers in the independent or voluntary sectors may be more adept at marketing and loyal to their services than are local authority employees and hence express more positive views. At Stage 2, most young people were considered to have made some educational progress, and this applied equally to those placed within the area and those living away. Perceived changes in educational attainment are shown in Table 7.10.

Table 7.10 Carers' or professionals' perceptions of changes in educational attainment during the follow-up period, by Stage 2 placement

Changes in educational attainment	Placed within area	Placed out of area	Total (%)
Never a problem	8	13	21 (20)
Resolved	2	2	4 (4)
Improving	17	18	35 (33)
No change	11	15	26 (25)
Fluctuating	4	4	8 (8)
Deteriorating	6	6	12 (11)
Total	48	58	106

Table 7.10 shows that the patterns of educational progress were very similar and, therefore, there is no evidence from our study that the educational experiences and attainment were significantly different if young people were placed out of area or lived locally. The same picture applies if we analyse by Stage 1 placements rather than those used at Stage 2.

Summary of Stage 2

Thus, approaching half of the sample had changed their educational provision during the nine-month follow-up period. But carers or professionals and young people alike felt that the changes had made a positive impact and that most were now receiving the right educational package. The children's homes group continued to experience particular problems: proportionately more changed schools and adults had more doubts about the new arrangements.

However, most young people interviewed (across settings) said that they experienced fewer school exclusions over the previous nine months than before. Furthermore, carers or professionals felt that approaching half of the group had made educational progress in the intervening period, a quarter had remained unchanged and only a few had deteriorated. There were no significant differences in progress between settings.

Summary points

- At the outset of the study (Stage 1), young people attended a range of educational settings, including combinations of academic and vocational learning.

- Many had posed previous educational challenges and had disrupted educational careers. Most were considered to have special educational needs, mainly BESD.

- Professionals were unaware of Key Stage 3 results for a quarter of the sample, especially within the children's homes group.

- Good study supports were made available to pupils, across care settings, including carer or professional input. This is likely to have improved recently with increased government and professional interest in the education of looked after children.

- Professionals reported that inter-agency and inter-professional working between social services departments, schools and education departments were mainly good.

- There were few individual differences with the educational experiences we examined by individual circumstances, such as gender or ethnicity.

- Many of the above findings applied to children across care settings but there was evidence that education for the children's homes group was particularly problematic. However, there was no evidence that educational *support* for this group was inferior to that available in the other categories.

- At follow-up (Stage 2), nearly half our sample had changed their educational provision in the previous nine months.

- Carers or professionals and young people felt that these changes had mainly a positive influence. But more problems continued to persist for the children's homes group.

- However, young people reported having reduced their number of school exclusions. Professionals reported that approaching half the sample had made educational progress during the follow-up and a quarter had remained unchanged. These findings applied to young people living in all groups of care setting.

- Similarly, there is no evidence from our study that the educational experiences and results were significantly different if young people were placed out of area or lived locally.

Chapter 8

Support Services
and Support Costs

The economic component of this study was carefully integrated with the rest of the research in terms of the overarching framework, the data collections and the analytic strategy. The particular aims for this element were to:

- describe the services and supports used by the young people in the study, with particular attention paid to the educational arrangements

- describe the costs associated with these services and supports

- compare and contrast service inputs and costs for young people in different placements

- compare and contrast the service inputs and costs for young people originating from the three local authorities

- explore the association between the costs of support and young people's characteristics, needs and changes in the level of those needs (final outcomes).

Methods

As with other elements of this research, the economic component builds on methods developed in the earlier preparatory study (Berridge *et al.* 2002). Then the aim had been to develop a method of identifying education and care costs for young people living in children's homes and residential schools in a way that meant like-with-like costs could be compared. Data was collected from establishments about the overall way the residents or pupils used a range of education, social work and other social care services, and (mental) health services.

In the pilot work, between 58 and 75 per cent of the costs of the seven residential BESD schools were absorbed by staff and for children's homes the figures were between 87 and 92 per cent. Staff responsibilities were one of the main ways costs were allocated to 'education' or 'care' functions. For residents of BESD schools, formal education-related costs absorbed 53 per cent of young people's likely care package costs, on-site care-related costs a further 47 per cent and off-site services just 1 per cent. Children's homes provided a stark contrast. In-house care staff costs accounted for over 90 per cent of the likely care package costs with education adding only a further 7 per cent. Residents of the six children's homes in that study used mainstream schools, which have lower costs per day, but, importantly, about half the young people were not attending school and neither were they receiving much by way of any other education services. Thus the lower costs were likely to lead to poorer educational outcomes.

In the current study our focus is on the supports used by young people in the period between the Stage 1 and Stage 2 data collections. The details of the methodologies used are given in the Appendix. But, in summary, the work entailed a lengthy preparation stage after the collection of service-use data and before statistical analysis could begin. Preparation work involved listing all services and supports used by the young people in the sample and estimating a unit cost for each one. For some, such as the main education and care placements, service-specific unit costs were estimated. For others, such as general practitioners or social workers, we used publicly available data, mainly from an annual compendium of nationally applicable data, *The Unit Costs of Health and Community Care 2005* (Curtis and Netten 2005). Data on the unit costs and the use made by each young person of each service was combined to arrive at the total cost of their support package. These individual level costs formed the basis of our analysis. Different types of appropriate statistical analysis were used. (Cost comparisons between groups, such as originating authority or age, were made using simple bivariate statistics (*t*-tests, analysis of variance, ANOVA), but the variations in the costs of supporting the young people were also explored. This used more complex multivariate analyses.)

Sample

The costs of support packages between Stage 1 and Stage 2 could be estimated for 103 of the original sample of 150 young people. Client Service Receipt Inventory (CSRI) interviews were not undertaken with 30 young people and additional data could not be collected for 12 pupils at residential BESD schools who were not in school when the Stage 2 interviews should have been completed. For five young people CSRI data was available but the costs of accommodation could not be estimated; one young person lived in an independent dual-registered establishment and four in independent sector foster care.

Table 8.1 compares the number of young people in each type of placement at Stage 1 for the full sample and for the 103 young people in the 'costs sample'. The distribution of placements is broadly similar between the two samples but Table 8.2 shows that most of the sample attrition came from the *Borough* authority. The cost sample had a slightly lower proportion of boys than the full sample (59% versus 62%), but the average age remained similar at 14.3 years and 14.2 years, respectively.

Table 8.1 Young people's placement at the start of the study

Placement at Stage 1	Full sample, n = 150 (%)	Costs sample, n = 103 (%)
Foster care[a]	51 (34)	33 (32)
Children's home	39 (26)	23 (22)
Dual-registered home/school	28 (19)	21 (20)
BESD residential school	32 (21)	26 (25)

BESD, behavioural, emotional and social difficulties.
[a] The foster care category includes placements with family and friends.

Table 8.2 Young people's local authority of origin at Stage 1

Local authority	Full sample, n = 150 (%)	Costs sample, n = 103 (%)
County	42 (28)	35 (34)
Metro	35 (23)	26 (25)
Borough	32 (21)	10 (10)
BESD residential school[a]	41 (27)	32 (31)

BESD, behavioural, emotional and social difficulties.
[a] Includes some placements later identified as 'dual-registered'.

Table 8.3 shows there are three slight differences in care history for the full sample and those for whom costs could be estimated. The proportion of young people not looked after is slightly higher in the costs sample, and the proportions of young people subject to Section 20 (Children Act 1989) or in the Stage 1 placement for less than six months are slightly lower. Otherwise the groups are very similar.

Table 8.3 Young people's care history at Stage 1

Care history	Full sample, n = 150 (%)	Costs sample, n = 103 (%)
Care status at start of study:		
not looked after	26 (17)	21 (20)
Section 20	38 (25)	23 (22)
Section 31	82 (55)	57 (55)
other order	4 (3)	2 (2)
Placement duration prior to screen:		
less than 6 months	39 (26)	24 (23)
6–12 months	30 (20)	22 (21)
over 12 months	81 (54)	57 (55)

The Strenghts and Difficulties Questionnaire (SDQ) total scores as rated by the young person and informant (see Chapter 6) were not significantly different for those whose costs could and could not be estimated, nor were age and gender. Perhaps importantly the 'costs sample' has a significantly lower proportion of young people who had any change of placement over the study period. In the full sample, 40 per cent had at least one change of placement, whereas for the 'costs sample' this dropped to 30 per cent, or 26 per cent taking into account the tighter nine-month definition used for the cost estimations (274 days from Stage 1 data collection). The local authority for which fewest CSRI were available (*Borough*) was also the one with the highest proportion of young people who changed placements (19/32).

Services and supports used by young people in the study
Education services
Chapter 7 considers in detail the impact of education on young people in our sample. Table 8.4 quantifies the data on use of education services with a view to assessing its costs. We have data on two-thirds of the young people participating in Stage 1 of the study and Table 7.1 allows a comparison of school attendance with the full sample of young people. The categorisations used in the two tables are not quite the same but similar patterns prevail.

Table 8.4 Use of education services at Stage 2, by original placement

Type of school	Number of children attending each school at Stage 2[a]			
	Foster care (n = 33)	Children's home (n = 23)	Dual-registered (n = 21)	Residential school (n = 26)
Mainstream school (LEA)	15	3	0	1
Special unit in mainstream school	1	0	0	0
BESD day school (LEA)	4	4	0	0
LEA special boarding school	1	0	0	5
P&V special day school	1	3	1	1
P&V special boarding school	1	0	17	20
One-to-one teaching assistance in school	1	0	0	0
Taught in small groups in school	0	0	0	0
Extra professional support[b]	7	0	3	3
Pupil referral unit	2	0	0	0
Further education college	6	3	1	8
Other education resource[c]	5	4	1	0
Individual tuition at home	0	1	2	0

LEA, local education authority; BESD, behavioural, emotionsl and social difficulties; P&V, private and voluntary sector.

[a] Figures include some children who attend a second educational setting for a half- or full-day per week.

[b] Includes learning support assistants, support worker from P&V fostering agency, private lessons, one-to-one help from children's home staff, a 'sewing afternoon', support from the school during period of exclusion.

[c] Includes work experience, basic skills teaching, resource centre, on-site resources, Fresh Start.

Children who were originally sampled from dual-registered establishments or residential BESD schools were most likely to attend on-site classes during the school term before the Stage 2 interviews (see Table 8.4). Most attended full-time, but eight pupils attending residential BESD schools spent a day each week at a local further education (FE) college and one young person from a dual-registered facility spent four days a week at an FE college.

Only two young people who had been living in foster care at Stage 1 were not attending any schools or colleges at Stage 2. Twenty young people had attended one school full-time, including one young person at a pupil referral unit (PRU). Five had mixed education packages; mainstream/PRU/FE college, boarding school/FE college, boarding school/mainstream school, FE college/work experience, or BESD day school/work experience (two plus two days). A further three young people attended FE colleges for two or three days each week, three spent between two and four days at resource centres or using on-site resources, and one was in full-time work experience. The two young people who were not attending any form of education classes were two of the oldest in this group at 16 years old and 15 years 10 months, respectively.

The picture for those originally sampled from children's homes was less encouraging, with the data from Stage 1 providing some insights; these young people had previously truanted more, they were the worst attenders, they were the worst behaved at school and they had the more problematic relationships with teachers (see Chapter 7). During the research period, just nine of the young people attended full-time at one school or FE college, three attended for four days each week (FE colleges or a resource centre) and one young person attended a BESD day school for three days each week. One young person attended a resource centre for two days each week and one received just four hours of basic skills teaching each week. Only one young person appeared to receive a mix of inputs, attending two days per week at a BESD day school and two at a resource centre. The remaining seven young people accessed very limited schooling or educational support.

Table 8.5 summarises the information on use of school or care placements and education supports, and gives the average and range of costs. The 'current placement' category includes the costs of the care placement and use of any on-site education (i.e. for placements in residential BESD schools or dual-registered establishments). Only those living in residential BESD schools used weekend or holiday placements – most commonly spending this time with their families. If the young people went 'off-site' for classes, perhaps to an FE college, these costs are included under community-based education. Thus, the education costs for young people in children's homes or foster care are also included in the community-based education and education support categories. A survey by

Ofsted (2003) of mainstream provision for special educational needs in 12 authorities reported that schools and local education authorities (LEAs) both found it hard to make appropriate provision for pupils with BESD and numbers were said to be increasing. Additional costs were not always easy to identify but were estimated to be around £3000 per pupil per year (Ofsted 2003). The costs in Table 8.5, therefore, may be an underestimate of the full costs borne by mainstream schools.

Table 8.5 Use and costs of services and supports over nine months

Service	All young people (n = 103)			
	n (%) using service		Mean cost £ (range)	
All accommodation and education	103	**(100)**	**65,281**	**(6352–164,563)**
Current placement[a]	103	(100)	54,415	(229–164,400)
Weekend/holiday	31	(30)	1537	(0–10,624)
Placement changes[b]	16	(16)	5496	**(0–92,335)**
Community-based education	54	(52)	3678	(0–21,772)
Educational support	5	(5)	119	(0–3661)
Education professionals	**70**	**(68)**	**38**	**(0–1348)**
Education psychologist	18	(17)	35	(0–490)
Education welfare officer	9	(9)	20	(0–1348)
SENCO	7	(7)	5	(0–218)
Connexions	49	(48)	51	(0–1122)
School nurse	18	(17)	5	(0–113)
Speech therapy	3	(3)	1	(0–58)
Other[c]	10	(10)	38	(0–981)
Hospital care	**47**	**(46)**	**255**	**(0–4676)**
Inpatient stays	11	(11)	145	(0–4676)
A&E attendances	36	(35)	87	(0–790)
Outpatient clinics	9	(9)	23	(0–474)
Community health	**97**	**(94)**	**73**	**(0–461)**
General practitioner	83	(80)	33	(0–324)
Nurse	31	(30)	2	(0–13)
Dentist	86	(83)	14	(0–102)
Optician	78	(76)	14	(0–36)
Other[d]	10	(10)	10	(0–316)

Table 8.5 cont.

Service	All young people (n = 103)			
	n (%) using service		Mean cost £ (range)	
Community mental health	**36**	**35**	**178**	**(0–1944)**
Counselling	28	(27)	120	(0–1296)
Other[e]	13	(13)	58	(0–1296)
Social care	**85**	**(83)**	**530**	**(0–5478)**
Social worker	79	(77)	313	(0–3564)
Fostering officer	21	(20)	93	(0–2673)
Youth/YOT worker	17	(17)	57	(0–1188)
Drug services	7	(7)	25	(0–1248)
Other services[f]	15	(15)	41	(0–1254)
All supports or services	103	(100)	66,317	(6418–164,772)

SENCO, special educational needs co-ordinator; CAMHS, child and adolescent mental health services.

[a] Accommodation or school.

[b] Changes in type of main placement in the 'statistical nine months' following Stage 1.

[c] Includes drop-in counselling, education support worker, looked after children's education worker, learning mentor, art therapy, anger management, CAMHS support.

[d] Includes paediatrician, other community doctor, community-based speech therapy, child development centre, genito-urinary medicine clinic, health visitor.

[e] Includes individual or family therapy, art therapy, anger management.

[f] Includes independent or children's rights visitors, Voice (voluntary group for children in public care), leaving care team, respite care, guardian ad litem.

As suggested in our pilot study, it is these complex and different connections between the care and education locations which mean like-with-like cost comparisons may be made only if care and education costs are considered together. The mean cost of care and education for these 103 young people was £65,000 for the nine-month period, or around £1670 per week. However, the range is wide with more than a 23-fold difference from the least to most expensive: from £180 per week per young person to £4200. As shown below, there are systematic cost differences by type of placement as well as cost variations within placement types.

Table 8.5 shows that, as well as support provided in school, just over two-thirds of the young people in the costs sample received support from education professionals who are funded from outside the school budget. Unsurprisingly, the Connexions worker was the most commonly seen professional, but the school nurse and the educational psychologist were used by one in six of the young people. Educational psychology support is most commonly related to special educational needs (SEN) assessments. More information on education was given in Chapter 7 but it is worth repeating that approximately four-fifths of the young people interviewed at Stage 2 said they received enough extra support at school.

It is perhaps surprising that little mention was made of inputs from the specialist educational support services set up by the three authorities (see Chapter 2). There are possibly two reasons for this. In the first place, the teams were likely to do most of their work establishing links with other professionals, providing training and management information; direct work with young people was more limited. Second, the teams were usually multi-disciplinary, so as young people and other informants reported service contacts they would not necessarily know that any specific professional or service was connected to the educational support service. There was, however, little evidence that this sample had received the intensive coaching or individual tutoring that was available through these teams; one young person had one-to-one teaching in school, one had private lessons and a handful were supported by learning assistants in school.

Health and social work or social care services

Table 8.5 also shows that a good range of health services were involved, although use of any one service, with three notable exceptions, was quite low. The exceptions are general practitioners (GPs), dentists and opticians. Four out of five children had contact with their GP, commonly once or twice in the previous nine months, although at the top end, one young person saw their GP almost monthly. More than three-quarters of the sample saw dentists and opticians. Only 13 of the young people in children's homes or foster care at Stage 1 had not seen a dentist and only 18 had not seen an optician.

A third of the young people used a hospital Accident and Emergency Department (A&E). Many of these were for usual incidents such as stomach pains, a burn or other minor injuries. However, two young people attended A&E for alcohol abuse, two for drug overdoses and one for solvent abuse. Very few had an inpatient stay but 4 of the 11 young people were admitted for treatment after drug overdoses, including one of the young people attending A&E. Three were young women originating from one authority: two lived in independent sector children's homes and one in semi-independent living. The fourth was a young man from a different authority, who was living in a kinship foster care placement in his local area.

The low use of mental health services is concerning. Just one-third of the young people used these supports, commonly counselling, although three young people also had anger management support at school. The child and adolescent mental health service (CAMHS) professionals provided staff support in some of the residential BESD schools and dual-registered establishments, although this often related to monitoring the use of medication. By contrast, all the young people in this sample were selected as having high levels of problem behaviour and informants rated nearly half (32/74) of the young people as being in the 'abnormal' range (total scores above 20) on the Strengths and Difficulties Questionnaire (SDQ) at Stage 1 (see Chapter 6). Problems are defined in different ways and certain 'discourses' may dominate (Foucault 1977), but it appears to us that there is a mismatch between young people's difficulties and needs and the extent of specialist mental health support available. For example, a young man living away at a dual-registered facility, who was a suicide risk, sought out a rope when his home visits had gone badly and carers had to remove dangerous items from his room. That said, we were aware of a number of cases where young people had been referred to the CAMHS but had refused to attend.

Turning to community-based social work or social care services, just 17 per cent of young people received no support. They were most likely to be those attending residential BESD schools (Table 8.6). Social worker contact was, unsurprisingly, the most commonly used of these supports and one in five young people reported contact with a fostering officer. More information is given on the social work support received by young people in Chapters 5 and 6.

Costs of support

The final two columns in Table 8.5 provide information on the costs of supporting the young people over the nine-month period. On average, each young person cost £66,300 with 92.7 per cent of this sum absorbed by the costs of their care or education placements (including weekend and holiday living circumstances) and 5.9 per cent by use of mainstream education services and education professionals. Community-based hospital, health and social work or social care services accounted for just 1.6 per cent of their total support costs, of which the latter absorbed about a third.

The final column of Table 8.5 shows the range of costs for each service; 0 indicates that at least one young person in the sample did not use that service. Indeed, comparing this data with the service use rates in the first column illustrates the long right-hand skew, meaning that one or two young people used a particular service at a relatively high intensity but many did not use it at all. Figure 8.1 shows this graphically for one service: A&E visits. This service use or cost pattern is not unusual and is the reason why the subsequent analyses focus on the costs for the service groups (hospital care, community-based health services, and

Table 8.6 Costs of accommodation, education and other supports, by original placement group

Service groups[a]	Foster care (n = 33)				Children's home (n = 23)				Dual-registered (n = 21)				Residential schools (n = 26)			
	Use service		Mean cost		Use service		Mean cost		Use service		Mean cost		Use service		Mean cost	
	(n)	(%)	(£)	(SD)	(n)	(%)	(£)	(SD)	(n)	(%)	(£)	(SD)	(n)	(%)	(£)	(SD)
Main accommodation or school	33	100	18,714	(28,686)	23	100	66,273	(37,677)	21	100	93,643	(2806)	26	100	57,555	(20,956)
Weekend or holiday	1	3	31	(175)	0		0	(0)	4	19	1154	(2709)	26	100	5119	(1584)
Other placements[b]	8	24	7436	(22,237)	5	22	11,600	(25,278)	2	9	2516	(9833)	1	4	42	(215)
Community-based education	27	82	5382	(5493)	18	78	7836	(8065)	3	14	1301	(4774)	8	30	230	(374)
Education profs.	19	58	144	(284)	11	48	159	(338)	18	86	144	(167)	22	85	175	(214)
Total accommodation or school			31,333	(35,260)			85,868	(23,616)			98,759	(24,004)			63,121	(21,086)
Hospital services	15	45	374	(938)	10	43	215	(399)	9	63	113	(188)	13	50	256	(438)
Health services	31	94	75	(92)	20	87	48	(40)	21	100	82	(61)	25	96	84	(53)
Mental health services	9	27	147	(390)	11	48	204	(356)	5	14	149	(387)	11	42	215	(425)
Social work/social care services	32	97	725	(100)	22	96	602	(618)	19	90	545	(371)	12	46	206	(389)
Grand total			32,655	(35,250)			86,937	(23,522)			99,648	(23,878)			63,882	(21,301)

SD, standard deviation.

[a] See Table 8.5 for services within these groups.

[b] Placement other than original placement between Stage 1 and Stage 2 interviews.

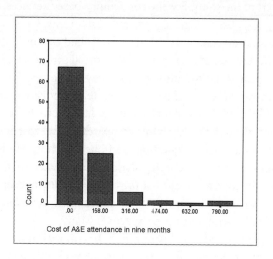

Figure 8.1 Distribution of costs for accident and emergency (A&E) visits

community-based social work or social care services) or total costs. Data on the various accommodation and education supports is given separately, however.

Comparing costs by placements at Stage 1

Table 8.6 shows the costs of the service groups by the original (Stage 1) placement groups. Looking at the total accommodation or education costs, dual-registered placements, commonly for 52 weeks per year, tend to be the most costly, followed by children's homes, but average (mean) costs for these two groups are not significantly different. However, accommodation and education for young people in dual-registered establishments or children's homes are significantly more costly than for those young people attending residential BESD schools, which in turn are more costly than children supported in foster care. The total cost figures also follow this pattern of statistical significance but no difference was found between groups in the costs of community-based hospital, health and social work or social care services.

Although 31 young people in this costs sample changed placements between Stage 1 and Stage 2, in Table 8.6 we show separately the costs where young people moved from one *type* of placement to another – perhaps from foster care to a children's home or to a dual-registered placement. The numbers are small but it is worth noting that this group of 16 young people includes one in four of those originally in foster care and just over one in four of those living in children's homes at the start of the study. For the community-based services, those in foster care had the highest observed average (mean) cost for hospital services and those in children's homes and residential BESD schools had the highest observed cost for mental health services. Mean social work or social care costs for young people in foster care appear to be the highest, and they are lowest for the residential schools group in which few of the young people are looked after.

The cost differential between foster and residential care has been the topic of many discussions, although research that compares the full cost of these locations is less common. A more recent question, and one which is very relevant to this research, emerged in the current legislation *Care Matters* (DfES 2007): can boarding schools be used as a means of providing stability and support for some children in care and to help improve their educational outcomes? The present study has provided an interesting perspective. Many of the residential BESD schools studied here provide weekly or termly boarding. Pupils therefore need a stable and consistent placement to return to at weekends and during school holidays. In the present study, most pupils could return to the family home (and thus retain good links with their families) but if a young person was 'looked after', it was usually the result of a family breakdown. If a pupil cannot return at weekends and during holidays to the family home then a place must be kept available in foster care or in a children's home. Any reduction in costs perceived to emanate from use of a residential BESD school placement rather than a children's home placement may disappear as both school and weekend or holiday placements must be funded. The alternative is to consider dual-registered placements. These appear to facilitate good school attendance and provide 52-week care. However, the present study found no cost advantage for dual-registered placements over children's homes. On the evidence of the current study, local authorities may end up spending more money when seeking to improve educational outcomes in this way.

Comparing costs by local authority of origin

Bearing in mind that in this 'costs sample' there are only ten young people who were sampled from the *Borough* authority, the discussion is focused on the samples from the *County* and *Metro* authorities. The data in Table 8.7 suggests that there are some differences in the utilisation rates for these local authorities, although some samples are still fairly small when looking at the service groups. About a quarter of the young people had more than one placement over the study period and around two in three attended community-based education, although those in the *Metro* sample appear more likely to have access to additional support from educational professionals. Young people from *Metro* also appear to be more likely to have used hospital and social work or social care services and the proportion of young people using mental health services was also higher. None of the cost differences between these local authority groups reached statistical significance, however, suggesting that these two authorities did not differ systematically in the way they supported difficult young people.

Cost associations

The *production of welfare* model provides a sensible ordering of variables to test for their influence on the costs of support (Knapp and Lowin 1998). This comprises four linked components. *Costs* are estimated using information on resource inputs, such as staff, buildings and equipment. In care services, staff costs commonly comprise the major part of the total cost of any given service. Second, *non-resource inputs* are less easy to measure but they may help to explain vital differences between ostensibly similar services. Examples would include the needs and characteristics of the young people, but also social features of the care environment and the characteristics, experiences, personalities of the main actors. *Final outcomes* are the eventual goal of the care system – these represent not the production of services but the 'production' of changes in the welfare in the young people. These should not be confused with the *intermediate or service-related outcomes* (often called 'outputs'); examples here would be levels of provision, turnover or volume of services. These four domains allow us to maintain an analytic focus on the young people, recognising that various young people will respond differently even if they receive similar combinations of resource inputs.

Following the *production of welfare model*, in the first instance we would expect the costs of support – which summarise the intensity of services and supports received over the statistical nine-month period – to be sensitive to the characteristics, needs and circumstances of the young people. These are the very factors that social workers and educational psychologists explore as they assess a child. In this study we have data on the following items.

- *Young people's characteristics*: age in years, gender, ethnicity (white or other minority ethnic).

- *Family characteristics*: source of household income (benefits or earned income), whether the family is 'high risk' due to factors such as mental health problems, substance abuse, criminality and so on.

- *Young people's needs assessed at Stage 1*: the problems score, the SDQ total score as rated by the young people, the 'ladders' completed by young people.

Table 8.7 Costs of accommodation, education and other supports, by original local authority

Service groups[a]	County (n = 35)				Metro (n = 26)				Borough (n = 10)			
	Use service		Mean cost		Use service		Mean cost		Use service		Mean cost	
	(n)	(%)	(£)	(SD)	(n)	(%)	(£)	(SD)	(n)	(%)	(£)	(SD)
Main accommodation or school	35	(100)	54,672	(45,130)	26	(100)	34,711	(38,892)	10	(100)	64,646	(46,897)
Weekend/holiday	3	(9)	401	(1791)	–	–	–	–	0	–	–	–
Other placements[b]	8	(23)	8890	(23,130)	7	(27)	9765	(23,178)	0	–	–	–
Community-based education	22	(63)	5075	(6732)	18	(69)	5291	(6635)	8	(80)	6995	(7420)
Education professionals	20	(57)	174	(335)	17	(65)	112	(160)	5	(50)	115	(300)
Total accommodation or school	**35**	**(100)**	**69,212**	**(43,322)**	**26**	**(100)**	**49,878**	**(37,164)**	**10**	**(100)**	**70,528**	**(49,516)**
Hospital services	13	(37)	124	(215)	12	(46)	527	(1071)	8	(80)	142	(90)
Health services	32	(91)	65	(61)	24	(92)	65	(87)	10	(100)	88	(93)
Mental health services	11	(31)	442	(6195)	9	(35)	159	(307)	5	(50)	237	(406)
Social work/social care services	32	(91)	754	(1012)	26	(100)	636	(528)	10	(100)	487	(301)
Grand total			**70,333**	**(43,157)**			**51,266**	**(37,096)**			**71,482**	**(49,559)**

SD, standard deviation.

[a] See Table 8.5 for services within these groups.

[b] Placement other than original placement between Stage 1 and Stage 2 interviews.

- *Proxy measure for young people's needs*: care status – looked after or not and whether accommodated under Section 20 or Section 31 (Children Act 1989), number of child-related reasons for placement, time spent away from home at Stage 1, duration of placement at Stage 1.

- *Education measures*: excluded (temporary or permanent) from school in the term prior to the Stage 1 interview, truancy from school prior to Stage 1, SEN provision, whether the young person has been assessed as having BESD and the level of effort the young person reports putting into their education at Stage 1.

It is also perfectly reasonable to expect that costs will vary with the level of *final outcomes* achieved; although rarely found in such statistical explorations, higher cost support packages, all else being equal, should generate better outcomes. The SDQ was also used at Stage 2 so the change in score from Stage 1 to Stage 2 gives a measure of outcomes. Two other outcome measures were used in the present analysis: the researcher-compiled composite measure of outcome reflecting change in BESD over the study period (see Chapter 6) and the informant-rated overall measure of how education is progressing at Stage 2 (coded as very/quite well, very/quite badly).

There are also several 'service-related' variables (*intermediate outcomes*) available which may help 'explain' cost variation once associations between costs and the young people's characteristics, needs and outcomes have been taken into account:

- whether the young person has had a change in accommodation in the follow-up period, or a change in education establishment

- original placement type

- originating local authority

- the overall measure of care quality compiled from young people's reports.

Cost associations: single variables

The discussion here becomes inevitably more complex but we try to explain it as straightforwardly as possible. We spell out at the end what it all means.

In the first instance each variable hypothesised to have an influence on costs was tested individually against two summary cost variables: the costs of accommodation and education support, and the total costs of the support packages. Given the high proportion of total cost that is absorbed by accommodation or education costs, it is not surprising that these summary costs are highly correlated. The cost of all hospital, health and social work or social care services was not associated with either the accommodation or education cost or the total cost measure. That is to say, there are no patterns of health and social work or social care service use that are associated with particular placement types.

Ten of the variables we identified were associated with costs (Table 8.8 and Table 8.9). Five variables related to young people's circumstances prior to Stage 1. Three factors reflect some of the needs and circumstances of the young people in the sample: whether they came from a high-risk family, had an unstable care history, and, in Table 8.9, having a greater number of problems. Two factors associated with costs relate to their education history: the stability of the young person's education experience and whether they had truanted in the past. The type of placement in which the young person was living at Stage 1 was also significantly associated with costs.

Table 8.8 Associations with summary cost variables

Variable[a]	Difference in accommodation or schooling cost	p value (CI)	Difference in total cost	p value (CI)[b]
Comes from high-risk family (55/83)	– £21,964	.012 (–39,820, –6022)	– £21,487	.014 (–36,834, –4472)
Had unstable care history (45/67)	+ £21,498	.040 (839, 42,093)	+ £21,321	.047 (1546, 39,963)
Had unstable education history (30/66)	+ £27,536	.006 (9275, 45,119)	+ £27,930	.005 (7677, 46,635)
Has truanted in the past (27/65)	+ £25,887	.010 (5374, 43,103)	+ £25,392	.011 (6534, 43,976)

[a] A positive cost difference means that young people with this characteristic have higher costs. (Number of young people with this characteristic or number of young people for whom the data is recorded.)

[b] The p value is a measure of whether our research findings could have arisen by chance. A p value of <.05 means this finding would have arisen by chance on fewer than 1 in 20 occasions and p <.01 would mean fewer than 1 in 100 occasions and so on. The confidence interval (CI) may be used to confirm statistical significance. If the two values pass through zero the difference is not statistically significant.

Table 8.9 shows that just one service-related measure assessed over the study period was associated with costs; the Quality of Care measure (see Chapter 5). One measure of outcome was also associated with costs, the SDQ total score at Stage 2 as rated by the young person.

Table 8.9 Associations with SDQ score, quality of care and placement type variables

Variable	Accommodation or schooling cost p value	Total cost p value
Higher young person's SDQ total score at Stage 1 ($n = 68$)	.042	.040
Number of problems at Stage 1 ($n = 99$)	.001	.001
Number of child-related reasons for placement ($n = 95$)	.042	.040
Higher young person's SDQ total scores at Stage 2 ($n = 74$)	.013	.011
Quality of care ($n = 73$) (between groups 2,3,4)[a]	.011	.010
Placement type ($n = 103$) (between groups 1,2,3,5)[b]	<.001	<.001

SDQ, Strengths and Difficulties Questionnaire.

[a] Quality of care rated as: 1 = poor; 2 = fair; 3 = good; 4 = very good. Care for only one child was rated poor, this case has been excluded. There was no cost difference between care rated as 2 and 3. Those with care rated as 4 were significantly less costly.

[b] Placement type at start of study rated as: 1 = dual-registered establishment; 2 = children's homes; 3 = foster care (combining 3 = foster care, 4 = placed with kin); 5 = residential BESD school.

Cost associations: multiple variables

The final aim for the economic element of this study was to explore the multiple effects of these characteristics and other factors. We did this because some factors may be inter-related – as, for example, gender and self-harm might be. Table 8.5 showed not just the mean cost for the various service groups – the figure of most interest to commissioners and service providers – but also the range of costs. These are wide, some young people are supported intensively (higher cost) and others less so. Table 8.6 showed that this cost variation remains even for young people placed in ostensibly similar facilities; most of the standard deviations (SDs) are quite large when set alongside the mean cost. Figure 8.2 illustrates this variation graphically for the total costs of support over the nine-month period.

Table 8.8 and Table 8.9 indicate that costs vary systematically with some characteristics, needs and circumstances of the young people in the study. The use of a statistical 'cost function' analysis identifies the relative contribution of these factors in the form of a mathematical equation (Knapp 1998).[1] Once a

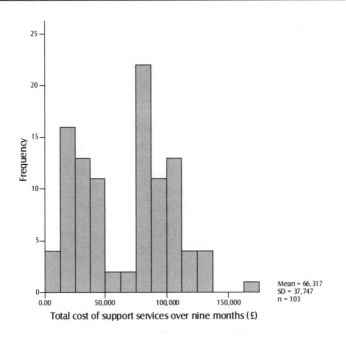

Figure 8.2 Total costs of support over nine months. SD, standard deviation

satisfactory equation was obtained by use of the data described in Table 8.8 and Table 8.9, the other measures we identified but which were found not to be associated with costs on their own were tested. It may be that inter-relationships between the variables would improve the (statistical) explanatory power of the equation. Finally, the service-level factors were included to assess their additional contribution. The accommodation or school subtotal and the total costs of support were tested as dependent variables but, as they generated similar equations, we report the findings using the total costs measure.

Not all the variables in Table 8.8 and Table 8.9 could be taken forwards to the multivariate regression analyses. Some variables were available only for young people in contact with social services. Initial investigations using the variables in Table 8.8, for example, reduced the sample to just 50 young people (i.e. those who had data for all of these variables). Importantly, if we used these variables more than two-thirds of the young people in residential BESD schools would have been excluded from the analysis. Other variables, such as the measure of quality of care and the SDQ scores, were dependent on the young people's willingness to be interviewed as part of the research. However, the final equation (Table 8.10) means that just four young people from our cost sample are excluded.

Table 8.10 Cost function analysis[a]

Characteristic	Equation A		Equation B	
	Coefficient	p value	Coefficient	p value
Constant	+ 38,852	<.001	+ 77,749	<.001
Number of problems, Stage 1	+ 8786	.001	+ 4168	.043
In residential school, Stage 1	–	–	– 55,339	<.001
In foster care, Stage 1	–	–	– 28,138	<.001
	$df = 98; R^2 = .112$; adjusted $R^2 = .103$		$df = 98; R^2 = .476$; adjusted $R^2 = .460$	

[a] Dependent variable is total costs of support package over the nine-month study period.

Equation A in Table 8.10 shows the findings from the exploration of the associations between the total costs of support and the needs, circumstances and characteristics of the young people in the cost sample. In these analyses, just one indicator of needs lay behind the cost variations described above: the number of problems the young person had at Stage 1. As we might expect, higher costs are associated with a greater number of problems. This variable 'explains' 10 per cent of the cost variation. No other measures of characteristics, needs or outcome entered the equation alongside this one. It is notable that young people were selected for this study if they had difficulties in at least two of the six 'problem' dimensions, yet the variation between the young people in terms of the complexity of their difficulties are still sufficient to have an influence on the total cost measure.

Equation B allowed the service-related variables to enter the equation. Placement type at the start of the study was found to be significantly associated with costs in the bivariate analyses: using 'yes/no' variables to identify the placement type for each young person (Table 8.9). The best equation (as measured statistically by the adjusted R^2) also included the variable identifying which young people lived in foster care (29%) and residential BESD schools (26%). Both of these were negatively associated with costs – these placement choices were associated, all else being equal, with lower costs. Together these three variables 'explained' nearly half of the observed cost variation.[2]

If we compare Equation A and Equation B we may see that the placement (service-level) variables have a strong influence on costs; the coefficients for living in schools or foster care are both quite large and the proportion of cost variation explained (as measured by the adjusted R^2) has risen from 10 per cent to 46 per cent. We can also look at what has happened to the other variable in the equation; the problem count at Stage 1. Its direction of influence has remained the same (i.e. in both equations the coefficient is positive – having more problems is associated with higher costs whether or not placement is taken into account), but in Equation B, the value of the coefficient is lower (so it has less impact on costs) and the p value fell to .04.

The problems count, however, remains an important consideration. For readers who are still with us, what this means is that the increase in the number of problems young people have is linked to their placement type, and also to an increase in placement cost. The most difficult young people were placed in the more expensive dual-registered facilities or children's homes (mean = 3.6 problems at Stage 1). Pupils at residential BESD schools had an average of 3.4 problems, and, for those in foster care, the least expensive placement option, the average number of problems was 2.6. Chapter 3 also showed systematic differences between the young people selected into the study who were living in the various placement types.

The proportion of variation explained is not unusual for this type of micro-level analysis in social work or social care services. Indeed, the few recent user-level cost analyses in social work or social care have found slightly lower levels of explanatory power from similar types of data; around one-fifth for six studies of a similar size (see Beecham and Sinclair 2007 for a summary). Across these studies, a similar range of variables was found to be important: absent or poor home environment, emotional and behavioural problems, mental health problems, socially unacceptable behaviour and disability (Beecham and Sinclair 2007, p.75).

However, just over half the cost variation – 54 per cent – in the present study remains 'unexplained'. Why might this be? There are two main sets of reasons: those that relate to the research and those that relate to the service context. Perhaps the outcome measures used by researchers are insufficiently sensitive for the small changes in welfare we should expect in this client group? Perhaps the cost measures are too rudimentary? Is the time-scale too short? Given the similarity of findings, there is no reason to suppose this research is any different from other research in this area. The unexplained variation may also be reflecting placement policies and practices within the local authorities that cannot easily be identified or picked up in the present type of study.

The match between costs and needs is by no means perfect, and there is no evidence from the present study to suggest that increased resources are generating improved outcomes. What is encouraging, however, is that an association between needs and cost does exist. The main message is that more resources do appear to be spent on those young people who have higher levels of needs. The problem score had a small, but important role in explaining cost variation. Alongside the systematic differences found between groups of young people in the placement types, this suggests that those making decisions about placements are allocating resources (services, money and so forth) with regard to the level of difficulties young people have to overcome.

Summary points

- Young people in the present study used a wide range of services and supports. The high utilisation rates of opticians and dentists for young people who were looked after were particularly encouraging. However, the low use of mental health services is concerning, particularly given that the sample was selected as having behaviours which pose considerable management challenges.

- There was better school attendance at residential BESD schools and dual-registered establishments that provided on-site education. Young people in children's homes were least likely to attend school full time, and nearly one in three received a very limited education service.

- Total support costs could be estimated for 103 of the young people originally sampled, at an average of £66,000 over the nine months. The range of support costs was wide, from £6500 to £165,000 over the study period.

- Education and care placement costs accounted for 92 per cent of the total costs of support.

- The total costs of supporting young people varied by placement. Those originally placed in dual-registered facilities, or children's homes, were more costly than those in residential BESD schools, which in turn were more costly to support than young people placed in foster care. However, pupils at residential BESD schools were able to return to their family at the weekend and during school holidays. If they did not, any cost advantage would be much reduced.

- Young people across placement categories made similar use of community-based supports: hospital, health and social work or social care.

- The costs of supporting young people originating from two authorities (*County* and *Metro*) were compared. Although there were some differences in service utilisation rates, the two authorities did not differ systematically in the level of support for these young people.

- Support costs varied within as well as between placement types. Young people's difficulties explained nearly half the variation in costs among our sample, mediated through choices made prior to the study about the placement for each young person.

- Those originally living in dual-registered facilities or children's homes were assessed at the start of the study as having more problems than pupils at residential BESD schools. In turn, these pupils had more problems than those living with foster carers. Costs varied accordingly.

Notes

1   Such an equation may suggest that, for example, the young person's age multiplied by 3.2 plus their Stage 1 SDQ score multiplied by 45.7 would 'explain' a proportion of the variation in the total support costs.

2   For the statistically minded, the standardised residual from both these equations was normally distributed. Bootstrap analysis confirmed the statistical significance of the component variables. Given the unusual bimodal distribution of the costs data the findings were also tested using a log-transformation of the dependent variable and this produced similar findings.

Chapter 9

Conclusion

Over the past decade looked after children have become a high political priority. This has not always been the case and the commitment to society's most vulnerable is to be welcomed. Government has pursued welfare reform and there has been a series of wide-ranging policy initiatives. Examples have been the Green Paper *Every Child Matters* (DfES 2003b), more recently the White Paper *Care Matters: Transforming the Lives of Children and Young People in Care* (DfES 2007) and, at the time of writing, the subsequent Children and Young Persons Bill (2007–2008). We return to these later. But these were preceded in 1998 by the White Paper, *Quality Protects*, which very much set the scene for New Labour's approach to social policy for children and families experiencing difficulties, including setting performance targets. This was announced initially as a three-year initiative, subsequently extended, bringing with it £375 million of extra resources.

This book has focused on the educational experiences of children looked after by local authorities. It is based on a study that was part of a research initiative linked to *Quality Protects*, evaluating its impact. We concentrated on its educational objectives, relating to school attendance, exclusion and achievement. These have been set more widely in the context of young people's care experiences, costs of services and outcomes. We began with a preparatory phase (Berridge *et al.* 2002). Our approach combined different academic disciplines: sociology, social policy, psychology and social care economics. We have applied these to child and family welfare services, and for comparative purposes to (residential) special education for pupils 'with behavioural, emotional and social difficulties' (BESD).

Our specific interest was in adolescents, who arouse special concern in the modern UK and have done so for a very long time in social history. Children's education has been a main focus in New Labour's social policy for looked after children (DfEE/DoH 2000), consistent with Prime Minister Tony Blair's early pledge in 1997 that Labour's three priorities would be 'education, education, education'. Indeed, success in the education system is potentially an important route to social mobility in the UK and this should apply, as much as to anyone, to those growing up at acute social and economic disadvantage or experiencing poor parenting, or both.

In this final chapter we bring together our main findings. Each of our chapters has ended with a summary of its main points and so we try to avoid undue repetition. However, we shall also develop some of the main themes stemming from this work and their policy implications. By no means is this the final word. For whatever reason, child welfare research has become increasingly challenging and we have examined some very complex situations. Our research design inevitably has been multifaceted (see Chapter 1 and the Appendix). The methods we adopted included an analysis of official statistics and local documentation, and interviews with social services and education managers in three local authorities (fictitiously titled *County*, *Metro* and *Borough*). Quantitative and qualitative approaches were combined.

The major, and certainly most time-consuming, element was a nine-month follow-up study of the care and educational experiences of 150 'difficult' adolescents. Initially, the young people were approximately 11–15 years of age, and were divided equally between those living in foster care, children's homes or residential 'BESD' schools. This reflects our particular interest in the differential impact on education of care settings: previously, little detailed research has occurred. Data was gathered from interviews with young people, social workers and carers. 'Difficulty' was defined in terms of antisocial behaviour, namely: poor school attendance; behavioural problems in school; regular use of alcohol or drugs; conviction for criminal offences; self-harm; and aggression or violence. Being aware of the dangers of 'moral panic' (Cohen 1972), we appreciate that young people are not all 'difficult', and looked after children are not difficult most of the time. However, social work research focuses particularly on social problems rather than those who are unproblematic. We tried to ensure that the three placement groups were broadly comparable but, as we have seen, there were marked differences.

Key findings

So what did we discover? Initially, a scrutiny of national Key Stage 4 GCSE or GNVQ results confirmed that the looked after group performs academically much more poorly than the general school population. Some improvements have occurred, but government targets have been missed. At the local level, we urged caution on the interpretation of these statistics, which may be misleading: groups are often small and populations differ both across authorities and over time. We are often not comparing like with like. Overall, academic achievements among looked after pupils fluctuated in our three study authorities; yet, encouragingly, there were very few permanent exclusions recorded at all.

Over the duration of the *Quality Protects* initiative, authorities received very little government grant linked specifically to its education objectives. Other sources of funding were available but, in light of this, we might expect any advances to have been modest. In fact an analysis of local documentation revealed that the implementation specifically of *Quality Protects* was accompanied by progress on inter-professional working and each of the three authorities (along with many others) had established forms of dedicated education support teams for looked after pupils (though sometimes these had been set up earlier). Within these broader developments, local managers were overwhelmingly positive about the impact of the *Quality Protects* initiative in helping to improve looked after children's education and in moving away from a narrow focus on an 'at risk' group.

Looking specifically at our study group of 150 young people, though there was probably some convergence owing to the requirement for evidence of behavioural difficulty, the looked after groups recruited via local authorities had quite different family backgrounds from those encountered at residential BESD schools. The former had experienced noticeably more adversity. The family members of looked after young people (mainly birth parents) were significantly more likely to demonstrate problems in relation to alcohol or drug misuse, criminal activity, mental health and domestic violence. The care group had been living away from birth parents from an earlier age than were the residential school students and had a much higher experience of abuse and neglect. But, as we argued earlier, it is the *combination* of adversities that brings with it particular stresses (Caprara and Rutter 1995): individual stressful experiences in themselves tend to inflict limited damage, but the effects of several are cumulative. Looked after young people were found to have much worse combinations of family adversity than those recruited from the residential special schools.

Indeed, professionals thought that almost nine in every ten of the residential schools' sample would identify the birth family as their 'home-base' compared with only half for the local authority groups. Three-quarters of the schools' sample had unrestricted access to their birth families but the comparative figure for the looked after groups was below a third. We would expect these differences in upbringing to influence current behaviour and educational achievement. There has been a tendency for commentators to claim that the looked after and residential BESD groups are very similar, or even interchangeable, but our evidence shows the opposite.

In terms of how services responded to these problems, a wide variety of provision was used. There was also much disparity within groups – such as the type of children's homes or dual-registered establishments. Interestingly, contact with birth parents was unrelated to distance and whether or not placements were local or out of area. Four in every ten young people in the sample changed placements during our nine-month follow-up period (between Stage 1 and Stage 2), although this includes 6 per cent who returned to parents in line with a (revised) social work or educational plan. This level of movement seems to us high but we need to remind ourselves that these young people have been selected because they are difficult adolescents and, expressed differently, six in every ten remained in the same placement. A quarter of the total sample changed categories of care, mostly from children's homes. Half the moves occurred because the placement broke down: either because it was impossible to contain the behaviour or, in view of this, to keep the young person out of trouble or safe. Residents of children's homes at Stage 1 were more likely to experience a move and the residential BESD group was the most stable. But these changes were also linked to the range of behavioural problems indicated at Stage 1, which were far greater for the former group. Furthermore, almost half of looked after young people had a change of social worker over the nine months – too many.

We developed our own instrument to 'measure' the quality of care that young people received during the follow-up period – a 'Quality of Care' Index (see Chapter 5). This concerned the overall 'care package', including wider professional involvement (such as social worker input and inter-professional working) and not just what occurred in the placement or residential school. We were able to apply this to the 75 young people who agreed to be interviewed by us at Stage 2. We must always be cautious of the effects of attrition, although the results do not seem to be particularly adversely affected, based on the comparative characteristics of the groups at Stage 1 and Stage 2. In response, young people were very positive about the care they had received. Thus, a clear majority – across foster care, children's homes, dual-registered facilities and residential BESD schools alike – said that they generally felt safe where they were living and that there was an adult who would stand up for them.

We are aware of the possible limitations of this methodological approach. Young people may have been too uncritical and, despite our efforts, not fully understood who we were and the implications of negative responses. Children may respond differently individually and collectively. The particular context of interviews in foster homes made privacy difficult. Therefore, we applied researcher ratings to this data taking into account a wider variety of information. The results were consistent with young people's original views but were less optimistic. There were no differences in the quality of care depending on young people's characteristics, but it did vary by placement. Most of the children's homes (without education) group had been provided with 'good' care but the quality of 'care packages' offered to those living in alternative settings was judged to be better. No doubt young people with particular difficulties are more challenging to work with than those who are more benign, and the children's homes and dual-registered home groups were catering for the most difficult. Yet there was no clear link between quality of care and young people's difficulties *per se* and some homes managed to offer a better care environment, greater security and a wider package of support than others. Furthermore, we also saw that children's homes were better resourced to deal with these greater challenges. An interesting specific finding was that half of the residential BESD school group we interviewed at Stage 2 (12/23) told us that they were prescribed Concerta® or Ritalin®, stimulants used to treat attention deficit hyperactivity disorder (ADHD). This strikes us as high. This is a controversial topic and one that merits closer examination beyond our current sample.

Although we judged that there were differences in the quality of care offered depending on where young people lived, this did not automatically translate into the degree of progress they made. We again applied researcher ratings and concluded that the majority of young people showed improvement in a general measure of behavioural, emotional and social difficulties. This occurred irrespective of placement. Indeed, it was complex to identify factors associated with progress. However, it was interesting to discover, using young people's overall perceptions, that there was an association between, on one hand, their judgement of the quality of care they received and, on the other, their satisfaction with schooling and general happiness. Furthermore, changes in placement were linked with lower levels of general happiness, less satisfaction with the school experience and, to some extent, with friendships. Of course we must bear in mind the familiar social science adage that correlation does not mean causation but these are interesting associations, nonetheless.

On education specifically, as we would expect, our sample had previously posed a range of educational problems. Most had special educational needs, mainly BESD. Good study supports were available to pupils across settings, including adult interest and involvement. These have improved over the past decade. Inter-professional working across children's services (at the time social services departments, schools and education departments) was also reported to have improved and now to be generally good. Education for the children's homes group was particularly problematic, although, as we have seen, there was no evidence that educational support for these residents was inferior. Nearly half of the total sample changed educational provision in the nine-month follow-up, although it was usually felt that this benefited pupils. The number of school exclusions was reduced during the follow-up, and nearly half the sample was judged to have made educational progress, with a quarter remaining unchanged: this applied to occupants of foster homes, children's homes, dual-registered and residential schools alike.

We set these experiences in the context of overall support services delivered and their costs. We live in an age which is increasingly conscious of the costs of public services, and local authorities are faced with difficult decisions about which services to provide and how are they to be funded. It has been estimated that the care system in England costs some £2.2 billion annually, a very significant sum (Beecham and Sinclair 2007). (Although, to keep this in perspective, rather less than the £24 billion made available by the government in 2007 for the collapsed bank Northern Rock, or the projected £9 billion plus budget for the London 2012 Olympics.) It is important that we know how much services cost so that we are aware of the possible alternatives; whether increased costs produce better services or whether equivalent outcomes may be achieved at lower cost. It is also useful when economic analysis is combined with broader child welfare evaluations, to their mutual benefit. Studies such as ours help provide relevant information and, it is hoped, contribute to the state of the art.

The economic component of the present study revealed that young people accessed a wide variety of services over the nine-month follow-up. Large numbers visited general practitioners (GPs), dentists and, interestingly, opticians. As many as one in three used hospital accident and emergency (A&E) services, and four of the costs sample were admitted following overdoses. Despite their considerable problems, only a third used mental health services. On average (mean), each young person cost £66,300 over the nine months to support, some nine-tenths of this sum going towards placement costs. Dual-registered homes (£99,648) and children's home (£86,937) placements were the most expensive, followed by residential BESD schools (£63,882) and foster care (£32,655). If looked after children are placed in residential special schools and require placements in foster care or a children's home during the weekends or school holidays, their educational attendance may improve but it will be at a higher cost to the local authority. There were no particular cost differences in supporting young people for the two of our authorities with sufficient numbers for detailed analysis. Multiple regression analysis revealed that overall costs were related to young people's needs, measured in terms of the number of problems each had at Stage 1 (see Chapter 3). The most difficult young people were placed in the more expensive facilities. This helps to explain the paradox that higher expenditure per child is associated with seemingly worse outcomes.

Some main themes

Let us now consider some of the main overall messages to emerge from this account of our research. We then look at the policy implications. Initially, we should remind ourselves of the constraints and limitations of our study. Though fascinating, it was complex and challenging. Social services departments, 'difficult' looked after adolescents and their social workers are not the most straightforward participants in social research, nor the recipe for an easy life. Gaining access was very time-consuming, as was making contact with interviewees. Several of our research instruments were developed by us specifically for the study and they have not been validated elsewhere. However, they each built on related, up-to-date research thinking. Despite our best efforts, we experienced some sample attrition in the follow-up, but this would have been anticipated with older adolescents and was not a major source of bias in terms of young people's characteristics (although there is always the concern over whether those who are lost are the most problematic or have the most negative experiences).

A larger sample would have enabled more statistical analyses but there would then be a trade-off with the quality of information that we felt we required for our particular research objectives. On the other hand, we have a large amount of qualitative information from young people and professionals that we have been unable to exploit fully and that we shall use, instead, as the basis for journal articles. Overall though, we feel that the research progressed well, we have some very good data and that the study should make a useful contribution.

General progress

A general message from our study is the positive nature of a number of the findings. This is at variance with most research and other commentary on the education of looked after children. Indeed, it is unusual to be in a position to produce conclusions that appear to be at odds with much received wisdom about the care system and young people's experiences within it. But it is the particular responsibility of academic research to produce objective and impartial evidence consistent with rigorous standards of social science theory, ethics and methodology. Hence our conclusions that official statistics on the educational achievements of looked after pupils are misleading and misunderstood; most young people we interviewed felt that they received good quality care; educational supports are generally good; most make some social, behavioural and educational progress across placement categories; and that, for the looked after children, the residential special school placements may be equally expensive as the other placement categories we scrutinised once other expenditure is included.

Of course this is not to deny that there are significant problems to be addressed. For example, there is much movement and instability and too much changeover of social workers. Questions remain about the role and functioning of the children's homes sector; this sector has long been professionally underdeveloped in the UK (Berridge and Brodie 1998). Furthermore, the majority of residents of children's homes in our sample were older girls, yet child welfare research and practice take insufficient account of the gender dimension (O'Neill 2001).

In assessing our overall findings: partly, the issue is about whether the glass is seen as half-full or half-empty. Young people make some progress but is it sufficient? As a social scientist, seeking an explanation for a social problem does not mean that we condone it. It also depends on how young people's problems are perceived in the first place and the position from which we start. Our brief case studies show the enormous complications in young people's lives, the social and psychological consequences of which are not easily remedied. As an extreme example, as we have seen, four members of the costs sample ($n = 103$) were admitted to A&E during the nine-month follow-up as a result of a drugs overdose. Some of these young people and their carers, therefore, were facing huge obstacles. As Sinclair (2000) reminds us, social work intervention may be quite marginal in their lives and we should not, therefore, be surprised that it has a limited effect.

Quality of care and relationships

Another overall reflection on the study concerns how to interpret our findings. We found few individual, child-related variables associated with care or educational outcomes. There were some gender patterns but not many. This could mean that it would have been preferable to have had an alternative study design, or that we should have asked other questions in a different manner. Our measures may be rudimentary, insufficiently sensitive and need refinement. Yet the overall pattern of findings is consistent with the general impression obtained during the course of the research, from the situations we observed and from the young people and professionals that we met. These adolescents' circumstances were very complex, and professional interventions were usually one influence among many. In some ways it is an encouraging message, in that it suggests that young people may not automatically be predestined to poor experiences or outcomes. How we intervene can make a difference.

There was some evidence that young people's general happiness and satisfaction with schooling were related to the quality of care they received. Of course it could be the other way round, and those of a more favourable disposition may have been more appreciative of efforts on their behalf. But it seems reasonable to assume that the elements of practice we incorporated in our quality of care measure are worth pursuing and may pay dividends.

This seems compatible with recent research by Sinclair and colleagues (2006), looking at issues of permanence and stability in the care system. These workers found that children's well-being did not vary overall between the 13 councils included in their study and was only slightly influenced according to the social work team. Other factors were responsible for the variation, the most important of which was quality of placements. This was consistent with another finding, by the same team, concerning the key influence exerted by the heads of children's homes in determining children's experiences (Sinclair and Gibbs 1998). One of the current authors has also conducted a systematic review of the literature on challenging and disruptive behaviour in residential child care (Kilpatrick *et al.* in press). Though there was a dearth of relevant, rigorous empirical research, the conclusions pointed to the importance of certain styles of working and staff features in minimising behavioural problems and benefiting residents generally, rather than particular types of structured intervention. This included staff coherence, prompt responses to disturbances and demonstrating accepting, warm and caring attitudes.

Our conclusions also fit in with the re-emerging interest in the importance of relationships *per se* in social work. Quinton (2004) acknowledged that relationships with professionals comprise an important form of family support. Indeed, Trevithick (2003) argued that relationships remain at the heart of social work and problems may be alleviated through a relationship with an understanding, committed professional. Linked to this, economics and social policy academics have recently argued for greater attention to be paid to well-being and happiness in people's lives rather than material prosperity. Jordan (2006) argued that relationships are more important than income for most people when determining well-being. He maintained that services for children, therefore, need to focus on promoting 'emotional flourishing' rather than delivering technically optimum packages for achieving specified target results (Jordan 2006, p.42). Relationships with professionals, which can supplement or replace dysfunctional or absent relations with kin, are central to nurturing children's emotions, happiness and self-worth. The work of Morrison (2007) links this to growing interest in the field of management with the concept of emotional intelligence ('EI'), which he relates to the centrality of relationships in social work. All of this resonates strongly with Bowlby's (1972) influential ideas on the importance for children of warm, continuous and supportive relations with adults. It also has important workforce implications, where the skills of practitioners are key for relationship-based social work rather than growing bureaucratisation (Gupta and Blewett 2007).

Following on from this, and in the context of what we have already said, our findings also generally indicate that certain placement categories are not necessarily superior to others. What seem more important are the attributes of the particular individuals with whom the young person lives and the quality of experience that they offer. No doubt management and leadership are very important. The delivery and impact of wider services are also key – school, social work, educational psychology, (mental) health and so on. Indeed, relatively little detailed attention is given by researchers to the *schools* dimension, which presumably has more impact on educational outcomes than many of the other social work variables that are commonly considered. Many young people also move across categories of placements, as we have seen, and so the *overall* care and educational package seems more important than a specific form of placement *per se.*

Educational disadvantage and looked after children

Chapter 1 opened by repeating some of the strong criticisms of children's services, including poor educational performance. Indeed, the former Prime Minister Tony Blair remarked that it is appalling that we spend £2 billion annually on children in care yet only 8 per cent of them get decent GCSEs and only 1 per cent go on to university (Wintour 2006).

In a number of respects, our findings here are at odds with the general thrust of these comments. Certainly, in the past, the education of looked after children received little attention and many pupils were probably, in effect, written off. It was wrongly felt that social work issues and, in particular, placements were the overriding priority, that looked after children were destined to academic failure and that focusing on education could be stressful and detrimental to children, in turn leading to worse social work outcomes. We now know this to be false and the efforts of Jackson (1987) and others, and recent government initiatives, have moved the situation on.

But there is a danger that the current position is now misunderstood. We argued in Chapter 1 that the current policy analysis of the low educational achievement of looked after pupils disregards a wide range of social research evidence (Berridge 2007a). For example, it is unwise to rely on official statistics on educational outcome indicators, which may be inaccurate, misleading or have a perverse effect. The socio-economic risk factors associated with family breakdown and entry to care, such as poverty and social class, also predict low educational achievement. As the link is so pervasive, it is probably more meaningful to talk of *poverty* determining *education* rather than the reverse. For example, research has revealed that the brightest children from the poorest homes are outperformed by the least-able children from wealthy homes by the time they are seven

(Blanden and Machin 2007). This is exacerbated by the fact that social mobility nowadays has declined significantly. Parental maltreatment is strongly linked with educational failure. Furthermore, over a quarter of all looked after pupils have special educational needs. This statistic is sometimes perceived as a negative *outcome* of the care system, rather than as recognition of the additional resources required to help address learning difficulties. Moreover, of all care leavers over 16 years of age who had the chance to sit GCSEs, half entered care when over the age of 13 and so authorities had limited time to turn the situation round. Other countries may do no better than England does (Weyts 2004).

All this is no excuse for complacency and we should make every effort, especially for those deprived of normal family life. But looked after children perform poorly at school for complex reasons, and those reasons are very much long term and structural in origin. It seems to us that the GCSE attainment gap between looked after children and all pupils is unlikely to narrow significantly, as the problems are deeply entrenched and not easily amenable to professional remedy. Probably the easiest way for authorities to appear to improve performance is by statistical manipulation of the group in question, which is unacceptable and probably detrimental to children.

Narrowing the social class attainment gap is a complex issue and current knowledge is limited about how to intervene effectively (DfES 2006d). However, the Joseph Rowntree Foundation is currently funding a programme of research on the link between poverty and educational disadvantage, which includes qualitative studies of children's experiences (Hirsh 2007). The results are likely to be very relevant to the experiences and achievements of looked after pupils, most of whom originate from poor families. Initial findings from this research programme confirm that low income continues to be a strong predictor of low educational performance. Just 14 per cent of variation in individual performance is accounted for by school quality. Though there are other disadvantages for minority ethnic groups, white boys face particular challenges. For poor parents, it can be difficult to balance the economic demands of raising a family with setting aside enough time to spend with children. Disadvantaged children received little help with homework, and crowded, noisy conditions are unconducive for study. It was not so much that parents did not value homework but that they were not well placed to help.

The Joseph Rowntree Foundation research programme is also showing how school achievement is influenced by attitudes towards education, which develop from an early age. Disenchantment with school may start early as a result of growing up in poverty and the problems confronting teachers in schools in deprived areas. Children are aware of their social position from an early age and different groups interact with the education system in different ways. Children themselves identify confidence and self-esteem as crucial. Disadvantaged children find themselves less in control in school as they may be undertaking tasks for which they lack confidence and feel ill-equipped. Out-of-school activities are potentially important but certain pre-conditions have been identified in order to succeed with disadvantaged pupils. If undertaken successfully, this can help disadvantaged pupils to identify learning as a partnership rather than an exercise in control.

Policy implications

All of the above have important policy implications if government is to have a major influence on looked after children's experiences and achievements. The problems, and their resolution, go much wider than the care system itself. Many observers would feel that educational inequalities are most likely to be addressed by government's laudable policy to eradicate child poverty by 2020, although progress has slowed and targets have been missed (Judd 2007). The ambitious *Sure Start* and subsequent children's centres initiatives would also be expected to strengthen the poorest families' educational experiences. There are emerging signs of improved experiences and outcomes for young children living in *Sure Start* areas (National Evaluation of Sure Start Team 2008). Extended schools, concentrating family support services in schools, are innovative but still in their early stages. In addition, government has developed its *Aim Higher* strategy to increase the involvement of under-represented groups in higher education, for example by encouraging campus visits for school pupils, residential summer schools and mentoring programmes.

Regarding the care system itself, government proposals are contained in a new Children and Young Persons Bill, currently proceeding through Parliament. Many researchers were concerned about the earlier Green Paper stage of *Care Matters* (DfES 2006a), which was felt to be too negative in tone, rhetorical and lacking an evidence base (Berridge 2007b; Stein 2006b). The subsequent White Paper demonstrated a stronger professional understanding and was more consistent with research. Many of the proposals are to be welcomed. Measures are included to encourage more regular visiting of looked after children and not to force them to leave care prematurely. There will be more emphasis on local accommodation and for placements to be near to school. Pupils should not change school during Years 10 and 11 unless in exceptional circumstances. 'Designated persons' (formerly designated teachers) in schools will be a statutory requirement. Personal advisers will be provided to encourage further education or training. Payments will be facilitated for university attendance. It is not that social work managers and practitioners previously did not want to operate in these ways, but that resource and other constraints may have prevented them from doing so.

Some other measures in the new Bill are more contentious, such as the potential outsourcing of social work services to independent sector providers. It is encouraging that many of the proposals in the new Bill are to be piloted and, it is hoped that evaluations will be rigorous and impartial.

Final thoughts

Based on our findings, what else should we consider to enhance the care and educational experiences of looked after young people? Further research is required on a range of issues. The role of schools is very important and we need to know more about exactly how teachers interact with looked after pupils. In addition, there is more contact than we would have anticipated for the looked after group with special education services (not just residential). But this can be variable and it touches on the meaning of 'BESD': how it is used and how do schools respond to challenging pupils? We do not know what the additional factor of being looked after adds to this. More generally, 'designated persons' (teachers) are an important group but there is often little space in the timetable for them to play a more proactive role. We know little about who they are, what they do and to what effect. Further education colleges are increasingly used for this group, yet we know little of the further education experience and its impact. In addition, we are aware that we are focusing on the final years of pupils' educational careers and what happens earlier is very important, especially for those with an unsatisfactory upbringing.

On the social work front, we need to understand more about the exact characteristics and practices of successful carers. Some work has been undertaken in foster care based on attachment theory (Schofield and Beek 2004). Positive outcomes may be difficult to predict, even when carers and child appear theoretically compatible. Work is also currently underway to explore successful linking and matching in adoption (Farmer, Dance and Ouwejan, personal communication). This all is very complex, but it is at the heart of effective care: there is something about the personal interactions that is very difficult to capture. The policy implications of this would include focusing more on how we recruit, support and retain professionals and carers; how much we pay them so as to attract and keep the best; how to bolster their professional status; and to examine the approaches and consequences of different forms of professional training.

Finally, we began this book by considering government proposals to improve the educational experiences and attainment of looked after pupils, especially the *Quality Protects* initiative. We conclude that these have been generally successful;

however, having an effect on the official educational outcome indicators is a quite different matter. Our findings need to be scrutinised by other researchers to discover whether similar messages emerge when approached in other ways, or in different contexts. We hope that our work makes a useful contribution to knowledge in this field and that it helps inform policy development for this committed group of staff and these highly deserving young people.

Methodological Details

Relative care and educational experiences and outcomes according to three types of setting

Chapter 1 included a brief outline about the methodology adopted for the present study. This Appendix now provides more detailed information.

The main body of the research, relating to research objectives two and three, identified towards the end of Chapter 1, entailed a follow-up, case study approach with a sample of 150 young people. These had each experienced one of three, broadly categorised, types of setting: foster care, children's homes or residential special schools for pupils with behavioural, emotional or social difficulties (BESD). The sample was gathered from the three participating local authorities and eight residential schools that were prepared to work with us. These had been identified mainly in our pilot phase (Berridge *et al.* 2002). This part of the study aimed to select a group of 'difficult adolescents', that is, young people whose behaviour was presenting challenges to those responsible for their care and/or education (this is elaborated later). We aimed to collect data at two time-points (Stage 1 and Stage 2), approximately nine months apart.

Stage 1 data collection included, with the agreement of professionals, parents and the young people, an interview with the young people themselves. These interviews focused on their current educational and social experiences, as well as views about their education and care. At this point, information about young people's background experiences and the extent of their behavioural difficulties was collected from a professional informant – a social worker or head of care.

At the follow-up (Stage 2) we revisited the same young people – where they agreed to this. The interviews focused, once again, on their views about the care and education they had received, as well as their assessments of their wider social experience. We obtained carer or professional perspectives of young people's progress in the nine-month period by interviewing a carer or social worker for each of the young people – whichever adult was felt to know the young person best. Information concerning the extent and type of service use was also collected on a case-by-case basis at follow-up in order to estimate the costs of the different services provided. As an additional research strand, a further questionnaire aimed to gather information from providers about the nature and extent of services delivered and the costs for each care or education facility represented in the study. This information was usually supplied by the manager of the unit in question or a head of care or education. This organisational information proved quite difficult to obtain in many cases and our approach is described later.

Instruments and measures

For the most part we relied on data collection instruments that had been specifically designed to gather information of interest to this study. The development of these schedules was informed by national and local policy documents, the findings of other studies in the field and, in particular, the pilot study (Berridge *et al.* 2002) discussed in Chapter 1.

Because the majority of instruments were study-specific, we give a brief overview of the purpose of each here. More detailed descriptions have been provided as needed within individual chapters.

The instruments used in the study included:

- a screening questionnaire, designed to identify young people who met the criteria for inclusion in the case study phase

- a structured interview schedule designed to collect systematic information about young people's earlier experiences, social workers' views on the suitability of the current placement and their experiences of working with other agencies

- two semi-structured interview schedules for use with young people at first meeting and then at follow-up approximately nine months later

- a structured interview schedule for use at Stage 2 to obtain outcome and service use information from adult informants (either a foster carer, a residential key worker, case manager or social worker)

- the Strengths and Difficulties Questionnaire (SDQ) (Goodman 1997) to be completed by young people and informants at Stages 1 and 2

- a questionnaire designed to deal specifically with the services provided by residential establishments, and the costs incurred by them in providing services

- an adapted version of the *Client Service Receipt Inventory* (CSRI) (Beecham and Knapp 2001) on which could be recorded information on supports and services (education, social work and health care) used by the young people over the previous nine months.

Sampling for the follow-up case study

Our intention was to identify and follow up a group of adolescents whose behaviour presented difficulties in either their care or educational settings. As previously stated, three local authorities and eight residential special schools for pupils with BESD were our points of access to young people.

The process of sampling for this study was not straightforward. From the outset the circumstances and histories of the three groups of young people (those in foster care, children's homes and residential BESD special schools) were likely to be very different. The requirement was to control, wherever possible, for the most dramatic of these differences in order that there should be some comparability between groups for the purposes of assessing quality of care, costs, effectiveness and service provision. The selection of cases for the case study phase was handled slightly differently for local authorities and schools.

With local authorities we used a staged approach, which entailed identifying and screening a cohort of young people in order to 'select' a sample whose current circumstances and experiences met specific criteria regarding the extent to which they presented a challenge in terms of care and/or education settings. In residential BESD schools, on the basis that all of the young people were likely to meet our criteria and the fact that all had a Statement of Special Educational Needs, we focused more on trying to balance the demands of participation across classes and subunits.

Although we wanted the sample to be representative of the national picture as far as possible, we were also interested to ensure that young people in particular circumstances were represented in adequate numbers, in order to be able to observe whether there seemed to be anything different about their experiences. For example, at any one time, children and young people of minority ethnic background comprise about 22 per cent of all looked after children (DCSF 2007a). In two of the areas in which we were working the proportions were nearer 13 per cent (DfES 2006b). Clearly such rates, *pro rata*, would be unlikely to give us a large enough sample to analyse separately; therefore wherever possible we oversampled with regard to minority ethnic group membership.

Identifying young people looked after by local authorities

When we set about collecting a sample of young people exhibiting challenging behaviour we were intent on ensuring that the level of difficulty that young people displayed was judged systematically, therefore we asked local authorities to provide anonymised data concerning all the young people in their care on a given date who were aged between 11½ and 15½ years. From this data we selected our sample, based on the following criteria:

- young people who were placed in foster care (including relatives or friends care) or residential children's homes (i.e. not placed for adoption or with parents)

- young people who had been living in the current placement for at least three months

- young people who had been living in the current placement for less than four years.

We chose the age-range to reflect the period of secondary education, although we reduced the upper age limit in the hope that all of the young people would still be in school at the point of follow-up and, it was hoped, easier to contact. We did not feel it would be appropriate to approach young people about participating in research while they were in periods of transition between placements and therefore we set a criterion of a minimum of three months in residence. The exclusion of those who had been in placement for more than four years was largely pragmatic: we needed to be able to identify a manageable sample for the fieldwork, there were relatively few young people in such a position, but the length of time in placement varied widely and we reasoned that the stability of these placements suggested that there was a lower likelihood of identifying young people who were exhibiting difficulties.

Within the *Borough* and *Metro* authorities we found that the application of the selection criteria resulted in quite manageable numbers of young people (76 and 71, respectively). *County*, however, had a much larger population of looked after young people in foster care and a random selection procedure had to be applied. Details of the precise numbers involved at each stage of the sampling process are given later in this Appendix, along with details of the statistical checks to ensure that selected cases did not differ noticeably from those omitted.

Identifying a sample of young people attending residential BESD schools

We knew from our experience in the pilot work for the present study that, although the ratios of boys to girls in care are quite similar (56:44), interestingly, girls comprise a small proportion of young people placed in residential BESD schools. In order to mitigate for this situation, we deliberately included four schools that were known to accept both girls and boys.

Our approach to sampling in the schools was somewhat different to that used for the looked after groups. We liaised with either the head teacher or the head of care in each school in order to identify young people who could be included in the screening process (according to our previously mentioned criteria).

The eventual sample for the screening stage comprised 349 young people. The three local authorities advised us of a total of 242 young people of whom, at the time of referral, 150 were living with foster carers or with relatives or friends and 92 were living in children's homes. Schools advised us of a total of 107 young people who met our age and duration of placement criteria (Table A.1).

Table A.1 Numbers of young people referred to the study, according to source of referral

	County	Borough	Metro	Residential BESD schools
Young people living in foster (or relatives or friends) care	58	47	45	–
Looked after young people living in residential care	38	28	26	107
Total young people referred	96	75	71	107

Selecting a sample of 'difficult adolescents' for follow-up: the screening process

Once we had established a group of looked after young people whose circumstances met with our initial criteria concerning the type and duration of their placement, we embarked on the task of screening the cases to establish the level of management challenge that each young person presented. This entailed a process of, initially, engaging with team managers and then contacting the named social workers for each of the young people. This part of the process took much longer than envisaged. Some team managers failed to respond to repeated letters and follow-up telephone calls for several weeks – because of annual leave or absence, for example – sometimes resulting in data collection opportunities being lost for several months. Undertaking research with vulnerable young people is complex, time-consuming and unpredictable but it is by no means clear to us that working with professionals is any more straightforward (Munro, Holmes and Ward 2005).

It was eventually possible to scrutinise 88 per cent of the cases. There was some variation between authorities as to the success of this screening process, with 96 per cent of cases in the *Metro* authority being fully examined, but 87 per cent and 84 per cent being examined in the *Borough* and *County* authorities, respectively (χ^2 test = 6.5; df = 2; p <.05). Of the 29 cases that were not fully scrutinised, there were five who proved to be inappropriate to the study because they had returned to the care of birth parents after relatively short stays in care, between notification to the study and our contacting their social workers. Table A.2 illustrates that there were differences between the three local authorities in the distribution of placements made, the legal arrangements under which the young people were looked after and in their ethnic composition. Specifically, the young people looked after in *Borough* were slightly less likely to be fostered with relatives, much more likely to be living in an independent agency placement and more often of minority ethnic background. With regard to legal status, the patterns across the three authorities were distinctly different with young people looked after by *Metro* much more likely to be subject to a full care order. Parker and Loughran (1990) cogently observed some time ago that national averages conceal wide differences between authorities.

Conceptualising and quantifying 'difficult to manage' behaviour

The next stage was to screen this group of young people to identify, systematically, a sample of young people who were presenting behaviour that was 'difficult to manage'. Alongside basic information about the young person's biographical and schooling characteristics, the screening questionnaire therefore included a series of questions designed to quantify the level of difficulty presented by the young people. This approach did not entirely avoid the problem of differing perceptions since the social workers we interviewed may have over- or underemphasised the levels of problems. But, by asking for examples with a note of frequency and severity of the difficulties, we hoped that the resulting researcher-based judgements would even out the variability across individual opinion and thereby provide some standardisation between the three placement categories.

Our criteria for rating the level of difficulty had been established in the pilot phase of this research (Berridge *et al.* 2002, 2003) and included the following:

Table A.2 Characteristics of the full group of 242 looked after adolescents

Characteristic	County (n = 96)	Borough (n = 75)	Metro (n = 71)	Analysis
Type of placement (%):				*Borough* had fewer relatives or friends placements but the difference is not significant (χ^2 test = 9.4; df = 4; p = .052)
children's homes	40	37	37	
foster care (unrelated)	44	59	45	
fostered with relatives or friends	17	4	18	
Local authority or agency placement (%):				Difference between authorities is significant – *County* accommodated far more young people within own resources, *Borough* far fewer (χ^2 test = 42.2; df = 2; p <.001)
agency placement	26	80	43	
local authority	74	20	57	
Legal status (%):				Difference between authorities is significant when 'other status' is omitted (χ^2 test = 10.7; df = 2; p <.01)
full care order (Section 31)	54	62	74	
accommodated (Section 20)	46	37	20	
other status[a]	0	1	6	
Ethnic background (%):				Difference between authorities is significant when comparisons are made between proportions of white, mixed ethnicity and 'any other background' (χ^2 test = 18.4; df = 4; p <.01)
white (all)	74	55	86	
mixed (any)	16	29	11	
Asian (all)	2	0	0	
black (all)	8	14	2	
Chinese or other	0	3	0	
Gender (%):				Not significant
Male	59	59	59	
Female	41	41	41	

[a] Other status included residence order, freed for adoption.

- *Poor school attendance:* we were concerned here with problems of both self-exclusion through truancy or school refusal, and with periods of imposed exclusion from school. Young people screened positively here if they had experienced a short-term or permanent exclusion in the previous three months, or had been absent without permission for more than one day in the previous three months.

- *Behavioural problems in school:* here we were concerned with reports from school that behaviour was difficult to manage in the classroom or during break-periods. We included instances of disruptive behaviour as well as violence or aggression (verbal as well as physical) to either peers or adults.

- *Regular use of alcohol or drugs:* we focused here on levels of behaviour that were of concern to the professionals involved with the young person. We did not include 'experimentation' with substances but we did include episodes of excessive drinking or regular use of drugs.

- *Conviction or caution for criminal offences:* self-explanatory.

- *Self-harm:* here our interest was on deliberate self-harm – such as gouging, cutting or overdose, although we are aware of the argument made by some professionals that some young people appear to harm themselves by other means – such as dietary control or smoking.

- *Aggression or violence:* this category included any type of violence or aggression (e.g. physical, verbal, sexual or violence to property).

Young people were deemed to 'screen-in', and therefore be potentially eligible for our study, if any *two* of these problems had been apparent within the previous three months. (A past history of problems was noted but, in itself, was not deemed to meet the criteria.) This produced a total of 199 young people.

As illustrated in Table A.3, the proportion of young people screening into our 'difficult' group varied between 52 and 75 per cent across our three local authorities and the BESD schools group. The difference, in particular between the schools and the two smaller authorities, is statistically significant. It is not surprising to find that three-quarters of young people resident at schools which cater for pupils with BESD problems should present current management difficulties as this is why they were referred. The proportions of looked after adolescents exhibiting difficult behaviours are substantial but, as we concluded previously (Berridge *et al.* 2003), it is noticeable that large minorities of looked after adolescents are not considered 'difficult to manage'.

Table A.3 Proportion of young people classified as difficult to manage, according to source of referral

	County	Borough	Metro	BESD schools	Analysis
Proportion of young people classified as difficult to manage (%)	65	52	52	75	χ^2 test = 13.8; df = 3; p <.005

Patterns of 'difficult to manage' behaviour for the follow-up sample

We selected our cases from the wider group of looked after young people by rating each individual on a series of behavioural indices. The extent to which each of these behavioural problems was represented among selected cases is presented in Table A.4.

Table A.4 Patterns of difficult to manage behaviour in the previous three months (n = 199)

	Local authority groups (n = 123)	Schools (n = 76)	Analysis
Violence and/or aggression (%)	80	72	NS
Behavioural problems in school (%)	79	91	χ^2 test = 4.9; df = 1; p <.05
School attendance problems (%)	62	21	χ^2 test = 31.4; df = 1; p <.001
Convictions or cautions (%)	50	20	χ^2 test = 17.2; df = 1; p <.001
Regular drug or alcohol use (%)	32	16	χ^2 test = 6.1; df = 1; p <.05
Self-harm (%)	25	19	NS
Other antisocial or difficult behaviour (%)	58	53	NS

NS, not significant.

As is clear from Table A.4, while experimentation was very common, *regular* or *worrying* use of alcohol or drugs among young people was evident for nearly one-third of the looked after sample. This tended to be more common among the older age group (F = 3.8; df = 2,118; p <.05). Self-harm was more common among girls and, perhaps surprisingly, among those who were accommodated voluntarily under Section 20 of the Children Act 1989.

Table A.4 reveals that the majority of selected cases in the local authority groups met the inclusion criteria by virtue of a tendency towards violence to people or property, behavioural problems or attendance problems at school, or a history of convictions or cautions. The 'other' antisocial or difficult behaviour includes behaviours that professionals found extremely challenging, such as running away or putting themselves at risk of sexual exploitation. The cases selected from schools also showed problems with violence or aggression and behavioural problems in the school setting. But these young people were much less likely to have difficulties associated with attendance at school, police contact for criminal activities or problems with alcohol or drugs.

It was of interest to explore the extent to which young people presented a multiplicity of problems and whether there was variation between our referral sources in this regard. Overall, nearly half of this sample (45%) was described as having four or more current problems at screening but there were differences across referral groups. Figure A.1 provides an illustration of the numbers of young people with two, three or four (and so on) problems according to which referral group they belonged. As may be seen, by tracing the pattern for any one group, there were differences in terms of the range of problems for individuals. The patterns for both the *County* and *Borough* authorities are quite flat, while in *Metro* there was a sizeable group who presented problems only in a couple of domains. The pattern for schools is very marked with the majority having no more than three problems.

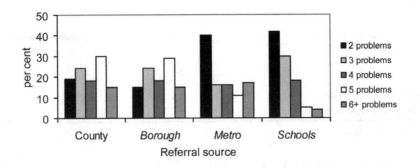

Figure A.1 Number of problems at screening, by source of referral

Some further information is provided later on how the characteristics compare of the 'selected' and 'not selected' samples of looked after young people.

Attrition

Although a total of 199 of the original 349 young people were selected for inclusion in our sample, there were a number with whom we were unable to proceed. Fifteen of the local authority group were omitted from the sample, because either we were unsuccessful in making contact with the social workers, or because their inclusion would have been too demanding on an individual worker who had other cases in the sample. Thirty-four of the schools group were lost because we were unable to obtain the written permission from parents for the young person to take part. (Several schools had insisted on an 'opt-in' rather than an 'opt-out' approach.) The final sample therefore comprised 150 young people.

As is so often the case in social work research, particularly with follow-up designs, we experienced some difficulties in engaging all those professionals and young people whom we had identified as appropriate for the research. There was also substantial change both in terms of the mobility of some young people and with regard to the professionals working with them. Thus, the process of making initial contacts and re-engaging with individuals at follow-up was, in some cases, not only complicated and time-consuming, but on occasion it proved impossible to achieve within a reasonable period. As a result we experienced some attrition between Stage 1 and Stage 2. The exact numbers for whom data was available at each time-point is illustrated in Figure A.2.

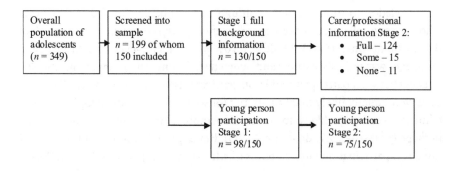

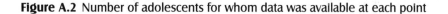

Figure A.2 Number of adolescents for whom data was available at each point

Although our aim was to engage directly with young people in the research, since we were primarily interested in outcomes in relation to experience, we felt it important to ensure that we were able to follow up, at least in some respects, all of the young people who had been identified – whether or not they themselves chose to participate. This choice does raise ethical issues, which we discussed with our advisory group, but it was important, when we came to look at outcomes, that we were able to assess whether and how the experiences of those taking part differed from those who declined and any resulting bias. We found that we were able to follow up, anonymously, non-participating young people through their social workers and, therefore, did not need to compromise our obligations.

Representativeness of participating young people

In considering the representativeness of the sample we confine ourselves, initially, to young people identified through our participating local authorities. This is because the selection process in schools was different and we did not have access to any information about those who declined, or whose parents refused permission.

We felt it important to check the extent to which participating young people represented the characteristics of the 'population' as determined by the screening process. We were obviously interested in characteristics such as gender, age and ethnicity. In addition, we also wanted to be aware of any bias in terms of type of placement, whether placements were within or outside of the authority area, young people's histories and, most importantly, whether all types of current difficulties were adequately represented.

In relation to those recruited through our authorities, we found that those who chose to take part in the research were slightly younger, on average, than those who declined ($F = 3.94$; df = 1,107; $p < .05$). However, this difference in mean ages was only six months and, when tested using categories of age, the differences between participants and non-participants was not significant. Girls and boys were equally likely to take part, but for some reason young people of mixed ethnicity were more likely to refuse than those with a white, Asian or black heritage (χ^2 test = 13.7; df = 2; $p < .005$). Being placed in or out of the area did not affect participation rates. In terms of whether young people's different histories were adequately represented, we found no differences according to the reason for care, its duration or the number of previous moves in care. Regarding young people's current difficulties, we were anxious that it might be more difficult to meet with the more troubled members of the group; in fact, there were no significant differences and, if anything, it was those with fewer problems who were least likely to agree to take part in Stage 1.

Looking at continuing participation of young people at follow-up, across the whole sample (i.e. including young people recruited through residential schools) we lost 25 per cent of our interview sample between Stage 1 and Stage 2. The only factors that we found to be statistically significant were a move of care placement during the study period (χ^2 test = 26.5; df = 1; p <.001) and worsening behavioural problems according to informants (χ^2 test = 7.0; df = 2; p <.05). There was some overlap between these two factors in that some of the young people who had moved had done so because of deterioration in their behaviour but each factor also exerted some independent influence. That is, we lost some cases whose behaviour had worsened although they remained in the same placement, and we lost some who had moved although there was no deterioration in behaviour.

Despite our best efforts, there were some young people for whom we were unable to access any systematic follow-up information from carer or professional informants either. Again, we were concerned that we should be aware if this might lead us to draw false conclusions from the data. We found we were more likely to have full follow-up information from informants when young people were placed in dual-registered establishments or residential BESD schools as opposed to local authority children's homes or foster care. This is undoubtedly related to the fact that young people and their carers in these settings are each relatively 'captive' participants. In relation to the group recruited through local authorities, in particular, we found that we were less likely to be able to engage informants for the *Borough* authority cases. We suspect that this is largely attributable to the high turnover of social work staff – along with the relatively high proportion of placement changes for *Borough* cases, which made it very difficult to conduct the follow-up phase in this London authority.

Methods for economic component
Unit costs
The present study aimed to look at the way each young person used services and supports over the research period. Building on methods used in the earlier pilot study, a version of the *Client Service Receipt Inventory* (CSRI) (Beecham and Knapp 2001) was used to record the frequency and duration of young people's use of all education, health and social work services and supports. Young people and adult or professional informants were each asked about service use. Informants tended to have good information on the services provided from within their own agency – often recorded on case files. Head teachers, for example, had good information

about school support, and social workers knew about many of the social work or social care services. Young people, however, tended to have a more all-round picture of the support they received and knew about their visits to the GP or the local A&E services as well as school or social work. In reporting service-use we have commonly relied on a combination of the two sources.

A list was made of all services and supports used and a unit cost estimated for each one. For many services, unit costs were taken from publicly available sources (e.g. Curtis and Netten 2005). In other cases, where services were the focus of the study and/or likely to absorb a significant proportion of the total costs of support packages, service-specific unit costs were estimated using an equivalent methodology (Beecham 1995, 2000). For example, unit costs for each residential school and children's home – per resident day – were carefully estimated to be the closest approximation of *long-run marginal opportunity costs* using descriptions of each establishment collected on the *Service Information Schedule* developed during the pilot study. This schedule recorded information on the number days the facility was open, the number of places and occupancy, staffing and support for staff (such as advice from psychologists), and location of education as well as data on annual income and expenditure, fees, location and acreage, and capital valuations. Where the head of school or home could not complete details (commonly financial information), the agency finance department or senior management were contacted. For foster care, the fees or allowances paid comprise the main part of the unit costs but we also included an element to reflect the costs to the social services department of running the fostering service and supporting foster carers.

A proportion of the costs of Social Services Management and Support Services (SSMSS) was allocated in line with the overall national spend on foster care fees resulting in an 'uplift' factor of 10.5 per cent. A similar approach to estimating overheads was used for the children's homes run by the local authority. In the 'private and voluntary' (independent) sector, income and expenditure accounts commonly included an amount for such organisational overheads. In the absence of income and expenditure data, fees were only used as a proxy for the costs of residential schools and homes where we had a sufficient description of the establishment to assess their validity (based on the pilot study) as long-run marginal opportunity costs.

To ensure that like-with-like comparisons were made across the groups of young people in different placements, the costs of weekend leave and holidays have been included for residential BESD school pupils. Most pupils return home at these times so costs have been estimated using data from the family expenditure survey (National Statistics 2005a). A few young people stayed in, for example, foster or respite care placements and where costs had not already been estimated, nationally applicable costs were used (Curtis and Netten 2005). The unit costs for mainstream schools have been estimated from routinely compiled unit costs data (National Statistics 2005b) and adjusted data from the DCSF Section 52 expenditure returns were used for special needs day schools. For both type of schools, an uplift factor for support from the local education authority (overheads) was included.

Some young people had placement moves over the nine-month period (see Chapter 5). In the absence of detailed information on the type and location of these 'other placements', if a young person remained in the same *type* of placement (local authority foster care, independent sector children's home and so on) it was assumed that the cost for the previous placement would be indicative of the costs of the current one. Where the type of placement changed, and service-specific costs could not be estimated, nationally applicable unit costs were used (Curtis and Netten 2005).

Support package costs

The unit costs and service use data was combined to calculate total support costs for each young person; a variable sum depending both on *which* services were accessed and *how much* of each service was used. The data collection and cost-estimation methods ensured that, once costs were calculated, they could be presented as a total cost per young person or in disaggregated form, perhaps by provider (education authority, social services and so on), accommodation type (residential school, foster care and so forth), or by the local authorities involved in the study. Costs could also be presented for different subgroups of young people, perhaps by age group, gender or severity of problems.

In the present study, the aim was to follow up young people over a nine-month period, but a particular challenge in estimating education costs was that data collection could cover any part of the year. For some young people, for example, the study period would include the long summer school holiday but for others it would not. This would have quite an impact on support package costs. To overcome this, information on use of education services was recorded on the CSRI with reference to the last *full* school-term, rather than the period between the interviews. These term-based patterns of use of education services have then been assumed to reflect the whole research period, unless a change in education placement was recorded.

To ensure some standardisation of time, a 'statistical nine months' has been used to calculate the costs of support packages so that attendance at school, school holidays, weekend leave and changes in placement may be taken into account. This statistical nine months covers the 274 days (365×0.75) from the Stage 1 interview of which 143 (190×0.75) would be spent in formal schooling.

The number of days spent in residential BESD schools or dual-registered facilities has also been adjusted for whether the home or school provides 52-week placements, or termly or weekly boarding.

Analysis of costs

Our analytic approach has three stages. First, we describe the patterns of service use and costs for the sample and groups of young people in the different placement types. Second, we test individual variables describing the needs, characteristics and circumstances of the young people for their association with cost using bivariate statistics (t-tests, simple analysis of variance (ANOVA) or non-parametric equivalents). The same criteria for statistical significance were used as described above and measures of distribution are reported as ranges, standard deviations (SDs) or confidence intervals (CIs). Third, only those variables significantly associated with costs were taken forward to the multivariate analyses ($p< .05$) The aim was to develop a 'cost function' that would identify associations between costs and other variables. Only those variables where more than 10 per cent of the sample had a valid answer were selected for this exploration of cost variations. And, while we were aware of the necessity not to select too many variables for the relatively small costs sample ($n = 103$ – see Chapter 8), the elements within the *production of welfare* model allowed us to identify clearly why an association with costs may exist. Multiple regression techniques allow us to assess the combined capacity of the variables to 'predict' costs statistically (Dunn *et al.* 2003; Knapp 1998). Given relatively small sample sizes and likely data skew, the statistical significance of predictors would be confirmed by use of bootstrapped confidence intervals (1000 repetitions; Efron and Tibishirani 1993).

Characteristics of young people screened in the three local authorities and differences between 'selected' and 'non-selected' cases

Although outside the remit of the current research, our process of screening for our sample in the three local authorities necessarily entailed collecting some basic information about those who did not meet the sample criteria on level of difficulties. We felt it would be of interest to present this information as it sets a balance against the relatively high level of problems discussed in main body of the report. As we have said, not all adolescents in care are difficult and what follows is the proof. The exercise also allows us to explore if and how our sample of selected 'difficult' adolescents differed from the larger group.

The screening questionnaire allowed us to collect basic information about young people (their age, gender, ethnicity, care status, date of placements and date of first living away from home in this care period) as well as understand something of their educational experience regarding type of schooling, attendance and attainment. Table A.5 below shows the background characteristics for selected and non-selected cases.

Table A.5 Characteristics of young people looked after by participating authorities, according to whether selected into the final sample

	Selected cases	Non-selected cases	All	Significance
Average age	13 years 8 months	13 years 3 months	13 years 6 months	$F = 5.6$; df = 1,214; $p <.05$
Average duration of this placement (months)	15	20	17	$F = 6.8$; df = 1,214; $p <.05$
Average duration of this care period (months)	45	39	43	NS
Gender:				
male (%)	59	60	59	NS
Care status:				
accommodated (%)	36	27	32	NS
care order (%)	64	73	68	NS
Ethnicity:				
white (all) (%)	77	64	72	χ^2 test = 7.9;
mixed ethnicity (all) (%)	18	19	18	df = 2; $p <.05$
any other ethnic background[a] (%)	5	16	10	
Type of placement:				
friends & family (%)	11	15	13	χ^2 test =
foster care (%)	33	71	49	41.2; df = 2;
residential unit (%)	56	14	38	$p <.001$

[a] 'Any other ethnic background' includes 17 black young people, two of Asian background and two of 'other' ethnicity.

'Difficult' young people who screened-in were slightly older, on average, than those who did not. Similarly, selected young people had, on average, spent significantly less time in their *current placement* at the point of screening, although the average duration of the current *care period* did not differ significantly between the two groups. As we might expect, difficulty is associated with placement instability (Berridge 2000).

Although there were more boys than girls in the group as a whole, boys and girls were equally likely to meet our criteria for presenting difficulties. There were no differences between selected and non-selected cases according to the legal arrangements for their being looked after; young people accommodated under Section 20 and those subject to care orders were equally likely to meet the criteria for selection. With regard to ethnicity we found that proportionately fewer young people of 'other' ethnic background met the selection criteria for our study – this is accounted for by 14/17 black young people *not* showing management challenges according to their social workers.

Young people in residential units at the time of screening were particularly likely to be classified as 'difficult to manage' by our criteria. This was not unexpected since it is recognised that residential establishments are likely to be used only when young people's problems exceed the potential of foster care provision. However, although numbers are relatively small, it was noteworthy that around half of young people in friends and family care also met our selection criteria. This raises questions about the extent of difficulties faced by relative carers and the degree of support provided (Farmer and Moyers 2008).

Schooling patterns for the looked after sample as a whole

As we have discussed in the main body of the report, we discovered very early in our data collection phase that there is a wide, and growing, range of educational provision for young people who are unable to access or engage with mainstream education. We have developed the categories listed below to try to give an indication of the type of provision but, in reality, there was a good deal of variety and complexity for some young people. For example, not all of these categories are always indicative of full-time education, some may be only for a few hours a week, and sometimes it was difficult to tell whether a case belonged to the home tuition or education centre grouping. These more complex packages are described in some detail in Chapter 7 and Chapter 8 but, for now, we felt it of interest to present some basic information about the schooling packages for difficult adolescents in the context of that provided for all young people (within our age-range) looked after by our local authorities. We also thought it important to examine the extent of special educational needs (SEN) among those who screened into the sample as well as those who did not. The proportions of selected and unselected cases in different types of education and their levels of SEN are presented in Table A.6.

We discovered that the majority of young people overall (60%) were educated in mainstream educational settings, although this was less likely for our selected cases group. The other 40 per cent of young people were in receipt of a

Table A.6 Type of educational provision and special educational needs provision for selected and non-selected cases

	Selected cases (n = 121) (%)	Non-selected cases (n = 94) (%)	All (n = 215) (%)
Type of educational provision:			
none	7	1	4
mainstream	49	74	60
special needs day provision	20	13	17
special needs residential	15	6	11
education centre	5	2	4
mixed academic and vocational	1	1	1
home tuition	4	3	4
Special educational needs:[a]			
none	35	57	45
school action	3	7	5
school action +	8	8	8
Stage 3 of code of practice	12	1	7
Statement of Special Educational Needs	43	27	36

[a] Differences between selected and non-selected cases in terms of special educational needs were significant (χ^2 test = 18.3; df = 4; p <.001).

range of different types of provision. Substantial numbers of young people were enrolled in special needs schools, as either day or residential pupils. The extent to which we were able to check the registration categories of schools and other educational settings at this point was limited by social workers' understanding of the establishments involved. For example, the same facility might be described to us as a children's home with education and as a residential school. While we may not be able to comment on how schools were actually registered, we do know that almost all of this provision was intended for young people with BESD.

Given the nature of our sample, we were somewhat surprised by the relatively small number of young people described as attending education centres. The proportions receiving home tuition or on a mixed academic and vocational package at this point were also fairly small. It was somewhat worrying that, although not a great number, a total of 4 per cent of the whole group were not receiving any formal educational input at the time of screening.

Overall, more than one-third of looked after young people (36%) were said to have a Statement of Special Educational Needs (SEN) and a further 20 per cent were receiving some sort of additional help in their schooling through school action, school action plus or were in the process of having their special educational needs (SEN) assessed. Once again, young people selected for inclusion in the study were more likely to require some form of additional help. Where a Statement was in place, they had almost always been issued because of BESD.

The other area of schooling that we thought it important to comment on for the group as a whole is that of attendance at school. The government's performance targets for looked after children include school attendance as a major component. As illustrated in Table A.7, we sought information about six forms of non-attendance. These percentages apply to the whole cohort and the information was provided by social workers during a telephone interview rather than from the local authorities' data management systems. As may be seen, in the three months preceding the screening interview, some 15 per cent of the young people in our cohort had experienced periods of at least four weeks without a school place; over one-quarter had been regularly absent without authorisation – either post-registration truancy or school refusal; one in five had received a fixed-term exclusion and nearly one in ten had been permanently excluded. Although we are talking of a slightly different time-period, these figures do not tally with the findings reported in Chapter 2, which analysed the publicly available statistics for our local authorities and found that there had been no permanent exclusions in the period studied.

Table A.7 Patterns of school attendance for looked after young people

	Never as known	In the past	In previous 3 months	Not known
No school place (%)	73	11	15	1
Authorised absence (%)	79	4	12	5
Unauthorised absence (%)	61	9	27	3
Fixed-term exclusion(s) (%)	61	14	20	5
Permanent exclusion (%)	76	10	9	5
Informal exclusion (%)	72	5	16	7

The final row in Table A.7 refers to 'informal exclusion'. Informal exclusion refers to situations in which a young person is asked to leave the school premises without recourse to proper, formal procedures, and return some time, or days, later. This was a feature identified in earlier research (Brodie 2001), which has been a cause of some concern for practitioners and carers, since the practice denies young people and their parents or carers any formal route for appeal. As can be seen, according to social workers some 16 per cent of young people had experienced this form of exclusion in the preceding three months. Problems with school attendance were a criterion for inclusion in the study sample, thus it may be taken as read that these experiences were disproportionately represented in the selected group.

In summary, it may be seen that young people classified as 'difficult' were slightly older, on average, than those not so classified, and the time spent in their current placements was slightly shorter (again, on average). Boys and girls were equally like to meet our criteria but a relatively high proportion of black young people did not. Not surprisingly, significantly fewer young people in foster care screened into the sample than was true for those in residential units. Across the group as a whole, only 60 per cent of young people were found to be in mainstream educational provision; alternatives were more common among our eventual sample but not significantly so. Over half of all looked after young people were receiving some extra help at school with over one-third having Statements of Special Educational Needs; these difficulties were significantly more frequent for those selected to the sample. Examination of the pattern of school attendance for the group as a whole revealed quite high rates of absence and exclusion from school.

Summary points

- The main part of this research consisted of a nine-month, follow-up study of 150 young people who lived either in foster care, children's homes or residential special schools for pupils with behavioural, emotional and social difficulties. They were identified from three local authorities (*County*, *Metro* and *Borough*) and eight residential schools. Semi-structured interviews were held with young people and professionals or carers.

- A screening process was used to identify the sample. At the outset, young people needed to be aged between 11½ and 15½ years and to have been living in their current care or educational settings for between three months and four years.

- The particular focus was on 'difficult' adolescents, which we defined as behaviour that was difficult to manage at home, school and/or in the community. This spanned six areas: poor school attendance or exclusion; behavioural problems in school; regular use of alcohol or drugs; offending; self-harm; or aggression or violence.

- Based on this definition, between 52 and 65 per cent of the three local authorities' potential groups were 'difficult', as were 75 per cent of those attending the eight residential special schools. Violence or aggression and behavioural problems in school were the most prevalent form of difficult behaviour. Almost half of those eligible demonstrated problems in four of the six areas.

- Our overall study sample was not particularly adversely affected by initial bias. Young people who declined to participate from the outset were more likely to be slightly older and of mixed ethnicity but did not display other differences.

- Despite our best efforts, we were unable to interview a quarter of our young people at Stage 2. As might be expected, these individuals were more likely to have moved between care settings in the interim and, according to adult informants, to have deteriorating behavioural problems.

- The economic component applied well-established methodologies in cost estimation and cost analysis to this research and service context. The costs of support packages over a nine-month period were estimated and the associations between costs, needs and outcomes explored.

References

Advisory Council on the Misuse of Drugs (2006) *Pathways to Problems: Hazardous Use of Tobacco, Alcohol and Other Drugs by Young People in the UK and Its Implications for Policy.* ACMD September 2006 Ref 275432. Available at www.drugs.gov.uk (accessed 21 April 2008).

Aldgate, J. and Tunstill, J. (1995) *The Children Act Now: Messages from Research.* London: Department of Health.

Barter, C., Renold, E., Berridge, D. and Cawson, P. (2004) *Peer Violence in Children's Residential Care.* Basingstoke: Palgrave.

Beecham, J. (1995) 'Collecting and Estimating Costs.' In Knapp, M. (ed.) *The Economics of Mental Health Care.* Aldershot: Arena.

Beecham, J. (2000) *Unit Costs – Not Exactly Childs Play.* Kent: Department of Health, PSSRU.

Beecham, J. (2006) 'Why costs vary in children's services.' *Journal of Children's Services 1,* 50–62.

Beecham, J. and Knapp, M. (2001) 'Costing Psychiatric Interventions.' In Thornicroft, G., Brewin, C. and Wing, J. (eds) *Measuring Mental Health Needs.* London: Gaskell.

Beecham, J. and Sinclair, I. (2007) *Costs and Outcomes in Children's Social Care: Messages from Research.* London: Jessica Kingsley.

Berridge, D. (1997) *Foster Care: A Research Review.* London: HMSO.

Berridge, D. (2000) *Placement Stability.* Quality Protects Research Briefing 2. London: Department of Health.

Berridge, D. (2007a) 'Theory and explanation in child welfare: education and looked after children.' *Child & Family Social Work 12,* 1–10.

Berridge, D. (2007b) 'To take more care of children, take more care with the facts.' *Parliamentary Brief 11,* 21–22.

Berridge, D., Beecham, J., Brodie, I., Cole, T. *et al.* (2002) *Costs and Consequences of Services for Troubled Adolescents: An Exploratory, Analytic Study.* Luton: University of Luton.

Berridge, D., Beecham, J., Brodie, I., Cole, T. *et al.* (2003) 'Services for troubled adolescents: exploring user variation.' *Child and Family Social Work 8,* 269–279.

Berridge, D. and Brodie, I. (1998) *Children's Homes Revisited.* London: Jessica Kingsley.

Berridge, D., Brodie, I., Ayre, P., Barrett, D., Henderson, B. and Wenman, H. (1997) *Hello – Is Anybody Listening? The Education of Young People in Residential Care.* Warwick: University of Warwick and Social Care Association (Education).

Berridge, D. and Cleaver, H. (1987) *Foster Home Breakdown.* Oxford: Blackwell.

Blanden, J. and Machin, S. (2007) *Recent Changes in Intergenerational Mobility in the UK.* London: Sutton Trust.

Blyth, E. (2001) 'The impact of the first term of the New Labour government on social work practice in Britain: the interface between educational policy and social work.' *British Journal of Social Work 31,* 563–577.

Borland, M., Pearson, C., Hill, M., Tisdall, K. and Bloomfield, I. (1998) *Education and Care Away from Home.* Edinburgh: Scottish Council for Research in Education.

Bowlby, J. (1972) *Maternal Care and the Growth of Love.* London: Penguin.

Brodie, I. (2001) *Children's Homes and School Exclusion: Redefining the Problem.* London: Jessica Kingsley.

Brodie, I. (2005) *Education of Children in Public Care.* Highlight No. 218. London: National Children's Bureau.

Cantril, H. (1965) 'Discovering People's Aspirations: The Method Used.' In Cantril, H. (ed.) *The Pattern of Human Concerns.* New Brunswick, NJ: Rutgers University Press.

Caprara, G. and Rutter, M. (1995) 'Individual Development and Social Change.' In Rutter, M. and Smith, D. (eds) *Psychosocial Disorders in Young People: Time Trends and Their Causes.* Chichester: Wiley.

Children and Young Persons Bill [HL] (2007–08).

Chrystal, K. and Mizen, P.D. (2001) *Goodhart's Law: Its Origins, Meaning and Implications for Monetary Policy.* London: City University Business School.

Cicourel, A. (1994) *Method and Measurement in Sociology*. New York, NY: Free Press.

Cleaver, H., Unell, I. and Aldgate, J. (1999) *Children's Needs – Parenting Capacity: The Impact of Parental Mental Illness, Problem Alcohol and Drug Use, and Domestic Violence on Children's Development*. London: The Stationery Office.

Cleaver, H. and Walker, S. (2004) 'From policy to practice: the implementation of a new framework for social work assessments of children and families.' *Child and Family Social Work 9*, 81–90.

Cliffe, D. with Berridge, D. (1994) *Closing Children's Homes: An End to Residential Childcare?* London: National Children's Bureau.

Cohen, S. (1972) *Folk Devils and Moral Panics*. London: MacGibb and Hee.

Cole, T., Visser, J. and Upton, G. (1998) *Effective Schooling for Pupils with Emotional and Behavioural Difficulties*. London: David Fulton.

Cole, T., Visser, J. and Upton, G. (1999) *Patterns of Educational Provision by Local Authorities for Pupils with Behaviour Problems*. Report for the Nuffield Foundation. Birmingham: University of Birmingham.

Coleman, J. (2000) 'Young people in Britain at the beginning of a new century.' *Children & Society 14*, 230–242.

Colton, M., Drury, C. and Williams, M. (1995) 'Children in need: definition, identification and support.' *British Journal of Social Work 25*, 711–728.

Commission for Social Care Inspection (CSCI) (2005) *Social Services Performance Assessment Framework Indicators 2004–05*. London: CSCI.

Curtis, L. and Netten, A. (2005) *The Unit Costs of Health and Social Care*. Kent: PSSRU, University of Kent.

Daniels, H. and Porter, J. (2007) *Learning Needs and Difficulties Among Children of Primary School Age: Definition, Identification, Provision and Issues*. Primary Review Interim Report, Research Survey 5/2. Cambridge: University of Cambridge.

Department for Children, Schools and Families (DCSF) (2007a) *Children Looked After by Local Authorities in England (Including Adoption and Care Leavers), Year Ending 31 March 2007*. London: DCSF.

Department for Children, Schools and Families (DCSF) (2007b) *Outcome Indicators for Looked After Children: Twelve Months to 30 September 2006, England*. London: DCSF.

Department for Education and Employment (DfEE) and Department of Health (DoH) (2000) *Education of Young People in Public Care: Guidance*. London: DfEE/DH.

Department for Education and Skills (DfES) (2000) *Quality Protects Research Programme*. Available at www.york.ac.uk/res/qualityprotects/index.htm (accessed on 2 July 2008).

Department for Education and Skills (DfES) (2003a) *Disabled Children in Residential Placements*. London: DfES.

Department for Education and Skills (2003b) *Every Child Matters*. Cm 5860. London: DfES.

Department for Education and Skills (2003c) *The Report of the Special Schools Working Group*. London: DfES.

Department for Education and Skills (DfES) (2004a) *Every Child Matters: Change for Children in Social Care*. London: DfES.

Department for Education and Skills (2004b) *Outcome Indicators for Looked After Children: Twelve Months to 30 September 2003, England*. London: DfES.

Department for Education and Skills (2004c) *Removing Barriers to Achievement: The Government's Strategy for SEN*. London: DfES.

Department for Education and Skills (DfES) (2004d) *Children in Need in England 2003*. London: DfES.

Department for Education and Skills (2005) *Outcome Indicators for Looked After Children: Twelve Months to 30 September 2004, England*. London: DfES.

Department for Education and Skills (2006a) *Care Matters: Transforming the Lives of Children and Young People in Care*. Cm 6932. London: DfES.

Department for Education and Skills (DfES) (2006b) *Children Looked After by Local Authorities Year Ending 31 March 2005*. London: DfES.

Department for Education and Skills (DfES) (2006c) *Outcome Indicators for Looked After Children: Twelve Months to 30 September 2005, England*. London: DfES.

Department for Education and Skills (DfES) (2006d) *Social Class: Narrowing Social Class Educational Attainment Gaps*. Supporting materials to a speech by Rt Hon. Ruth Kelly MP, Secretary of State, 26 April 2006. London: DfES.

Department for Education and Skills (DfES) (2006e) *14–19 Education and Skills: Implementation Plan*. London: DfES.

Department for Education and Skills (DfES) (2007) *Care Matters: Transforming the Lives of Children and Young People in Care.* London: DfES.

Department of Health (DoH) (1996) *Focus on Teenagers: Research into Practice.* London: DoH.

Department of Health (DoH) (1998a) *Modernising Social Services.* Cm 4169. London: DoH.

Department of Health (DoH) (1998b) *Caring for Children Away from Home: Messages from Research.* Chichester: Wiley.

Department of Health (DoH) (2001) *Outcome Indicators for Looked After Children: Twelve Months to 30 September 2000, England.* London: DoH.

Department of Health (DoH) (2002) *Outcome Indicators for Looked After Children: Twelve Months to 30 September 2001, England.* London: DoH.

Department of Health (DoH) (2003) *Outcome Indicators for Looked After Children: Twelve Months to 30 September 2002, England.* London: DoH.

Department of Health (DoH) (2005) *Research Governance Framework for Health and Social Care.* London: DoH.

Department of Social Security (DSS) (1999) *Opportunity for All: Tackling Poverty and Social Exclusion.* London: The Stationery Office.

Dunn, G., Mirandola, M., Amaddeo, F. and Tansella, M. (2003) 'Describing, explaining or predicting mental health care costs: a guide to regression models.' *British Journal of Psychiatry 183*, 398–404.

Efron, B. and Tibishirani, R. (1993) *An Introduction to the Bootstrap.* New York, NY: Chapman & Hall.

Farmer, E., Dance, C. and Ouwejan, D. 'An Investigation of Linking and Matching in Adoption: Research in Progress.' School for Policy Studies, University of Bristol, personal communication.

Farmer, E. and Moyers, S. (2008) *Kinship Care: Fostering Effective Family and Friends Placements.* London: Jessica Kingsley.

Farmer, E., Sturgess, W. and O'Neill, T. (forthcoming) *The Reunification of Looked After Children with their Parents: Patterns, Interventions and Outcomes.* London: Jessica Kingsley.

Foucault, M. (1977) *Discipline and Punish: The Birth of the Prison* (trans. Alan Sheridan). London: Allen Lane.

Frost, N. and Stein, M. (1989) *The Politics of Child Welfare. Inequality, Power and Change.* London: Harvester.

Galloway, D., Armstrong, D. and Tomlinson, S. (1994) *The Assessment of Special Educational Needs: Whose Problem?* London: Longman.

Gilligan, R. (1997) 'Beyond permanence? – the importance of resilience in child placement practice and planning.' *Adoption and Fostering 21*, 12–20.

Goodman, R. (1997) 'The Strengths and Difficulties Questionnaire: a research note.' *Journal of Child Psychology and Psychiatry 38*, 581–586.

Goodman, R., Meltzer, H. and Bailey, V. (2003) 'The Strengths and Difficulties Questionnaire: a pilot study on the validity of the self-report version.' *International Review of Psychiatry 15*, 173–177.

Goffman, E. (1961) *Asylums: Essays on the Social Situation of Mental Patients and Other Inmates.* New York, NY: Doubleday.

Gordon, D., Parker, R. and Loughran, F. (2000) *Disabled Children in Britain: A Reanalysis of the OPCS Disability Survey.* London: The Stationery Office.

Grimshaw, R. with Berridge, D. (1994) *Educating Disruptive Children: Placement and Progress in Residential Special Schools for Pupils with Emotional and Behavioural Difficulties.* London: National Children's Bureau.

Gupta, A. and Blewett, J. (2007) 'Change for children? The challenges and apportunities for the children's social work workforce.' *Child and Family Social Work 12*, 2, 172–181.

Hargreaves, D. (1967) *Social Relations in a Secondary School.* London: Routledge.

Harker, R., Dobel-Ober, D., Berridge, D. and Sinclair, R. (2004) *Taking Care of Education: An Evaluation of the Education of Looked After Children.* London: National Children's Bureau.

Heath, A., Colton, M. and Aldgate, J. (1994) 'Failure to escape: a longitudinal study of foster children's educational attainment.' *British Journal of Social Work 24*, 241–260.

Hester, M. and Pearson, C. (1998) *From Periphery to Centre: Domestic Violence in Work with Abused Children.* Bristol: Policy Press.

Hirsh, D. (2007) *Experiences of Poverty and Educational Disadvantage.* York: Joseph Rowntree Foundation.

Howe, D., Brandon, M. and Schofield, G. (eds) (1999) *Attachment Theory, Child Maltreatment, and Family Support: A Practice and Assessment Model.* Basingstoke: Macmillan.

Jackson, S. (1987) *The Education of Children in Care.* Bristol: University of Bristol, School for Applied Social Studies.

Jackson, S. (1998) *High Achievers: A Study of Young People Who Have Been in Residential or Foster Care.* Swansea: University of Wales, Swansea.

Jensen, P., Hinshaw, S., and Swanson, J. (2001) 'Findings from the NIMH Multimodal Treatment Study of ADHD (MTA): Implications and applications for primary care providers.' *Journal of Developmental and Behavioral Pediatrics 22,* 60–73.

Jordan, B. (2006) 'Well-being: the next revolution in children's services?' *Journal of Children's Services 1,* 41–50.

Judd, J. (2007) 'Hard lessons.' *Search 47,* 10–13.

Kilpatrick, R., Berridge, D., Sinclair, R., Larkin, E. *et al.* (in press) *Working with Challenging and Disruptive Situations in Residential Child Care: Sharing Effective Practice.* London: SCIE.

Knapp, M. (1984) *The Economics of Social Care.* London: Macmillan.

Knapp, M. (1998) 'Making music out of noise: the cost function approach to evaluation.' *British Journal of Psychiatry 173 (Suppl. 36),* 7–11.

Knapp, M. and Lowin, A. (1998) 'Child care outcomes: economic perspectives and issues.' *Children & Society 12,* 169–179.

Lacey, C. (1970) *Hightown Grammar: The School as a Social System.* Manchester: Manchester University Press.

Layder, D. (1993) *New Strategies in Social Research.* Cambridge: Polity Press.

Layder, D. (1998) *Sociological Practice: Linking Theory and Social Research.* London: Sage.

Malek, M. and Kerslake, A. (1989) *Making an Educational Statement: An Analysis of the Admission of Children with Emotional and Behavioural Difficulties to Residential School.* Bath: University of Bath/Children's Society.

Martin, P. and Jackson, S. (2002) 'Educational success for children in public care: advice from a group of high achievers.' *Child and Family Social Work 7,* 121–130.

Meltzer, H., Gatward, R., Corbin, T., Goodman, R. and Ford, T. (2003) *The Mental Health of Young People Looked After by Local Authorities in England.* London: Office for National Statistics.

Morgan, S. (1999) *Care About Education: A Joint Training Curriculum for Supporting Children in Public Care.* London: National Children's Bureau.

Morrison, T. (2007) 'Emotional intelligence, emotion and social work: context, characteristics, complications and contribution.' *British Journal of Social Work 37,* 2, 245–263.

Munro, E. (2004) 'The impact of audit on social work practice.' *British Journal of Social Work 34,* 1075–1095.

Munro, E., Holmes, L. and Ward, H. (2005) 'Researching vulnerable groups: ethical issues and the effective conduct of research in local authorities.' *British Journal of Social Work 35,* 1023–1038.

Nacro (2005) *A Handbook on Reducing Offending by Looked After Children.* London: Nacro.

National Evaluation of Sure Start Team (2008) *The Impact of Sure Start Local Programmes on Three Year Olds and Their Families.* London: HMSO.

National Statistics (2005a) *Family Spending; A Report on the 2004–05 Expenditure and Food Survey.* London: ONS.

National Statistics (2005b) *Statistics of Education: Education and Training Expenditure Since 1995–96.* London: DfES.

Ofsted (2003) *Special Educational Needs in the Mainstream.* Available at www.ofsted.gov.uk/publications/index.cfm?fuseaction=pubs.summary&id=3408; (accessed on 12 January 2007).

O'Neill, T. (2001) *Children in Secure Accommodation: A Gendered Exploration of Locked Institutional Care for Children in Trouble.* London: Jessica Kingsley.

Osler, A. (1997) *Exclusion from School and Racial Equality.* London: Commission for Racial Equality.

Parker, R. (1990) *Away From Home: A History of Child Care.* London: Barnardo's.

Parker, R. and Loughran, F. (1990) *Trends in Child Care.* Bristol: Bristol University, School of Applied Social Studies.

Parker, R., Ward, H., Jackson, S., Aldgate, J. and Wedge, P. (1991) *Assessing Outcomes in Child Care.* London: HMSO.

Pinney, A. (2005) *Disabled Children in Residential Placements.* London: DfES.

Pitts, J. (2001) *The New Politics of Youth Crime: Discipline or Solidarity?* Lyme Regis: Russell House Publishing.

Quinton, D. (2004) *Supporting Parents: Messages from Research.* London: Jessica Kingsley.

Reder, P. and Lucey, C. (1995) *Assessment of Parenting: Psychiatric and Psychological Contributions.* London: Routledge.

Robbins, D. (1999) *Mapping Quality in Children's Services: An Evaluation of Local Responses to the Quality Protects Programme*. London: Department of Health.

Robbins, D. (2000) *Tracking Progress in Children's Services: An Evaluation of Local Responses to the Quality Protects Programme. Year 2*. London: Department of Health.

Robbins, D. (2001) *Transforming Children's Services: An Evaluation of Local Responses to the Quality Protects Programme. Year 3*. London: Department of Health.

Schofield, G. and Beek, M. (2004) *Providing a Secure Base in Foster Care*. London: BAAF.

Sinclair, I. (2000) 'Methods and measurement in evaluative social work.' *Theorising Social Work Research Series*, Seminar 6. York: University of York.

Sinclair, I., Baker, C., Lee, J. and Gibbs, I. (2006) *The Pursuit of Permanence: A Study of the English Care System*. Final Report to DfES. York: Social Work Research and Development Unit, University of York.

Sinclair, I. and Gibbs, I. (1998) *Children's Homes: A Study in Diversity*. Chichester: Wiley.

Sinclair, I., Wilson, K. and Gibbs, I. (2004) *Foster Placements: Why They Succeed and Why They Fail*. London: Jessica Kingsley.

Sinclair, R., Garnett, L. and Berridge, D. (1995) *Social Work and Assessment with Adolescents*. London: National Children's Bureau.

Social Exclusion Unit (1998) *Truancy and Social Exclusion*. London: The Stationery Office.

Social Exclusion Unit (2003) *A Better Education for Children in Care*. London: Social Exclusion Unit/Office of the Deputy Prime Minister.

Social Research Association (2005) *Ethical Guidelines*. London: SRA.

Stein, M. (2006a) 'Missing years of abuse in children's homes', *Child and Family Social Work 11*, 11–21.

Stein, M. (2006b) 'Wrong turn', *The Guardian*., 6 December.

Thoburn, J., Chand, A. and Procter, J. (2005) *Child Welfare Services for Minority Ethnic Families: The Research Reviewed*. London: Jessica Kingsley.

Timimi, S. and Taylor, E. (2004) 'ADHD is best understood as a cultural construct. "In Debate" feature, edited by Mary Canon, K. McKenzie and A. Sims.' *British Journal of Psychiatry 184*, 8–9.

Trevithick, P. (2003) 'Effective relationship-based practice: a theoretical explanation.' *Journal of Social Work Practice 17*, 163–176.

Triseliotis, J., Borland, M., Hill, M. and Lambert, L. (1995) *Teenagers and the Social Work Services*. London: HMSO.

Ward, H., Munro, E. and Dearden, C. (2006) *Babies and Young Children in Care: Life Pathways, Decision-making and Practice*. London: Jessica Kingsley.

Webb, S. (2001) 'Some considerations on the validity of evidence-based practice in social work.' *British Journal of Social Work 31*, 57–59.

Weyts, A. (2004) 'The educational achievements of looked after children: do welfare systems make a difference to outcomes?' *Adoption & Fostering 28*, 7–19.

Whitaker, D., Archer, L. and Hicks, L. (1998) *Working in Children's Homes: Challenges and Complexities*. Chichester: Wiley.

Wilson, K., Sinclair, I., Taylor, T., Pithouse, A. and Sellick, C. (2004) *Fostering Success: An Exploration of the Research Literature in Foster Care*. London: SCIE.

Wintour, P. (2006) 'Blair admits failing most needy children.' *The Guardian*, 16 May.

Young, J. (1999) *The Exclusive Society*. London: Sage.

Subject Index

Note: page numbers in *italics* refer to diagrams and information contained in tables and boxes.

Accident and Emergency (A&E) *156*, 158–9, *161*, 178, 180
accommodation
  B&B *82*
  costs *156*, *160*, 161, *164*, 165, *166*
  'homeless' *84–5*, *109*
  legal arrangements for 61–2, *61*
adoption 61–2, 185
adults
  relationships 90, *91*, *95*, 97, *98*, 103–5, *104*, 112, 114–16, 125
  trust in 114
age, and BESD change *106*, 112–13
agency care 71
  see also private sector care; voluntary sector care
aggressive behaviour 103–4, *104*, 113, *121*, 145–6, 194, 196, *196*
alcohol abuse 24–5, 57, 67, *82*, 103–5, *104*, 108, 111–12, 115, *121*, 125, 158, 174–5, 194–6, *195*
ambition 139–40
analysis of variance (ANOVA) 151, 202
anonymity 26–7, 46
Asian pupils 24
Asperger Syndrome 131, *132*
aspirations 139–40
asylum-seeking children *32*, 45
attachment theory 185
attention deficit hyperactivity disorder (ADHD) 131, *132*
  medication for 114, 177
attrition rates 197–8, *197*
audit cultures 33
autistic spectrum disorder (ASD) 22
  see also Asperger Syndrome

B&B accommodation *82*
Behaviour Support Plan 40
behavioural, emotional and social difficulties (BESD) 18–19, 22, 28, 43, 49, 173, 177, 185, 205–6
  case studies *108*, *109*, *121–3*
  and education costs 26, 156
  and education outcomes 131, *132*, 140
  fluctuations in 102, 112–15, 165
  nature of 104–11, *106–7*, *108*, *109*
  outcomes 101–28, 177
  and quality of care 89, 100
  services for 41
  single outcome measures 115–19
  see also BESD residential schools
BESD residential schools 23–6, 70–1, *70–1*, 174, 176–9, 187, 189
  and BESD outcomes 102, 103, 104, *106*, 109
  characteristics of young people in 75, *75–6*, 77
  costs 151, *152*, *154*, 155, 159, *160*, 161–2, 168–70, 178, 202
  curricula 51–2
  and difficult behaviour 194
  education outcomes *130*, 131–3, *132–4*, 136, *141*, 142, *143–4*, 147
  identifying samples 190–1, *191*
  and placement characteristics 72, *74*, 80, 81, *81*, *85–6*
  and pupil life histories 54, 56, 59–64, *63–4*, 66, 175
  and quality of care 92
  and sample representativeness 199
  time in *78*
black pupils 24, 109
Blair, Tony 173–4, 182
Borough council 25, 31, 174

agency provision 71
BESD problems 108
  costs 152, *152*, 153, 162, *164*
  Key Stage 4 achievement 35–7, *36*
  looked after children's backgrounds 54, *55*, 58, 60, *61–2*, 62, 65, *65–7*
  out-of-borough education 51
  placement stability 82
  policy and practice development 45–6
  quality of care 100
  sample representativeness 199
  sample selection 190, *191*, 192
  school absenteeism 33, *34*
  statistical information on children in need 32, *32*, 33
boundaries 114
bullying 97, 134, 140

cannabis use *85*, 108, *108*, *121*, *123*
care environment 17–20
care histories
  and costs 152, *153*, 166, *166*
  unstable 166, *166*
care managers 54, 101
  interviews with 46–52
care packages
  consistency of *85*, *86*, 114
  intermediate outcome assessment 89, 98
care staff
  quality 181
  see also specific staff
care system, as risk factor for children's educational achievement 28
care leaving 38, 52
  and GCSE results 14–15
  teams 52
career plans 140
carer–user relationships 20
carers 50
  and BESD change 101, 103, 110–11, 113–14, 116
  expectations 16

Author Index